D0966395

Between the American Civil War and the outbreak of World War I, global history was transformed by two events: the United States's rise to the status of a great world power (indeed, the world's greatest economic power) and the eruption of nineteenth- and twentieth-century revolutions in Mexico, China, Russia, Cuba, the Philippines, Hawaii, Panama, Nicaragua, and elsewhere. *The American Search for Opportunity* traces U.S. foreign policy between 1865 and 1913, linking these two historic trends by noting how the United States – usually thought of as antirevolutionary and embarked on a "search for order" during this era – actually was a determinative force in helping to trigger these revolutions.

Walter LaFeber argues that industrialization fueled centralization: Post–Civil War America remained a vast, unwieldy country of isolated, parochial communities, but the federal government and a new corporate capitalism now had the power to invade these areas and integrate them into an industrializing, railway-linked nation-state. The furious pace of economic growth in America attracted refugees from all parts of the world. Professor LaFeber describes an influx of immigration so enormous that it led to America's first exclusionary immigration act. In 1882, the United States passed legislation preventing all Chinese immigrant labor, skilled and unskilled, from entering the country for the next ten years.

Racism in domestic affairs, exemplified by the hundreds of lynchings in the United States during the 1890s and the rampant anti-Asian outbreaks of the era, influenced foreign policy as well. Racism was particularly important in the Philippine and native-American cases. In the late 1880s, U.S. military forces consolidated white power by destroying the last major Indian opposition. This success in empire building at home led to attempts in the late 1890s to create a new empire of commerce and insular possession in the Caribbean and across the Pacific Ocean.

The struggle for markets in Asia and elsewhere drove U.S. foreign policy during this era. The Cuban crisis of 1898, which sparked the Spanish-American War, provided the opportunity to annex the Philippines and thereby secure one of the most strategic positions in the Asian region. America's rise to the status of a world power necessitated the development of its naval forces to protect the nation's commerce. Such a navy, in turn, required overseas coaling bases and rest stops.

These years were the beginning of the "American century." The roots of that century, and its two great products – U.S. power and revolutions abroad – are analyzed here, as well as the "imperial presidency" that U.S. officials developed to control the revolutionary outbreaks and restore order for the sake of further American opportunity. The book includes a valuable bibliographic essay on the large historical literature of American foreign relations during the period.

The Cambridge History of American Foreign Relations

Volume II
The American Search for Opportunity, 1865–1913

THE CAMBRIDGE HISTORY OF AMERICAN FOREIGN RELATIONS

Warren I. Cohen, Editor

Volume I: The Creation of a Republican Empire, 1776–1865 – *Bradford Perkins*
Volume II: The American Search for Opportunity, 1865–1913 – *Walter LaFeber*
Volume III: The Globalizing of America, 1913–1945 – *Akira Iriye*
Volume IV: America in the Age of Soviet Power, 1945–1991 – *Warren I. Cohen*

THE CAMBRIDGE HISTORY
OF
AMERICAN FOREIGN
RELATIONS

Volume II
The American Search for Opportunity, 1865–1913

WALTER LaFEBER

CAMBRIDGE
UNIVERSITY PRESS

Published by the Press Syndicate of the University of Cambridge
The Pitt Building, Trumpington Street, Cambridge CB2 1RP
40 West 20th Street, New York, NY 10011-4211, USA
10 Stamford Road, Oakleigh, Melbourne 3166, Australia

© Cambridge University Press 1993

First published 1993

Printed in the United States of America

RO122428509
SSCCA

HOUSTON PUBLIC LIBRARY

Library of Congress Cataloging-in-Publication Data
LaFeber, Walter
The Cambridge history of American foreign relations / Walter LaFeber.
p. cm.
Includes bibliographical references and index.
Contents: v. 1. The Creation of a Republican empire, 1776–1865 – v. 2.
The American search for opportunity, 1865–1913 – v. 3. The globalizing of
America, 1913–1945 – v. 4. America in the age of Soviet power, 1945–1991.
ISBN 0-521-38209-2 (vol 1). – ISBN 0-521-38185-1 (vol 2)
1. United States – Foreign relations. I. Title.
E183.7.P45   1993
327.73 – dc20   92-36165
                                    CIP

A catalog record for this book is available from the British Library

ISBN 0-521-38185-1 hardback

This book is dedicated to Max Miller, in memory of a devoted father, great teacher, wide-ranging scholar, committed political activist, long-suffering Dodger fan, and always unwavering friend.

Contents

Maps

General Editor's Introduction

My goal for the Cambridge History of American Foreign Relations was to make the finest scholarship and the best writing in the historical profession available to the general reader. I had no ideological or methodological agenda. I wanted some of America's leading students of diplomatic history, regardless of approach, to join me and was delighted to have my invitations accepted by the first three to whom I turned. When I conceived of the project nearly ten years ago I had no idea that the Cold War would suddenly end, that these volumes would conclude with a final epoch as well defined as the first three. The collapse of the Soviet empire, just as I finished writing Volume IV, astonished me but allowed for a sense of completion these volumes would have lacked under any other circumstances.

The first volume has been written by Bradford Perkins, the preeminent historian of late eighteenth- and early nineteenth-century American diplomacy and doyen of currently active diplomatic historians. Perkins sees foreign policy in the young Republic as a product of material interests, culture, and the prism of national values. He describes an American pattern of behavior that existed before there was an America and demonstrates how it was shaped by the experience of the Revolution and the early days of the Republic. In his discussion of the Constitution and foreign affairs, he spins a thread that can be pulled through the remaining volumes: the persistent effort of presidents, beginning with Washington, to dominate policy, contrary to the intent of the participants in the Constitutional Convention.

The inescapable theme of Perkins's volume is presaged in its title, the ideological commitment to republican values and the determination to carry those values across the North American continent and to obliterate all obstacles, human as well as geological. He sees the

American empire arising out of lust for land and resources rather than for dominion over other peoples. But it was dominion over others – native Americans, Mexicans, and especially African Americans – that led to the last episode he discusses, the Civil War and its diplomacy. This is a magnificent survey of the years in which the United States emerged as a nation and created the foundations for world power that would come in the closing years of the nineteenth century.

Walter LaFeber, author of the second volume, is one of the most highly respected of the so-called Wisconsin School of diplomatic historians, men and women who studied with Fred Harvey Harrington and William Appleman Williams and their students, and were identified as "New Left" when they burst on the scene in the 1960s. LaFeber's volume covers the last third of the nineteenth century and extends into the twentieth, to 1913, through the administration of William Howard Taft. He discusses the link between the growth of American economic power and expansionism, adding the theme of racism, especially as applied to native Americans and Filipinos. Most striking is his rejection of the idea of an American quest for order. He argues that Americans sought opportunities for economic and missionary activities abroad and that they were undaunted by the disruptions they caused in other nations. A revolution in China or Mexico was a small price to pay for advantages accruing to Americans, especially when the local people paid it. His other inescapable theme is the use of foreign affairs to enhance presidential power.

The third volume, which begins on the eve of World War I and carries the story through World War II, is by Akira Iriye, past president of the American Historical Association and our generation's most innovative historian of international relations. Japanese-born, educated in American universities, Iriye has been fascinated by the cultural conflicts and accommodations that permeate power politics, particularly as the United States has confronted the nations of East Asia. Iriye opens his book with a quick sketch of the international system as it evolved and was dominated by Europe through the seventeenth, eighteenth, and nineteenth centuries. He analyzes

Wilsonianism in war and peace and how it was applied in Asia and
Latin America. Most striking is his discussion of what he calls the
"cultural aspect" of the 1920s. Iriye sees the era about which he
writes as constituting the "globalizing of America" – an age in
which the United States supplanted Europe as the world's leader and
provided the economic and cultural resources to define and sustain
the international order. He notes the awakening of non-Western
peoples and their expectations of American support and inspiration.
In his conclusion he presages the troubles that would follow from
the Americanization of the world.

Much of my work, like Iriye's, has focused on American–East
Asian relations. My friend Michael Hunt has placed me in the
"realist" school of diplomatic historians. Influenced by association
with Perkins, LaFeber, Iriye, Ernest May, and younger friends such
as John Lewis Gaddis, Michael Hogan, and Melvyn Leffler, I have
studied the domestic roots of American policy, the role of ideas and
attitudes as well as economic concerns, the role of nongovernmental
organizations including missionaries, and the place of art in international relations. In the final volume of the series, *America in the Age
of Soviet Power, 1945–1991,* I also rely heavily on what I have learned
from political economists and political scientists.

I begin the book in the closing months of World War II and end it
with the disappearance of the Soviet Union in 1991. I write of the
vision American leaders had of a postwar world order and the growing sense that the Soviet Union posed a threat to that vision. The
concept of the "security dilemma," the threat each side's defensive
actions seemed to pose for the other, looms large in my analysis of
the origins of the Cold War. I also emphasize the importance of the
two political systems, the paradox of the powerful state and weak
government in the United States and the secrecy and brutality of the
Stalinist regime. Throughout the volume, I note the importance of
the disintegration of prewar colonial empires, the appearance of
scores of newly independent states in Africa, Asia, and Latin America, and the turmoil caused by American and Soviet efforts to force
them into an international system designed in Washington and
Moscow. Finally, I trace the reemergence of Germany and Japan as

major powers, the collapse of the Soviet Union, and the drift of the United States, its course in world affairs uncertain in the absence of an adversary.

There are a number of themes that can be followed through these four volumes, however differently the authors approach their subjects. First, there was the relentless national pursuit of wealth and power, described so vividly by Perkins and LaFeber. Iriye demonstrates how Americans used their wealth and power when the United States emerged as the world's leader after World War I. I discuss America's performance as hegemon in the years immediately following World War II, and its response to perceived threats to its dominance.

A second theme of critical importance is the struggle for control of foreign policy. Each author notes tension between the president and Congress, as institutionalized by the Constitution, and the efforts of various presidents, from 1789 to the present, to circumvent constitutional restraints on their powers. The threat to democratic government is illustrated readily by the Nixon-Kissinger obsessions that led to Watergate and Reagan's Iran-Contra fiasco.

Finally, we are all concerned with what constitutes American identity on the world scene. Is there a peculiarly American foreign policy that sets the United States off from the rest of the world? We examine the evolution of American values and measure them against the nation's behavior in international affairs. And we worry about the impact of the country's global activity on its domestic order, fearful that Thomas Jefferson's vision of a virtuous republic has been forgotten, boding ill for Americans and for the world they are allegedly "bound to lead."

WARREN I. COHEN

Preface

This account of U.S. foreign policy from 1865 to 1913 divides into two parts. The first six chapters describe how Americans[1] developed the world's most powerful economic machine and how that machine, combined with the era's racism and missionary impulse, shaped the United States of 1865–96 and its foreign policies. The final four chapters are intended to demonstrate how that new American system helped trigger a set of revolutions that, in turn, were crucial in shaping twentieth-century international affairs. At home this system produced a quarter century of economic depression, strikes, riots, and radicalism after 1873. Abroad, the system helped produce revolution in the Caribbean, Central America, Mexico, Hawaii, the Philippines, and China.

Hence the thesis: that Americans, often viewed as ardently antirevolutionary, acted as catalysts for revolution as they searched for economic and missionary opportunities around the world; then, as they willingly sacrificed order for the sake of opportunity, they supported a new presidency that emerged with this imperialism.[2] Indeed, the president's chief function in foreign affairs became his use of constitutional commander-in-chief powers to use force, when necessary, to restore enough order so opportunities could again be pursued.

1 "America" and "Americans" are sometimes used in the text to refer to the United States or persons in the United States. The terms are used, with apologies to neighbors north and south, for word variation.
2 "Imperialism" is used as the dictionary defines it: a policy of extending the rule or authority of a nation over foreign countries, and, in some instances, acquiring colonies or dependencies. A more detailed and quite useful definition is in John Gallagher and Ronald Robinson, "The Imperialism of Free Trade," *Economic History Review,* 2d ser. 7, no. 1 (1953): 5–6, which begins: "Imperialism perhaps may be defined as a sufficient political function of this process of integrating new regions into the expanding economy."

That capitalism can be awesomely destructive, especially when pushed by state powers, is not news. In 1776, Adam Smith warned against establishing "a great empire . . . for the sole purpose of raising up a nation of customers who should be obliged to buy from the shops of our different producers."[3] Classical analysis of late nineteenth-century imperialism, however, had surprisingly little to offer in explaining the links between the new capitalism and revolution abroad. Their primary interest was in the sources of the capitalism (or imperialism) and in how that capitalism changed domestic society. Marx and Engels understood that British policies were transforming India, but they believed the destruction of India's old order was for everyone's good, including India's. When Engels witnessed Western and Japanese imperialism overwhelming China in 1894, he prophesied not a Chinese revolution but a Chinese capitalism whose scale could "furnish the impulse for the overthrow of capitalism in Europe and America."[4]

A more helpful theorist was also a policymaker after 1898. Charles A. Conant was an economist (who understood the ramifications of the new Industrial Revolution and its need for foreign outlets) and a government official (who negotiated gold exchange standards with the Philippines and China to maximize foreign investment opportunities). The seminal work of Carl Parrini and Martin Sklar has resurrected Conant's importance.[5] Between 1896 and

---

3 Adam Smith, *An Inquiry into the Nature and Causes of the Wealth of Nations,* 3 vols. (London, 1822), 2:517–18.
4 Engels to Sorge, November 10, 1894, in Karl Marx and Friedrich Engels, *Letters to Americans, 1848–1895: A Selection* (New York, 1953), 266; Jorge Larrain, *Theories of Development: Capitalism, Colonialism, and Dependency* (Cambridge, 1989), p. 57. Other analysts referred to include Joseph A. Schumpeter, *Imperialism and Social Classes* (New York, 1951), esp. 12–19, 83–6; V. I. Lenin, *Imperialism* (New York, 1939), esp. 88–125; and J. A. Hobson, *Imperialism: A Study* (London, 1902), 74–6, but also p. 11 where Hobson notes in passing that imperialism's "attack upon the liberties and the existence of weaker or lower races stimulates in them a corresponding excess of national self-consciousness." Then: "Imperialism is an artificial stimulation of nationalism in peoples too foreign to be absorbed and too compact to be permanently crushed."
5 Carl P. Parrini and Martin J. Sklar, "New Thinking About the Market, 1896–1904 . . . ," *Journal of Economic History* 43 (September 1983): 559–78; Carl

1900, Conant clearly saw, and publicly discussed, the relationship between the new American industrialism and the new American empire. Of equal interest, in 1908 he wrote a short essay, "The Influence of Friction in Economics," in which he heaped scorn on those still naïve enough to believe that "free trade" and "'the open door' in the East" could work. Protectionism and "competing nationalities" destroyed such illusions. Economic exchange, Conant warned, was "not man's sole impulse" even in "developed civilized society," let alone in societies "where commerce is feebly developed, where the church or the state, or immemorial custom prescribes a routine of each man's life, and where competition in our modern American sense is almost a thing unknown." Friction of the most violent kind often resulted: "As Bagehot truthfully declared of the conditions under which capital is transferred, 'You can not have it unless you have a strong government which will keep peace in the delicate line on which people are moving.'"[6]

Friction grew, especially in the late 1890s, as imperialism not only marked the Europeans' policies but became global, as Japan and the United States joined the pursuit of overseas expansion.[7] The dangers generated by the clash between Conant's "civilized" and less industrialized societies now were heightened by clashes among a number of imperial powers. Those clashes sometimes produced among the less industrialized societies a rising nationalism and, ultimately, revolution.[8] As such "friction" increased, Americans

Parrini, "Theories of Imperialism," in Lloyd Gardner, ed., *Redefining the Past: Essays in Diplomatic History in Honor of William Appleman Williams* (Corvallis, Oreg., 1986), 67–74; Martin J. Sklar, *The United States as a Developing Country* (New York, 1992), 212–15, an especially important analysis of the Progressive Era.

6 Charles A. Conant, "The Influence of Friction in Economics," *Science* 27 (January 7, 1908): 99–104.

7 Heinz Gollwitzer, *Europe in the Age of Imperialism, 1880–1914* (New York, 1969), 34–5.

8 As noted in note 4, Hobson understood how imperialism was destroying "internationalism" and becoming an "artificial stimulation of nationalism" (*Imperialism*, 10–12). One might argue with the adjective "artificial." In a widely noted essay, Isaiah Berlin has argued that despite nationalism's mighty force in the nineteenth century, "no influential nineteenth-century thinker" foresaw its

looked to a new presidency to restore order and opportunities. A centrifugal-centripetal effect set in: As Americans moved to pursue opportunity abroad, they centralized power at home to protect themselves in that pursuit.[9]

In writing this book I have incurred so many obligations over so many years that my acknowledgments must be selective. Robert Beisner and Robert Hannigan are highly respected scholars of the 1865–1913 era who improved this account greatly by commenting on the entire manuscript. I am especially indebted to these two friends. Martin Sklar, Joel Silbey, Michael Kammen, Richard Polenberg, Tim Borstelmann, Sherman Cochran, Shannon Smith, Evan Stewart, Eric Edelman, and David Langbart provided materials and criticism, as well as valued friendship. Lizann Rogovoy, Leslie Hilgeman, and Steven Gimber were exceptionally helpful research assistants. Fred Harrington, Tom McCormick, Lloyd Gardner, and the late William Appleman Williams educated me about the arguments in this book, and about more important matters, for over three decades. Warren Cohen and Frank Smith have been helpful and patient editors, and I am especially grateful to Warren and to Nancy Tucker for their advice and, above all, their friendship and encouragement. Sandra, Scott, and Mary Kay LaFeber and Suzanne and Tom Kahl have, as usual, made it all worthwhile and possible.

growth. Hobson bridged the centuries and wrote *Imperialism* in 1902; he started the book by noting in one section how imperialism stimulated some nationalism, an effect often neglected or downplayed by students of both nationalism and imperialism. Berlin's essay is "Nationalism: Past Neglect and Present Power" in his *Against the Current: Essays in the History of Ideas* (New York, 1980), esp. 337, 350.

9 The centrifugal-centripetal effect after 1787 is traced in Walter LaFeber, "The Constitution and United States Foreign Policy: An Interpretation," in David Thelen, ed., *The Constitution and American Life* (Ithaca, N.Y., 1988), 35–57.

1. Springboards and Strategies

The Civil War created the beginnings of a new world for United States foreign policy, but it was another generation before that future could be realized. Out of the deaths of 600,000 Americans emerged, slowly but with certainty, a different nation, which replaced Jacksonian decentralization with centralization, the presidencies of James Buchanan and Rutherford B. Hayes with those of William McKinley and Theodore Roosevelt, the Jeffersonian agrarian-ideal commercial farmer with the Andrew Carnegie–J. P. Morgan ideal of the billion-dollar U.S. Steel Corporation, and the 1840s laissez-faire capitalism of James K. Polk's Democrats with the late 1890s corporate capitalism of Senator Mark Hanna's Republicans. Of special importance, the nation built on these four domestic transformations to construct a foreign policy that replaced the Monroe Doctrine of 1823 with the Open Door policy of 1899–1900; that is, Americans were finished with land expansion from sea to sea. They were confident now in their supremacy over much of the Western Hemisphere and embarked on an imperialist course in parts of Asia and Africa.

These historic changes, of course, did not start cleanly in the 1860s. Jefferson and Polk, for example, had demonstrated the incredible potential for presidential power long before Theodore Roosevelt's birth. The faith that supplying China's market could put depression-ridden Americans to work dated back to the mid-1780s, not the mid-1890s. Even the once firmly held belief that the Civil War gave birth to the industrialized United States has been disproved. The annual growth rate of U.S. manufactures was 7.8 percent between 1840 and 1860, but 6 percent between 1870 and 1900. Between 1860 and 1870, the value added by manufacturing increased by only 2.3 percent annually, the lowest rate of increase in the nineteenth century. Some economists explain this surprisingly

1

low rate by arguing that the roots of industrialized America stretched back well before the Civil War, and by noting that the conflict itself was not the first modern war but one of the last major preindustrial clashes.[1]

That was one reason, no doubt, why later Americans glorified this struggle waged by foot soldiers and men on horseback who fought at close quarters to protect a plot of earth they knew well. As Lincoln's reflections at Gettysburg announced, and as Edmund Wilson's *Patriotic Gore* a century later realized, a sense of self-sacrifice, moving in part (as Wilson noted) from Calvinist realism, added a new dimension to the already healthy sense of mission held by Americans. Few Civil War soldiers were quoted as saying they were willing to march into near-certain death at Antietam because they were just "doing their job." The American belief in Calvinism and mission was not decades old but two centuries old when it moved soldiers on 1860s battlefields or missionaries in 1890s China. If a difference appeared, it was, as Albert Weinberg has observed, that in 1776 Americans assumed the natural rights that blessed them were universal, whereas by the 1890s these rights were considered national – and even then limited largely to males and certain Caucasians. The Civil War officially ended the slavery of African Americans, but the Emancipation Proclamation was not a commitment as well to raise the former slaves to equality. The mission and the racism that characterized U.S. imperialism in 1900 thus had different emphases and objectives than before the Civil War, but their roots reached deep into American history.[2]

New Government, New Wealth

The 1860s not only marked the climax of a historic sense of mission and the emergence of a different kind of racism – a racism of neither slavery nor equality. The Civil War and the acts of Reconstruction also turned the United States into a nation-state. The phrase

1 Stuart Bruchey, *Enterprise: The Dynamic Economy of a Free People* (Cambridge, Mass., 1990), 255–6.
2 Edmund Wilson, *Patriotic Gore* (New York, 1962), esp. 61.

was no longer, as it had been before the 1860s, "the United States are," but "the United States is." The country's unification occurred at the same time that Germany, Japan, Italy, and (with Alexander II's reforms) even Russia were also evolving into modern nation-states that could serve as springboards to empire. Industrialization, or in some early stages the aspiration to industrialize, acted as a catalyst in the development of these nation-states.[3]

In the United States, industrialization fed on the need to supply vast armies in the early 1860s. Those who could concentrate capital and set up spidery distribution systems could produce previously unimagined wealth in such businesses as meat processing and oil production. Many of the industries spawned by the Civil War helped shape U.S. foreign relations in the late nineteenth and early twentieth centuries. In 1865, Phillip Armour already enjoyed a $2 million income from his meat-processing firm. By 1907 Armour and Company's foreign sales manager watched over separate departments responsible for South America, Asia, Africa, Europe, England, Germany, and France. The first U.S. oil had been discovered in 1859; by 1865 this six-year-old industry already provided the sixth-largest U.S. export. In 1870, John D. Rockefeller and several partners named their refining operations (already the world's biggest) Standard Oil. By 1883–5, Standard shipped 70 percent of its major product, kerosene, to Europe, and another 21.6 percent to Asia where the Rockefellers were building the equivalent of their own diplomatic corps as they prepared for an epic battle with Russian oil.[4]

Such industries and others also generated capital that was not only burgeoning (especially with the help of the federal government, which during the war issued several billion dollars more in paper than it took in through taxes) but becoming concentrated. One New

---

3 The "are" to "is" is especially emphasized in Garry Wills, *Lincoln at Gettysburg: The Words That Remade America* (New York, 1992).

4 Barbara J. Fields, "Ideology and Race in American History," in J. Morgan Kousser and James M. McPherson, eds., *Region, Race and Reconstruction: Essays in Honor of C. Vann Woodward* (New York, 1982), 162–4; Alfred D. Chandler, Jr., with the assistance of Takashi Hikino, *Scale and Scope: The Dynamics of Industrial Capitalism* (Cambridge, Mass., 1990), 86–7, 92–3, 167–8.

York newspaper observed that in the 1840s not more than twenty citizens had a worth of $1 million, but now in the 1860s New York alone had several hundred worth that amount, and some claimed $20 million. This nascent finance capitalism had been helped by the fleeing of foreign investment when the war broke out. The nation thus simultaneously multiplied and concentrated the capital resources necessary to compete later with the European cartels and government-sponsored firms that spread over the nonindustrialized world. Capital moves "in larger masses than formerly," the *New York Commercial and Financial Chronicle* noted in 1866. Small firms cannot compete and are "absorbed into them. . . . It is one of the signs of the time and will probably exert no small influence over the future growth of our industrial and commercial enterprise."[5]

This multiplication and concentration of wealth was not born of laissez-faire principles. The secession of the South in 1861 suddenly removed many members of Congress who had opposed systematic governmental help to the business sector. (Their opposition had good reasons; with the expanding northern population giving that section control of Congress, southerners knew that the help would flow especially to railroads and new manufacturing, both of which were relatively scarce in the slaveholding region.) As historian Charles Sellers phrased it, "Only on the battlefields of the Civil War did the progressive bourgeoisie of free-labor exploitation finally prevail over resistant farmers, workers, and the anachronistic [southern] planter." Thus the low tariffs of the post-1832 era were replaced in 1861 after passage of the Morrill Act, and over the next five years average ad valorem rates on dutiable imports shot up 250 percent. Such tariffs, combined with the military's bottomless needs, opened the quickest path possible to creating a rich home market for industrialists. Nor did the new higher-tariff policy significantly change until the end of this era in 1913. Not content with merely creating a new protected market, Congress used more direct methods to unify and systematize it. In acts passed during 1862 and 1864, money, vast amounts of land, and rich timber and mineral rights were freely

5 Thomas C. Cochran and William Miller, *The Age of Enterprise* (New York, 1942), 116.

given to companies that would lay rail links. By 1869 the first transcontinental railroad existed. An industrialist spelled out one meaning for foreign affairs: "The drills and sheetings of Connecticut, Rhode Island, and Massachusetts and other manufactures of the United States may be transported to China in thirty days [instead of months]; and the teas and rich silks of China, in exchange, come back to New Orleans, to Charleston, . . . to Philadelphia, New York and Boston in thirty days more." Replacing pre–Civil War Jacksonian Democracy with Republican centralization radically changed the nation's foreign opportunities.[6]

Congress created a historic opportunity for wealth by passing a Homestead Act in 1862 that gave 160 acres of unoccupied land to anyone who would cultivate it for five years or pay $1.25 per acre within six months. The cash provision opened the riches of the western lands to wealthy speculators who seized good land, then sold it at profit. In 1864, Congress dealt with the growing labor shortage by passing the contract labor law, which allowed business agents to travel to Europe and bring back workers under contract. By 1865, the number of immigrants grew to twice that of 1861. Many were used to break strikes between 1864 and 1868, when the law expired. Unions had flourished in the early war years.[7] When immigrants were not used to break strikes, blacks often were, and the resulting clashes (especially between African Americans and Irish) turned bloody. The racism and xenophobia shaped the ideology of following generations, including those who made U.S. foreign policy. Of equal importance, the clashes between capital and labor previewed later confrontations that, as they grew sharper during the post-1873 depression, led U.S. officials to search for foreign policies that might end the upheavals.

6 Charles Sellers, *The Market Revolution* (New York, 1991), 6n; David Pletcher, "Growth and Diplomatic Adjustment," in William H. Becker and Samuel F. Wells, Jr., eds., *Economics and World Power* (New York, 1984), 132–4; quoted in Charles A. Beard and Mary Beard, *The Rise of American Civilization*, 2 vols. (New York, 1927), 2:128–9; on Civil War statism, and the emerging finance capitalism: Richard Franklin Bensel, *Yankee Leviathan: The Origins of Central State Authority in America, 1859–1877* (New York, 1990).

7 Cochran and Miller, *Age of Enterprise*, 107–10.

Post–Civil War America remained a vast, unwieldy country of isolated, parochial communities, but the federal government had demonstrated its power to invade these areas and integrate them into an industrializing, railway-linked world that had global boundaries. When, for example, Congress moved in 1863 to try to systematize the banking system, it followed with an 1865 law that taxed state bank notes and created a more uniform national currency under Washington's control. The growth of executive power more than kept pace with the legislature's. By reasoning that the country faced an unprecedented emergency, and then employing the Constitution's provision that the president is commander in chief of the nation's military, Abraham Lincoln raised and committed an army to oppose the South's secession without even consulting Congress. Lincoln did ultimately ask Congress in mid-1861 to judge his actions, but never during the next four years did Congress successfully rein in his growing prerogative. In E. S. Corwin's classic formulation, Lincoln's success produced two results. One was that future presidents could directly deal, without undue concern for congressional or state objections, with conditions that the president believed presented actual or potential violence and, in his judgment, endangered the nation's interest. A second result was that later presidents could more generally use, as Corwin phrased it, "Lincoln's acts as if they supported the thesis of presidential autonomy – in other words, presidential autocracy – in all fields of presidential power." Not the least of those fields would be foreign affairs, especially when the commander-in-chief authority could serve as a rationale. Presidential power could not be separated easily into domestic and foreign compartments.[8]

The line from the 1860s to the foreign expansionism of the 1890s was not unbroken. Lincoln exerted unusual control over Congress and demonstrated how the executive's broad powers could be stretched. Immediately after the war and his death, however, the Supreme Court moved to limit these powers by arguing that consti-

---

8 Edward S. Corwin, "The Aggrandizement of Presidential Power," *Annals* 218 (November 1941): 122–31; "island community" is a key theme of Robert Wiebe, *The Search for Order, 1877–1920* (New York, 1967).

tutional restraints worked "equally in war and in peace," and that to suspend those restraints even during an emergency could lead "directly to anarchy or despotism." Lincoln's successor, Andrew Johnson, tried to stop Congress's Reconstruction program that aimed to use military force, if necessary, to protect African Americans' rights (and therefore Republican power) in the former Confederacy. The clash climaxed in 1868 when Congress came within one vote of removing Johnson from the presidency. For the next quarter century, Congress usually maintained its domination over the executive. Lincoln's use of power, however, could not be permanently undone. The institutionalized centralization of power only required the rise of foreign affairs to a high place in the nation's agenda, along with recurring crises resulting from those affairs that, as most presidents believed, the president could best handle.[9]

Seward and Imperial Reconstruction

Lincoln's and Johnson's secretary of state was William Henry Seward of New York. As a leader of the former Whig party, Seward had bitterly opposed strong Democratic presidents such as Jackson and Polk. In a switch not uncommon in American politics, however, he became a strident defender of executive authority when his new Republican party occupied the White House. The New Yorker indeed constantly preached the need to centralize and rationalize the far-flung continental system so that it could compete with other powers. He developed, moreover, an imperial strategy that was unrealizeable in his lifetime but was to be realized in the next two generations. In a later American society in which marketplace competition is assumed and the ideology subsumed, Seward becomes the vital link between the pre- and postindustrial United States.

He argued that the federal government had to take the lead in this consolidation by passing higher tariffs to ensure the home market and thus create new industries that could grow safely until they were

9 Especially important is Eric McKitrick's essay in William N. Chambers and Walter Dean Burnham, *American Party Systems,* 2d ed. (New York, 1975), 139; Arthur Schlesinger, Jr., *The Imperial Presidency* (Boston, 1973), 69–70.

able to sell abroad; a more centralized banking system; a land act that rapidly filled the interior; and the 1864 contract labor law and an 1868 treaty that Seward negotiated with China to provide the necessary labor power, as well as inhabitants to populate western lands. He apparently shaped his views about immigration after reading the theorist of the earlier British Empire, Francis Bacon. Above all, Seward believed in the magic of new technology and transportation to tie the nation together and make it efficient. As governor of New York he had successfully pushed to build the foundations of the state's railway system. As a senator in the 1850s, he helped legislate a national federal improvements program of railways, canals, highways, and ships. As he proclaimed in 1853, "open up a highway through your country to San Francisco," fill the continent with farms and manufacturers, for "the nation that . . . sells the most of productions and fabrics to foreign nations must be, and will be, the great power of the earth."[10]

Seward combined this vision with another: the Stars and Stripes flying above Canada and Mexico. His passion for landed expansion, however, cooled before 1861 when he understood it could lead to the expansion of slavery and the South's power. By the early 1850s he had switched his passion from landed to commercial expansion and from the Western Hemisphere (where the South hoped to expand its "peculiar institution") to Asia. He declared disingenuously that the Monroe Doctrine had been realized. It was time to prepare for conquering Asian markets, a call to action that a friend promptly tagged "the Seward Doctrine." The conventional wisdom believed that trade followed the flag. Not necessarily so, Seward argued: "Political supremacy follows commercial ascendancy." He believed Mexico and Canada would join the Union, but peacefully, in time, without the hatreds of conquest. He feared, moreover, that "mixed

10 William Henry Seward, *The Works of William H. Seward,* ed. George E. Baker, 5 vols. (Boston, 1853–83), 5:5, 3:109, 616, 618; Ernest N. Paolino, *The Foundations of American Empire: William Henry Seward and U.S. Foreign Policy* (Ithaca, 1973), 5–6, 35–6. A different view of Seward is well argued in Robert L. Beisner, *From the Old Diplomacy to the New, 1865–1900,* 2d ed. (Arlington Heights, Ill., 1986); and Charles S. Campbell, Jr., *The Transformation of American Foreign Relations, 1865–1900* (New York, 1976), pp. 23–4.

races," such as those in Mexico, could not yet govern themselves. "The empire of the seas," not land, "alone is real empire," Seward trumpeted, and Asia, not the Western Hemisphere, was to be "the prize," "the chief theatre of events in the world's great hereafter."[11]

Americans' growing belief that they were using new technology to rationalize their continent so they could conquer that "prize" has aptly been termed "continentalism," and it opens insights into the entire era from the 1840s to World War I.[12] In 1864–5, Seward faced a pivotal test of his theory. Napoleon III of France had taken advantage of the Civil War crisis to send both troops and Archduke Maximilian of Austria to conquer Mexico and its liberal government of Benito Juarez. Napoleon instantly threatened to establish a French empire, block U.S. expansion, and balance British power in the hemisphere. Pressure grew on the beleaguered Seward to respond. On May 5, 1864, he counseled patience: "Five years, ten years, twenty years hence, Mexico will be opening herself as cheerfully to American immigration as Montana and Idaho are now." No European army could resist "the martial and moral influences of emigration." The next day he told the U.S. minister in Madrid that the United States desired no further "conquest" because it already had "abundant territory and all that [Americans] can improve." Seward's remarks signaled that nearly three hundred years of American landed expansion was ending. After the Civil War, U.S. armies mobilized on the Mexican border, but they were unneeded. The Mexicans executed Maximilian and destroyed Napoleon's dreams.[13]

The question became whether Seward was correct in prophesying that technological and commercial expansion would replace landed conquest in the nation's next historical phase. One answer appeared when the restored Mexican government welcomed U.S. investors.

11 Paolino, *Foundations*, 27, 28–30; Seward, *Works*, 3:618, 5:246; Frederick H. Stutz, "William Henry Seward, Expansionist" (Master's thesis, Cornell University, 1937), 26, 53.
12 Charles Vevier, "American Continentalism: An Idea of Expansionism, 1845–1910," *American Historical Review* 65, no. 2 (1960): 323–35.
13 Frederic Bancroft, *The Life of William H. Seward*, 2 vols. (New York, 1900), 2:429; Richard Van Alstyne, "The Monroe Doctrine," in Alexander DeConde, ed., *Encyclopedia of American Foreign Policy*, 3 vols. (New York, 1978), 2:590–1.

The future was glimpsed: Reactionary European colonialists were replaced by Americans who would "value dollars more, and dominion less," as Seward succinctly put it. Another answer appeared when he learned in 1867 that Egyptians had convened a legislative assembly in Cairo. The assembly demonstrated, Seward concluded, "that popular govt. follows in the track of the steam engine and the telegraph," even this "soon in Africa."[14] Yet another answer appeared between 1866 and 1868 when the secretary of state embarked on a breathtaking plan to build his own "highway" to Asia by obtaining naval bases and isthmian canal rights in the Caribbean region, seizing a foothold on Hawaii, and applying military pressure on Asia.

Seward's grand plan, however, crashed into roadblocks on the "highway" to Asia. He was nearly killed by a colleague of the assassin who shot Lincoln in April 1865. Recovering slowly, Seward watched as the new president and congressional Republicans clashed over Reconstruction policies. Johnson, born to poor white stock in Tennessee, had little sympathy for freed African Americans and wanted the South to return immediately to the Union. Leading congressmen were determined to punish the South and protect the former slaves. Seward not only sided with Johnson but persistently urged him to move rapidly in readmitting the old Confederacy. The secretary of state's motives were mixed. He respected the former Confederate leaders, many of whom had been prewar colleagues in the Whig party, and he believed they formed a safe, cooperative core for southern state governments. It might have been that the 65-year-old Seward viewed these friends as part of a new political party that would catapult him into the presidency in 1868. There is no doubt that he believed that African Americans were unable to govern themselves, let alone govern whites, and that (as he told southerners) perhaps slavery could be replaced by a kind of involuntary apprenticeship on the plantations. "The North has nothing to do with the negroes [*sic*]," Seward told liberal friends in April 1866. "I

14 Draft of reply to Charles Hale, January 5, 1867, Papers of William H. Seward, University of Rochester, Rochester, N.Y.; Thomas Schoonover, *Dollars over Dominion* (Baton Rouge, 1978), 252–4, 282.

have no more concern for them than I have for the Hottentots. . . .
They are not of our race. . . . The North must get over this notion
of interference with the affairs of the South."[15] That letter illustrated, among other things, why Seward and many other Americans
wanted no more landed expansion southward that might bring more
non-Caucasians (a number of Americans narrowed this to non–
Anglo-Saxons) into the Union.

Furious Radical Republicans speculated that Seward was the evil
genius back of Johnson's policy. In late 1866 the secretary of state
admitted that in his long, combative public life he had never been so
maligned.[16] The elections that autumn gave the Radical Republicans sufficient control of Congress to pass their program over Johnson's vetoes. Within a year they threatened not only to isolate the
president but to impeach him. Seward's foreign policy plans were
stymied, however, not only because of the political Armageddon
that threatened.

As indicated by powerful *New York Tribune* editor Horace Greeley
(a Seward nemesis who had once uttered the famous advice of "Go
west, young man, go west"), some Americans wanted no more land
of any kind, even warm harbors for commercial bases. "Our country
has already an ample area for the next century at least," Greeley
wrote. On the other hand, the editor added, Canada was always
welcome to "form at last one great, free nation" – a remark that
further underlined the racial views that shaped U.S. policies. Others, such as the powerful Massachusetts Senator Charles Sumner,
opposed taking such areas as Hawaii precisely because the native
people would lose their independence and, probably, protection.
The *New York Evening Post* opposed expansion because incorporating
such extracontinental areas as Alaska would replace our "present
system" with "a colonial policy," and do so "just at the time when
England is getting tired of colonies and [is] convinced of their
unprofitableness." In addition, others warned that the United States
was so deeply in financial debt because of the Civil War that it could

15 Seward, *Works*, 5:519–21; Fawn Brodie, *Thaddeus Stevens* (New York, 1959),
  285; Eric Foner, *Reconstruction: America's Unfinished Revolution, 1863–1877* (New
  York, 1988), 190, 219.
16 Seward, *Works*, 5:8.

not afford to buy any more territory.[17] The political atmosphere could not have been chillier as Seward set out to acquire stepping-stones to empire.

Seward and the Course of Empire

Against these odds, the secretary of state signed a treaty with Russia in 1867 to purchase Alaska for $7.2 million, and then convinced Sumner and other Radical Republicans to help him push the pact through the Senate. The deal had long been gestating. At least as early as the 1830s the Russians understood they had lost control of Alaska's trade and even its food supply to the ubiquitous New England traders who had been exploiting the region for decades. Nor could the territory be defended against a British attack from neighboring Canada, or against Americans intent upon repeating the settlement-and-conquer process that had turned Texas into part of the Union in 1845. As one influential, knowledgeable Russian official (I. A. Shestakov) warned, Europeans may be cynical about "the Monroe Doctrine or the dogma of Manifest Destiny," but in North America "this principle enters more and more into the veins of the people and . . . the latest generation imbibes it with its mother's milk and inhales it with the air." Officials around Tsar Nicholas I wanted to end the shaky hold on Alaska and concentrate on developing the potentially rich Amur River region in Asiatic Russia. By the mid-1850s the tsar was moving to sell, but obstacles arose, not least the Civil War. During that conflict Americans viewed Russia as a strong supporter of the Union, quite in contrast to the tsar's enemy, Great Britain, with whom Lincoln endured a series of crises between 1861 and 1863. The afterglow of Russia's support helped warm the political atmosphere as Seward, after signing the treaty late on the evening of March 30, 1867, at his home with Russian Minister Edouard de Stoeckel, prepared to battle the Senate.

The battle was intense, but quickly won. At the start Seward

17 Campbell, *Transformation of American Foreign Relations,* 16; Donald M. Dozer, "Anti-Expansionism During the Johnson Administration," *Pacific Historical Review* 12 (September 1943): 253–75.

gained high ground by emphasizing Russia's friendship and flooding the Senate with information that fulsomely described Alaska's riches and strategic position. The global ambitions of U.S. technology provided much of his information. During the war Seward had worked closely with Perry M. Collins and Hiram Sibley (president of Western Union) to lay a telegraph line through the United States, across Alaska, the Bering Straits, and Siberia. The Collins Overland Line intended to dominate global communications. The line would "extend throughout the world American ideas and principles of public and private economy, politics, morals, philosophy, and religion," Seward exalted. Cyrus Field's success in laying the Atlantic cable in the mid-1860s, however, destroyed Collins's plans. The negotiations with Russia nevertheless both paved the way to talks about Alaska and provided large amounts of material on the possible wealth in "Seward's Icebox," as it was soon known. The part of Alaska Americans paid less attention to was the people. Some Russian authorities were quite interested in the Eskimo and Aleut population, but U.S. officials seemed to see Alaska much as they had seen their own continental "frontier": as a potential for power and not as a home for native peoples. [18]

In his three-hour Senate speech supporting the treaty, Sumner stressed Alaska's worth, not simply Russian friendship. He, Seward, and many newspapers also emphasized that strategically the Alaska purchase could mean the inevitable annexation as well of British Columbia, now squeezed between two parts of the United States, if not the taking of much more of Canada. (The British minister in Washington reported home that the pact signaled a U.S.-Russian move against England's power and could mean as well the British loss of all Canada.) On April 9, 1867, the Senate ratified the treaty 37–2. [19]

---

18 Authoritative is N. N. Bolkhovitinov, "The Crimean War and the Emergence of Proposals for the Sale of Russian America, 1853–1861," *Pacific Historical Review* 59 (February 1990): 15–49; Seward to Cassius Clay, July 13, 1863, Instructions, Russia, National Archives, Department of State, Record Group 59, Washington, D.C. (hereafter NA, RG); Seward to Clay, March 28, 1867, ibid. Charles Vevier, "The Collins Overland Line and American Continentalism," *Pacific Historical Review* 28 (August 1959): 237–53.

19 Nikolai Bolkhovitinov, "How It Was Decided to Sell Alaska," *International*

The House, however, refused to pass the necessary appropriations measure until 1868. The Radical Republicans, who controlled the body, were taken up with Reconstruction and impeachment struggles, not Seward's grandiose plans. In foreign policy President Johnson was a second violinist in the secretary of state's one-man band, but the second violinist could at least disrupt the music. After the House moved to impeach Johnson, it finally passed the pact 113–43, with 44 members not voting. Nathaniel Banks (R.-Mass.), chair of the House Foreign Affairs Committee, led the protreaty forces. Not a Radical Republican, he tended to agree with Seward that the South should be brought back in quickly and foreign expansion expedited. With a keen eye for advancing his home state's commerce, a firsthand knowledge of the burgeoning American West, and warm friendship for Seward, Banks argued that the Aleutians, the "drawbridge between America and Asia," could give the United States new power in the Pacific Ocean area, which would be the "controller of the destiny of nations and the progress of mankind." Another House member added that the purchase would "cage the British lion" and hasten the day when "the two great Powers on earth will be Russia and the United States." To ensure passage, the tsar's minister apparently distributed money to key members, although the importance of the payments has been disputed by recent scholarship. Certainly Seward's raising of the Stars and Stripes at Sitka six months earlier helped his cause. "Palsied be the hand that would dare remove it," one House member exclaimed.[20]

Alaska had been seen as crucial in extending the U.S. reach into Asia. Seward's son, Frederick W. Seward, worked closely with his father and later recalled that it was argued that the purchase would give Americans "a foothold for commercial and naval operations accessible from the Pacific States." The secretary of state's view

Affairs (Moscow), no. 8 (August 1988): 116–26; Campbell, *Transformation of American Foreign Relations*, 20.

20 Fred Harvey Harrington, *Fighting Politician: Major-General N. P. Banks* (Philadelphia, 1948), 170–85; Paul Holbo, *Tarnished Expansion: The Alaska Scandal . . . 1867–1871* (Knoxville, 1983), 105–9; Campbell, *Transformation of American Foreign Relations*, 21–3.

literally knew no bounds. In May 1867, after the Senate ratification, he wrote a poem:

> Our nation with united interests blest
> Not now content to poise, shall sway the rest;
> Abroad our empire shall no limits know,
> But like the sea in boundless circles flow.[21]

Perhaps. But not in Seward's lifetime. Throughout 1867–8 he tried to parlay the Alaska triumph into a systematic expansionist policy. Time and again he was stopped by congressional hatreds or opposition to more expensive territory, or by the native peoples he had targeted.

He focused on the Caribbean. During the Civil War, the U.S. Navy discovered its need for a dependable Caribbean base. Europeans led by Spain, moreover, had taken advantage of the crisis to try to regain control of Santo Domingo. After the rising power of Prussia defeated Denmark in 1864, rumors circulated that the Prussians or Austrians would take the Danish West Indies (the Virgin Islands). North-South relations in the hemisphere, moreover, seemed to be warming. The Confederacy's defeat meant the end of proslavery filibustering expeditions. Emancipation had also finally aligned the United States with all of Latin America, which, except for Cuba and Brazil, was free of slavery. The climate cooled when Spain threatened Chile and Peru in 1866, and Seward, instead of wheeling out the Monroe Doctrine, looked the other way. His interests were more specific: the gateways for U.S. commercial and strategic supremacy that bases in the Caribbean and the Central American isthmus could open.[22]

In July 1867 Seward signed a treaty with Denmark to purchase the Virgin Islands for $7.5 million if the inhabitants agreed in a plebiscite. The plebiscite passed, but the treaty crashed against Senate opposition to spending such money (all of Alaska had cost

21 Frederick W. Seward, *Reminiscences* . . . (New York, 1916), 360; Seward to Philip Tomppert, May 10, 1867, Seward Papers.
22 On Spain, there is a long, important analysis in Richard Olney to George F. Hoar, September 13, 1895, Papers of Richard Olney, Library of Congress, Washington, D.C.

only $7.2 million), and the opponents felt confirmed in their wisdom when a hurricane hit the islands. Seward backed off, but he warned Europe that "no transfer of colonies in the West Indies between European powers can be indifferent to the United States." That declaration reinforced the "no-transfer" principle first issued by President James Madison in 1811. (The United States finally obtained the Virgin Islands in 1917.) Seward also tried in 1866 to deal through U.S. adventurers who had gained power in Santo Domingo to obtain land at Samana Bay in return for several million dollars. He wined and dined Radical Republican leader Thaddeus Stevens until the House gave him money for the negotiations. This action was notable given that Stevens hated Johnson's Reconstruction measures and had called Seward the president's "chief clown." The treaty, however, failed because some in Santo Domingo wanted more money and others feared that giving land away might lead to mass revolt. In Washington, Seward ran into ancient enemies within the Republican party. Navy Secretary Gideon Welles opposed obtaining a Caribbean naval base because Seward "has become almost a monomaniac on the subject of territorial acquisition, that being the hobby on which he expects to be a candidate for President."[23]

Stopped in the Caribbean, Seward worked with a group of New York businessmen to obtain rights to build the long-coveted isthmian canal. A first treaty with Nicaragua in mid-1867 passed the Senate because it gave nonexclusive rights and so did not break the Clayton-Bulwer Treaty, made with Great Britain in 1850, that provided the two countries would jointly develop any canal. In January 1869, however, Seward sent one of his best diplomats, Caleb Cushing of the Massachusetts mercantile community, to sign a treaty giving the United States (or a private company such as Seward's New York friends) rights to build a twenty-mile-wide canal through Colombia's Panama province, and to build it under U.S. control. It marked the first time the United States indicated that it intended to control, not merely share, any canal. The Senate refused to accept this deal, in part

---

23 Charles C. Tansill, *The United States and Santo Domingo, 1787–1873* (Baltimore, 1938), 226–77; W. Stull Holt, *Treaties Defeated by the Senate* (Baltimore, 1933), 104–6.

because of the 1850 commitment. Fourteen years later, however, another exclusive treaty was negotiated, this time with Nicaragua, and twenty years after that the United States indeed exclusively controlled a canal that linked the two great oceans.[24]

During the burst of activity in 1867–8, Seward also tried to gain a foothold on Hawaii. Massachusetts interests, with Sumner in the fore, worked with him to pull Hawaii into the U.S. orbit with a commercial reciprocity treaty. Seward instructed the U.S. negotiator that reciprocity was fine, but if Hawaiians were interested, quick annexation would be even better. In 1863, the secretary of state had raised the U.S. presence to the ministerial (or highest diplomatic) level. Minister Edward McCook now echoed his superior with his explanation of the treaty's meaning: "When the [U.S. transcontinental] Pacific Railroad is completed, and the commerce of Asia directed to our Pacific ports, then these islands will be needed as a rendezvous for our Pacific navy, and a resort for merchant ships, and this treaty will have prepared the way for this quiet absorption." Senate power Justin Morrill (R.-Maine) disagreed. A high-tariff fanatic who had been one of two senators to oppose the Alaska Purchase (his Senate colleague from Maine was the other), Morrill wanted no break in his tariff wall. Other members feared, correctly, that by giving the president the power to negotiate reciprocity provisions, Congress would lose some of its own power. Morrill's side defeated the treaty, but Seward's vision triumphed when an 1875 pact was signed, and the results were just as Minister McCook had prophesied. Meanwhile, on Washington's instructions, a U.S. Navy officer had taken possession of the uninhabited Brooks Island, twelve hundred miles west of Hawaii. Congress went along because it cost nothing. In 1903 the renamed Midway Island became a permanent U.S. naval base that played a prominent role in twentieth-century history.[25]

Seward had great plans for Asia, but his power never caught up with his vision. The gap led him to introduce two new principles in

24 Seward, *Works,* 5:33–4; Michael L. Conniff, *Panama and the United States* (Athens, Ga., 1992), 43.
25 Sylvester K. Stevens, *American Expansion in Hawaii, 1842–1898* (Harrisburg, Pa., 1945), 95–107.

U.S.-Asian policies, principles that shaped those policies through most of the next eighty years. Indeed, a distinguished historian of U.S.-Asia relations, Tyler Dennett, wrote in 1922 that "absolutely no new principles have been added to American Far Eastern policy since 1869." The foundation of that policy had been laid with the Sino-U.S. treaty of 1844, which pledged an Open Door and equal opportunity for Americans. The policy was maintained by following along back of British and French demands and, in a kind of scavenger diplomacy, demanding from China trade rights equal to those extracted by the Europeans. In the 1860s, however, Civil War needs reduced the U.S. naval presence to a single ship. Unwilling to pull back from Asia, even while waging war to save the Union, Seward formulated a policy of upholding equal U.S. opportunities by following the principle of cooperation (rather than being the go-it-alone scavenger), and the principle of using force if necessary. The two principles were carried out by U.S. Minister Anson Burlingame, a former Massachusetts congressman who wanted China to respect foreign rights, but was equally determined to uphold China's territorial integrity (a basic precondition, of course, to being able to trade in all of China). Burlingame's sensitivity later led the Chinese to have him represent them in Western capitals; Seward negotiated the Burlingame Treaty in 1868 with him to allow Chinese laborers into the United States.[26]

The principles of cooperation and use of force were quickly applied. In 1864 Japan, still trying to close itself off from the West, apparently burned the U.S. legation (although the actual cause of the fire was disputed), and closed the Strait of Shimoneseki to all foreign shipping. Seward had a visceral reaction to any nation that tried to shut itself off from trade; he saw it as an unnatural and immoral act. Seward especially grew angry because the Japanese opposed the proselytizing and practicing of Christianity. The U.S. minister to Japan, R. H. Pruyn, revealed another notable U.S. perspective when he wrote Seward in 1862 that all Western diplo-

---

26 Tyler Dennett, "Seward's Far Eastern Policy," *American Historical Review* 28 (October 1922): 45–64; Seward to Burlingame, March 6, 1862, Instructions, China, NA, RG 59.

mats "in Japan are sentinels in this outpost of civilization. It is here as with our Indian tribes . . . the bolt [sneak attack] comes out of an unclouded sky." In this Far West, the natives only understood force. Thus the U.S.S. *Wyoming* joined British, French, and Dutch ships who blasted their way into the strait and then, in 1866, dictated trade treaties. When the Civil War ended, Seward dispatched three more warships to Asian waters. After Korea murdered passengers and crew of a U.S. merchantman in 1866, he again wanted to use force, but France refused to cooperate. He also sent his nephew George F. Seward to open Korea much as Admiral Matthew Perry had opened Japan in 1853. The younger man failed; he also refused to use force, as the secretary of state suggested he might, to open the so-called Hermit Kingdom.[27]

Seward not only added new principles but discovered a new dilemma that plagued U.S. policies in China (and elsewhere) for decades. On the one hand, he instructed the U.S. legation in Peking on September 8, 1868, that China must be pushed to "make all . . . concessions" as rapidly as possible for trade, railway construction, and telegraphs. On the other hand, these demands were not to be pressed so as to endanger "the stability of the present Government or the internal peace and tranquillity of China."[28]

The quest for order was at first undermined, and in two generations destroyed, by the American quest for trade and power. Neither Seward nor any other official could ever discover how to extract extensive concessions from weaker nations without ultimately undermining the order, if not the sovereignty, of that nation. As Americans realized many of Seward's visions for the Caribbean, Pacific, and Asian regions in the post-1893 years, they also faced the dilemma he outlined in September 1868. Indeed, his dilemma became a trap for later Americans. Not able to have both equal opportunity and order in their foreign policies, they chose the former and risked the latter.

In early 1869 the departing Seward had to be content with some

---

27 Seward to Burlingame, April 9, 1866, Instructions, China, NA, RG 59; Paolino, *Foundations,* 171–4.
28 Seward to J. R. Browne, September 8, 1868, Instructions, China, NA, RG 59.

distant islands and Alaska. In November 1867, the House had resolved that it might pass the Alaska purchase appropriation, but "in the present financial condition of the country any further purchases of territory are inexpedient." President Johnson responded in his 1868 annual message: "Comprehensive national policy would seem to sanction the acquisition and incorporation into our Federal Union of the several adjacent continental and insular communities as speedily as it can be done peacefully, lawfully." Seward doubtless wrote those words. In August 1869, after he left office, Seward declared at Salem, Oregon, that expansionism that voluntarily brought in adjoining lands and turned them into "new states" was not only inevitable, but "essential for the security of civil and religious liberty" in the United States. His close friend, and distinguished minister to Great Britain, Charles Francis Adams, drew the appropriate conclusion in his eulogy of the former secretary of state:

The idea of a popular form of government which he had built up in his own mind was one of the most expansive kind. He applied it to our system, and saw at once the means of its development almost indefinitely. . . . In this he was a conservative, that he sought to change, only the better to expand on a wider scale.[29]

All true. The larger question became whether expansion "on a wider scale" might ultimately destroy order and stability rather than be conservative. The more immediate question was how quickly Americans could create the power to realize Seward's visions and test that larger problem. As he left the State Department in 1869, they were well on their way.

29 Seward, *Works*, 5:572; Campbell, *Transformation of American Foreign Relations*, 17; Charles Francis Adams, *Address on the Life, Character and Services of William Henry Seward. Delivered . . . at Albany, April 18, 1873*, Albany, 1873.

2. The Second Industrial Revolution
at Home and Abroad

The basis of U.S. global power in the early twentieth century was economic. From the 1890s on, the nation had emerged as the world's greatest and most competitive player in the marketplace. Fearful Europeans warned of an "American invasion" (an overwhelming offensive of U.S.-made goods and multinationals), long before they worried about the challenge of U.S. military, political, or cultural power. The invasion, moreover, proved deadly not only because of its magnitude but also because it was fueled by a growing crisis inside the United States, which was, ironically, caused by that very economic success. The crisis's depth and disorder marked a historic turning point in the development of both American capitalism and the American empire. The imperial visions of Seward and others who followed the New Yorker were primarily made real not by "large-policy" officials, bureaucratic processes, public opinion, or frustrated Progressive reformers. Those visions were realized by the architects of the Second Industrial Revolution, such as Andrew Carnegie, John D. Rockefeller, Cyrus McCormick, J. P. Morgan, and E. H. Harriman, who redesigned the productive system.

The first Industrial Revolution occurred in late eighteenth-century England, depended on coal, and remained dependent on the old craft system in many respects. The Second Industrial Revolution emerged from new technology produced by inventors such as Alexander Graham Bell and Thomas A. Edison. Certainly electricity profoundly changed the economy's structure. Until the immediate pre–Civil War years, U.S. producers had only three alternatives for turning out more goods: adding more laborers (difficult because of labor scarcity), redistributing work into area homes (difficult over long distances because of primitive communications), or producing more power by finding more water, wood, animal, coal, or wind

21

sources. The engines of the late nineteenth century began to exemplify the possibilities of oil and natural gas. [1]

The key to American economic leadership, however, did not rest only on technology. It required investment, that is, the entrepreneur's ability to tap the incredibly high American savings rates, which had been an impressive 10 to 12 percent of national output in the 1850s but soared to an unbelievable 18 to 20 percent between 1865 and 1914. It also depended on exploiting traditional sources of foreign investment. This amounted to $3 billion in the late 1880s; in the British case alone, it was a net $1.5 billion of investment in the United States between 1870 and 1895. American technology became American power, as Alfred D. Chandler has demonstrated, because citizens decided to invest these monies to obtain cost advantages of scale and scope in production; to create an efficient, targeted marketing system; and to build teams of salaried managers who made the operations work. In Chandler's words, "It was the investment, not the innovation, that transformed the structure of industries and affected the performance of national economies. It was investment that created the new institution – the modern industrial enterprise" of "the second industrial revolution."[2]

The domestic corporation and then, after it made its first significant appearance in the 1880s, the multinational corporation, became the organizations of choice. They could best gather and target needed investment, as well as generate profits and market share that produced future investment. The successful, lonely inventor was rapidly becoming a figure of the past. Edison's laboratory of the 1870s became the General Electric Corporation of 1901 because the corporation could be immeasurably more successful in obtaining capital, political help, and market share both at home and, increasingly, abroad. American universities meanwhile developed schools of engineering and business courses to supply the needs of the new

1 T. Jackson Lears, *No Place of Grace: Antimodernism and the Transformation of American Culture, 1880–1920* (New York, 1981), 8–9; E. J. Hobsbawm, *The Age of Empire, 1875–1914* (New York, 1987), chap. 2.
2 Alfred D. Chandler, Jr., with the assistance of Takashi Hikino, *Scale and Scope* (Cambridge, Mass., 1990), 62–3; Stuart Bruchey, *Enterprise* (Cambridge, Mass., 1990), 311–13.

corporation. And the political parties, led by such men as James G. Blaine and William McKinley, quickly adapted. Those who did not adapt either disappeared (as did the Populists and the Knights of Labor) or lost national power (as did the Democratic party). There was no reason to believe that foreign policy, which is the overseas representation of these domestic interests, would be an exception to' the iron rule of the new corporation.[3]

The rate of change seemed to be accelerating so rapidly that Henry Adams, perhaps the best American mind of the age, worked out theories based on science, mathematics, and productivity to demonstrate that change was not only faster than it had been in Adams's "troglodytic" eighteenth-century Boston but roaring ahead at a faster pace than the sociopolitical system could hope to match. In the America of 1860 no steel and little oil was produced. Forty years later Americans had created a global empire of steel and oil. In 1871 two railroads met at an Alabama crossroads grandly named Birmingham; within thirty years the city's plants exported 300,000 tons of top-quality steel in only six months and successfully competed in markets once dominated by the powerful steelmakers of Birmingham, England. The era began in 1860 with 30,000 miles of U.S. railways (which did amount to half the world's rail mileage) and ended not only with 259,000 miles of railroads but the Wright brothers' airplane as well. Edith Wharton quoted Wilbur Wright saying, "I can conceive that aeroplanes might possibly be of some use in war, but never for any commercial purpose or as a regular means of communication."[4]

The South from Colony to Empire

America of 1865 might have been dominated by isolated, parochial communities, but by 1900 many had been linked by the Second Industrial Revolution. As U.S. officials were putting together a new global empire, these communities were becoming, often unwilling-

3 Mira Wilkins, *The Emergence of the Multinational Enterprise* (Cambridge, Mass., 1970), 68–9; Carroll M. Pursell, Jr., ed., *Technology in America* (Cambridge, Mass., 1981), 3–5.
4 Edith Wharton, *A Backward Glance* (New York, 1934), 319.

ly, part of an international marketplace. The defeated South was among the first to be brought into the revolution. C. Vann Woodward has suggested that during the 1865–77 Reconstruction era, the eleven former Confederate states might "be thought of as so many Latin American Republics simultaneously in the throes of revolution, with the Colossus of the North hovering over them, one of its proconsuls and its military guard in each, and each state with its own ties to the current [United] Fruit or Standard Oil." The proconsul era proved to be relatively short because the South understood that it had to choose one of two paths: "The right fork led to the East and the left fork to the West. . . . The Conservatives and right-fork won in 1877." Rich rewards were reaped for making the right choice. Between 1880 and 1900 the tide of capital investments alone rose from $250 million to $1 billion, worker population doubled, and profits of 22 percent were average.[5]

Before the Civil War the South's cotton exports had made the region a part of the world marketplace, although not the "King" that many southerners assumed. But the story had only begun. During the birth of the U.S. Industrial Revolution in the 1840s, the South had begun its own cotton mill complex. Between 1870 and 1891 production more than doubled in cotton from 4.3 million bales to 9 million. Such fecundity forced the price down from eighteen cents per pound in 1871 to seven cents in 1900. Northern capital flooded in to combine cheap cotton with laborers making twelve cents per day (many of whom were bankrupt tenant farmers forced into the mill towns to survive). The competitiveness allowed owners to exploit new markets in Asia or take old ones away from New England mills. The South so successfully did both that northern mills tried to cut off capital to the South's mills. A Bostonian admitted, "Southern mills are now exporting more cotton fabrics to China than all New England." The post-1873 depression accelerated the export drive, even as (indeed, because) the richly capitalized mills produced more goods, forced prices down, and helped sharpen

5 C. Vann Woodward, "Unfinished Business," in *New York Review of Books,* May 12, 1988, 22; C. Vann Woodward, *Origins of the New South* (Baton Rouge, 1951), 22, 49–50.

the economic downturn. Between 1875 and 1880, exports of U.S. cotton goods increased three times over those of 1871 to 1875. One estimate concluded that about 20 percent of all its manufactures had to be exported if the U.S. cotton-goods industry was to survive. Between 1887 and 1897, as the domestic market agonized under the weight of depression, textile exports to China rose 120 percent. Foreign and domestic policy implications were understood; southern textile representatives, for example, unsuccessfully opposed the 1882 act excluding Chinese immigrants from the United States for ten years because China could cut off imports in retaliation. Congressman Hernando D. Money of Mississippi observed in 1876 that since "the march of empire is westward," and since "every people who have enjoyed Asiatic commerce have grown rich and prosperous," the United States must possess Hawaii as a way station to the Asian markets.[6]

Money talked but James "Buck" Duke acted. The impoverished Duke seized an invention to manufacture cigarettes by a little-known Virginian, James A. Bonsack. He added imagination and capital and, by the mid-1880s, set out to monopolize the tobacco industry as Rockefeller monopolized oil refining. By 1912, Duke had grown so powerful in China's seemingly bottomless cigarette market that both the Chinese government and Japanese competitors declared economic war on him. For textile owners and Duke's American Tobacco Company, exploiting the China market was neither a mirage nor mere rhetoric, but necessary for their prosperity, if not survival.[7]

The South's producers were becoming so dependent on Latin American and Asian customers that the *Chattanooga Tradesman* worried about building too many factories that depended wholly on export trade. Not unnaturally, such southerners as Senator John T.

6 Patrick J. Hearden, *Independence and Empire* (DeKalb, Ill., 1982), 8–14, 25–8, 43–6, 55–8, 60, 66, 89–106; Parker T. Moon, *Imperialism and World Politics* (New York, 1938), 533.

7 Sherman Cochran, "Commercial Penetration and Economic Imperialism in China," in John K. Fairbank and Ernest R. May, eds., *America's China Trade in Historical Perspective* (Cambridge, Mass., 1985), esp. 204–8; William Hesseltine, *A History of the South, 1607–1936* (New York, 1938), 399–411.

Morgan of Alabama led the fight for the building of an isthmian canal (to which Mobile, New Orleans, and other regional ports would have a geographical advantage). Southerners might have had an aversion to the federal government's interference before 1860, but by the 1880s they demanded that Washington provide a canal, a merchant fleet, better diplomatic service, and other amenities necessary for survival in the global marketplace. The *Chattanooga Tradesman,* which spoke for much of the South's business community, was revealing. Latin American "trade is ours by *natural laws,*" it trumpeted in 1888, but then the paper felt it best to buttress God's laws by adding, "and a wise and liberal policy on the part of our government will secure it."[8]

The South actually had a limited ability to help itself. It was poorer per capita in 1880 than in 1860. By 1900 its per capita income was only half the nation's average. It could not accumulate enough capital of its own to keep up with the North. The region's labor was plentiful but terribly poor. The region was thus twice dependent: on the North for the necessary capital to compete, and on Latin American and Asian markets for survival.[9]

International Chattels

The story of the era was told in three sets of figures. One set revealed that in 1860 U.S. imports amounted to $354 million and exports to $316 million, thus producing a deficit balance of merchandise trade. By 1897 imports had doubled to $765 million, but exports more than tripled to $1.03 billion. After 1874, exports surpassed imports every year except 1875, 1888, and 1893, until the turn downward after 1971. Three hundred years of unfavorably balanced American trade reversed course in the 1870s, and the United States headed for world economic supremacy. The second set of figures showed that the U.S. share of world trade was 6 percent in 1868 but 11 percent in 1913. The increase was almost entirely in industrial

8 Bruchey, *Enterprise,* 272–3; Hearden, *Independence and Empire,* 60–2.
9 Edward C. Kirkland, *Industry Comes of Age* (New York, 1961), 278–9; Bruchey, *Enterprise,* 382.

products, so much so that the United States, it was said, had replaced Great Britain as the "workshop of the world." The American invasion, one Britisher wrote, "goes on unceasingly and without noise or show in five hundred industries at once. From shaving soap to electric motors . . . the American is clearing the field." The third set of figures showed that in 1880, 84.3 percent of all goods exported were agricultural, but by 1900 agriculture accounted for only two-thirds of all exports. Again, after three hundred years, the United States was becoming an industrial, urbanized nation, instead of an agrarian one.[10]

Farmers did not go into decline quietly. Between 1870 and 1900 more U.S. land was settled (430 million acres), than in all the previous three hundred years (407 million acres). Mechanization produced gigantic staple-crop farms, such as the wheat-producing facilities encompassing thousands of acres in the Red River Valley area. Between 1870 and 1910 the doubling of the nation's population provided an ever growing market for producers. Yet farmers suffered severely. By the 1890s the Red River Valley giants had virtually disappeared, thousands of farmers left homesteads in the Plains states, farm tenancy and foreclosures reached historic highs. Despite the huge domestic market, 20 percent of agricultural production had to find foreign markets; these markets could be tapped best by highly mechanized and capitalized producers, and even they discovered tough competition from Russian wheat, Latin American wheat and meat producers, and the determination of such imperial powers as Germany and France to become as self-sufficient as possible by subsidizing domestic producers or developing their colonies' agriculture. The ever alert *Chattanooga Tradesman* noted during the depths of the 1893 economic crash that southerners were producing more cotton than ever, but so were Russians, Latin Americans, and Egyptians. The prices of cotton and wheat in particular were not set in New York or Chicago, but in London financial markets. Wheat, as well as cotton, growers in the United States demanded Washing-

10 Bruchey, *Enterprise*, 296–300, 383; James D. Richardson, *A Compilation of the Messages and Papers of the Presidents, 1789–1897*, 10 vols. (Washington, D.C. 1900), 9:739.

ton's help in opening Latin American markets in part because they were trying to pull free of London's hold. The government did little, but in the 1890s it created a bureau in the Department of Agriculture that acted as a clearinghouse for information on foreign markets.[11]

It was, of course, insufficient. The one escape route that had served in the past, moreover, was closing: With the official announcement by the Bureau of the Census in 1890 that the frontier line had finally closed after four hundred years, it dawned on observers that the best and most accessible land was disappearing. Others had long drawn the conclusion. An 1886 article in the widely read *North American Review,* for example, noted the exploding population, the rise of farm tenancy, the similarities of America's problems and ancient Rome's decline (a favorite subject of these years), and lamented, "The pressure has already come. For all practical purposes, the public domain of the United States is now exhausted." Novelist Harold Frederic was more explicit: "Farmer's wives continued to break down and die under the strain, or to be drafted off to the lunatic asylum; the farmers kept hanging themselves in their barns, or flying westward before the locust-like cloud of mortgages; the boys and girls turned their steps townward in an ever-increasing host." Jefferson's ideal farm family seemed to be turning into international chattels.[12]

International Corporations and the Depression

In the 1880s, U.S. multinational corporations began to replace the farmers as players of the most important role in the nation's foreign economic policy. Singer Sewing Machine, Eastman Kodak, McCormick Harvester, the New York Life Insurance Company (which by the 1890s was doing business in fifty-six countries), and Standard Oil were international household names. By 1914, Russia's largest

11 Bruchey, *Enterprise,* 296, 300, 383; *Chattanooga Tradesman,* November 1, 1893, 39.
12 Thomas P. Gill, "Landlordism in America," *North American Review* 142 (January 1886): 60; Lazar Ziff, *The American 1890s* (New York, 1966), 210.

integrated commercial enterprises were Singer Sewing Machine and International Harvester.[13]

Three domestic events turned this stream of the 1880s into the post-1895 flood of American invasion so dreaded by Europeans. The first was the 1890 Sherman Anti-Trust Act, which forbade agreements in restraint of trade. Some of its sponsors hoped the measure would restore competition at home. It instead drove competitors to cut competition by merging. Between 1897 and 1904, not only the greatest corporate merger movement in the nation's history occurred, but these new giants actively moved overseas. A second event was the success of gold standard advocates in ending the bitter debate over silver coinage in the 1890s, and stabilizing the currency on gold. Some Americans had hoped that the British and French would lead an international effort to reach a more inflationary bimetallist (i.e., coinage of more silver) agreement. These efforts collapsed, and when the post-1893 crash threatened American overseas exports and investments, the so-called goldbugs moved. President Grover Cleveland, a Democrat, modified the 1890 Sherman Silver Purchase Act. Then Republican President William McKinley, after triumphing over silverite William Jennings Bryan in the 1896 election, pounded the final golden nail in silver's coffin by passing the Gold Standard Act in 1900. Corporations invested abroad with the certain knowledge that the monetary question had been decided at home, and they could deal with certainty with the other gold standard nations, above all, Great Britain.[14]

The "goldbugs" thus refused to agree that the economic crisis could be solved by manipulating the money supply. They argued instead that the crisis was due to overproduction, and that by finding new overseas markets U.S. producers could maintain their competitiveness and prosper. Very few in government considered using federal authority to redistribute income, especially after 1895 when the Supreme Court killed an attempt to impose an income tax. The

---

13 Wilkins, *Emergence of the Multinational Corporation*, 68–71; Bruchey, *Enterprise*, 386; Thomas C. Owen, "The Population Ecology of Corporations in the Russian Empire, 1700–1914," *Slavic Review* 50 (Winter 1991): 823–4.

14 Wilkins, *Emergence of the Multinational Corporation*, 73; Walter LaFeber, *The New Empire* (Ithaca, 1963), 154–9.

growing consensus around overproduction as the explanation for the crisis led Americans to search for buyers abroad. But to compete abroad required ruthless cost cutting at home. The cycle seemed closed. [15]

Thus appeared the third important influence on the multinationals' development: the twenty-five-year depression itself. This crisis did not cut production. The opposite occurred. In both the farm and industrial sectors production soared until gluts of goods threatened to suffocate the system. Prices steadily fell. If the 1873 price index is taken as 100, it plummeted to 78 by 1890 and 71 by 1896. This decline meant that only the most efficient survived, which meant, in turn, that those with the needed capital to purchase the new technology could produce most cheaply and weather the economic storms. Those storms overhung most of the post-1873 Western industrializing world. Europe's suffering was also due to increased and cheaper productivity, and driving down of prices and the driving out of labor, and intermittent banking scandals that, as in the United States, spiced the era's economic history. In the 1880s alone production of steel doubled in France, tripled in Great Britain, and quintupled in Germany and the United States. Between 1873 and 1886 the world's supply of cotton shot up 50 percent; in 1890–1 the United States alone produced three million more bales than the entire world could consume. As prices sunk in wheat as well as cotton, broken farmers became cheap labor in mills and factories, if they found jobs at all. [16]

Amid this twenty-five years of boom hidden in twenty-five years of bust, the United States rode one of the worst economic crises to the peak of world economic power. The price immediately paid was disorder, indeed the threat of class-driven revolutionary outbreaks, which were previously little known in the United States. The 1870s witnessed the birth of the first American socialist party. Influenced by the Paris Commune of 1871, its organization demonstrated that

15 Key is David A. Wells, as noted in Thomas McCormick, *China Market* (Chicago, 1967), pp. 27–32.
16 Walter Nugent, "Frontiers and Empires in the Late Nineteenth Century," *Western Historical Quarterly* 20 (November 1989): 394; Bruchey, *Enterprise,* 320, 337–8.

not only cotton prices were susceptible to events in the international arena. In 1877 the first general strike threatened the nation. Generated by railway problems, one hundred strikers were killed as the movement spread across West Virginia into the Midwest. The judge in Indianapolis who moved to end the strike was Walter Quintin Gresham. "Our revolutionary fathers . . . went too far with their notions of popular government," Gresham wrote a friend. "Democracy is now the enemy of law and order and society itself and as such should be denounced. I wish Grant was President." (In 1893 Gresham became secretary of state under President Grover Cleveland.) Many others also wanted Grant, a man on horseback, to have a third presidential term and end this "Communism and currency inflation," as one supporter phrased the problem. The crises had merely begun. The Haymarket Riot of 1886, the Homestead strike of 1892, and Cleveland's use of federal troops to break Chicago strikes in 1894 were only the most visible outbreaks of the long depression. [17]

The need to compete in the international marketplace was causing bloodshed in the domestic marketplace. Some reacted after the strikes of the mid-1870s by searching more immediately for armories, which served as fortresses and training grounds for local militias who were to protect the cities' middle class against angry workers and immigrants. As a Cleveland judge said in 1893, the new local armory was to be "an impregnable fortress . . ., a refuge and sanctuary . . ., in times of public commotion."[18] Others, such as Carnegie and Rockefeller, were making the United States the world's leading power while also making such armories necessary.

Carnegie's "Law of Surplus," "Triumphant Democracy," and the Navy

Andrew Carnegie later admitted that he used the 1873 to 1875 depression years to buy cheaply and save 25 percent of his costs when

17 Robert V. Bruce, *1877: Year of Violence* (Indianapolis, 1959), 310–17.
18 Gregory Bush, "Containing the Gilded Age Mob," *Reviews in American History* 19 (March 1991): 48–53.

building the first modern Bessemer steel plant in the United States. By the 1880s, iron and steel's great market, the new railways, was nearly exhausted. Again, however, Carnegie exploited the economic downturn of the 1880s to expand. He found fresh markets in the machine and construction industries and, not least, in the U.S. and foreign navies that were building armor-plated war fleets. Steelmakers also found markets in Russia where the vast Trans-Siberian Railway, as well as the nation's navy, was being built. In 1880 U.S. steel production reached 1.1 million tons, in 1890 4.3 million tons, and ten years later it was 10.1 million.[19]

Carnegie also later admitted that the 1870 tariff, which protected iron and steel producers for the first time, was a major reason why he entered the steel business. The producers gave generously to protectionist politicians, understandably so since observers estimated that the federal government's help gave the steel industrialists added profits of between $7 million and $25 million each year. By 1890, however, the industry had become so efficient that the tariffs began to drop. The focus was shifting. As Carnegie noted in 1895, he now wanted lower tariffs so the United States could obtain cheaper raw materials from countries that would then lower their tariffs for American goods. The tariff policy for the United States was moving into the twentieth century.[20]

Other than discovering how to make money from economic crises and behind tariff walls, Carnegie made another major contribution. He saw that he could be most competitive by systematically integrating his operations vertically so he could control the product from the iron-ore range of Minnesota and the coal of Pennsylvania through the furnaces of Pittsburgh. Such integration and new technology required so much capital and other overhead that these costs could best be paid off by continually running full, or as Carnegie phrased it, "running hard." His "law of surplus" required that his plants "run hard" even when few markets were in sight. Carnegie thus produced more goods, at lower and lower cost, then undersold

---

19 Andrew Carnegie, *The Miscellaneous Writings of Andrew Carnegie*, ed. Burton J. Hendrick (Garden City, N.Y., 1933), 2:31; Bruchey, *Enterprise*, 329.
20 Carnegie, *Miscellaneous Writings*, 1:306.

other competitors in the market. Taking a temporary loss was preferred to closing down the expensive furnaces. Between 1888 and 1898 the largest increase in U.S. exports thus occurred in iron and steel; in 1888 they amounted to $17.7 million and ten years later to $40 million. This 230 percent jump by 1898 also gave Americans a favorable trade balance of $30 million in these goods. Economist Edward Atkinson observed at the end of 1897 that "the portentous event of the year has been the recognition . . . that the paramount dominion in the making of iron and steel has passed from the other side of the Atlantic to this country." The nation that controls the iron and steel markets at the cheapest price, yet pays high wages, Atkinson concluded, "may control the commerce of the world" whenever it decides to follow a freer trade policy.[21]

When the tsar's government began building the Trans-Siberian across Russia in 1892, U.S. steelmakers envisioned limitless markets. By the mid-1890s iron and steel goods were replacing cotton as the most important U.S. export to Russia. Steel rails, Baldwin locomotives, bridges, and cars moved into Siberia as Americans underbid other producers. Count Sergei Witte, the godfather of the Trans-Siberian, grasped the meaning of all this for diplomacy. After nearly a century of friendship, U.S.-Russian relations were cooling, especially as they competed for ascendancy in China. Witte went out of his way to buy American and assure U.S. producers he wanted a good relationship. Carnegie's initiative in the early 1870s was helping to shape the world's power balance by the late 1890s.[22]

In 1886, Carnegie published *Triumphant Democracy,* which argued that his "law of surplus," among other capitalist principles, was as good for democracy as it would become for Russian railroads. The nation's democracy had produced the new industrial revolution, and it, in turn, had provided the wherewithal to reinforce individual freedom. Capitalism produced democracy as well as, and because of, profits. The message reached British thinkers who were mulling over the problem of how to maintain democratic institutions amid

21 *World,* Dec. 12, 1897, 35; Kirkland, *Industry Comes of Age,* 8–11, 172–3.
22 George S. Queen, *The United States and the Material Advance in Russia, 1881–1906* (New York, 1976), 122, 224–5.

their growing empire. They did not want to follow Rome's history of losing liberty to empire. The English Imperial Federation movement of the 1880s believed the United States federal system provided the model. *Libertas et imperium* could be reconciled, it was decided, by "the United States of the Britannic Empire." Or, as one believer declared, "What [Americans] have done, we can do. The Americans are a generation before us in the growth of democracy."[23] Carnegie agreed, although having been born in Scotland, he constantly both condemned the British Empire and warned Americans not to follow the British example of *imperium*. America's democracy appeared to be as seductive as its steel. Of course, Carnegie could argue that they were simply two sides of the same system.

Carnegie was doing well while doing good. He was one of many iron and steel producers, but he usually turned out one-quarter of the nation's product. By the 1890s his works enjoyed a $40 million annual profit. His workers were less happy. They labored around some of the hottest areas on the face of the earth and for twenty-four hours at a time when shifts changed. The horrendous conditions had helped labor organizers build one of the strongest unions in the new American Federation of Labor, at Carnegie's Homestead Plant outside of Pittsburgh. In 1892 the members demanded wages that matched their increased productivity.[24]

Carnegie had always worked with the union, but he was in Scotland and had given his partner, William Clay Frick, full rein. Frick cut wages, forced a strike, built a three-mile-long wall to keep the workers out, brought in "scab" labor, and hired three hundred Pinkerton National Detective agents to protect the strikebreakers. In mid-1892 warfare erupted. Nine Pinkertons and seven laborers died. The state governor sent in the militia to protect the nonunion laborers.[25] The strike was broken and Homestead again abided by

23 Andrew Carnegie, *Triumphant Democracy* (New York, 1886); Raymond F. Betts, "Immense Dimensions: The Impact of the American West on the Late Nineteenth-Century European Thought About Expansion," *Western Historical Quarterly* 10 (April 1979): 154.

24 A. C. Buell to Cramp, January 8, 1892, Papers of Benjamin Tracy, Library of Congress, Washington, D.C.

25 Nell Irvin Painter, *Standing at Armageddon: The United States 1877–1919* (New York, 1987), 110–14.

the law of "running hard." "Triumphant Democracy" appeared less triumphant.

In order to "run full," Carnegie had by 1892 also compromised another of his beliefs. In 1881, the U.S. Navy was a pathetic fleet whose five major ships were a quarter century old and obsolete. Since 1865 British plants had built the world's greatest navy with armorplate as thick as twelve inches. The next year, 1882, Congress appropriated funds to build four modern warships, and, without much prompting, gave preference to domestic steelmakers. (Humorist Finley Peter Dunne, or "Mr. Dooley," later observed that a secretary of the navy's first qualification was that he not have seen saltwater outside of a pork barrel.) Carnegie was of two minds. With a strong pacifist streak, he bragged in *Triumphant Democracy* that the great American power was not military: "Her navy, thank God! is as nothing." When Washington asked him to bid on warship contracts he told his wife he would not do so; she said she was proud of him. After more pressure from the Navy and his steel partners, he decided to make only armor plate, not guns. (He and the partners realized "there may be millions for us in armor.") By 1890 Carnegie was not only taking over contracts earlier given to competition. He was building special plants to produce the world's best armor. He also had placed his own agents in the U.S. Navy Department to give him inside information on construction plans so he could underbid competition. By the 1890s, Carnegie and Bethlehem Iron Works stopped bidding and simply split contracts. He was now producing armor at $175 per ton and selling it to the United States government at $450. Accused of exploiting his adopted homeland (and of selling it some defective goods), Carnegie indignantly refused to bid on contracts in the mid-1890s — at least until the price was right.[26]

He quickly found foreign markets. In 1891 he worked through Secretary of State James G. Blaine to take Russian Navy contracts for armor plate away from the British. By 1898, he was dividing this Russian market, as well as other overseas sales of armor, with friends. The U.S. Navy was not pleased when it heard that Carnegie

---

26 Carnegie, *Triumphant Democracy*, 6; Joseph F. Wall, *Andrew Carnegie* (New York, 1970), 645–54; Daniel R. Headrick, *The Tools of Empire: Technology and European Imperialism in the Nineteenth Century* (New York, 1981), 175.

was selling armor to the Russians for $249 per ton, or about half the price paid by Americans. The steelmaker was unrepentant. As the powers began to build the great fleets that would fight World War I, the profits became so attractive – especially amid the economic crisis of 1893 to 1896 – that Carnegie wanted to begin making gun forgings as well. His partners refused because the profits did not promise to be high enough. Others instead developed the new generation of highly efficient weapons, including rifles and machine guns, that revolutionized warfare and was made possible by the new steelmaking processes.[27]

In 1898–9 Carnegie financed the fight against President McKinley's annexation of the Philippines. In a gesture that was appropriate in fin de siècle America, the steel magnate stormed Washington to offer $20 million to buy the islands himself so he could give them their independence, thus sparing the United States the ignominy of resembling the British Empire. But he by no means opposed expansion. Carnegie accepted the taking of Hawaii. In 1898, he wrote, "I am no 'Little' American, afraid of growth . . . provided always that the new territory be American and that it will produce Americans and not foreign races bound in time to be false to the Republic in order to be true to themselves."[28] Seward would have agreed, not least with the racial views, as he would have applauded the new U.S. war fleet and the conquest of Russia's industrial markets. Seward, however, like McKinley, understood the desirability of having a few well-placed naval bases to safeguard the trip from U.S. factories to Eurasian customers.

Rockefeller's Thirty Years' War

By 1902, the United States produced more iron and steel than Great Britain and Germany combined. Production of primary steel, moreover, was more centralized in the United States than in either Great Britain or Germany. In 1901, Carnegie sold his firm to a combina-

27 Carnegie to Blaine, May 9, 1891, Papers of Andrew Carnegie, Library of Congress, Washington, D.C.; Schwab to Carnegie, March 7, 1898, ibid.; Wall, *Carnegie*, 652–4.
28 Wall, *Carnegie*, 694–5.

tion led by J. P. Morgan who (partly with stock-deal hocus-pocus) put together U.S. Steel, the earth's first billion-dollar corporation. Only John D. Rockefeller's Standard Oil Corporation approached it. Rockefeller developed the industry that first helped light that world of steel, and then fueled the machines, including the modern navies, that Carnegie had helped build. Instead of selling out to a banker, Rockefeller became his own so he could have the resources to compete, especially with Russian oil. For while Carnegie sold to the Russians, Rockefeller was fighting what German authors called the thirty years' war against Russia's powerful financial supporter, the Rothschilds of Paris.

Already the globe's greatest oil refining operation in 1870, Standard's power rested on growing U.S. petroleum production (1 million barrels in 1866, 20 million in 1896), and John D. Rockefeller's ruthless business practices that shaved costs, rationalized production, and drove out competition. In the 1890s Standard still did about 80 percent of the nation's refining. By then, however, its product was changing. As electrification spread over Europe and the United States, the company's primary product, kerosene, found outlets primarily in Asia, especially China. But simultaneously, new engines to drive warships, factory machines, and the automobile demanded oil and gasoline. The engines grew miraculously; the largest at the 1893 Chicago World's Fair had 35 horsepower, but at the Paris Exposition seven years later the largest generated 1,000 horsepower.[29]

From the 1860s to the 1880s, three-quarters of Standard's main product, kerosene, required overseas markets. Rockefeller linked the oil fields to the Atlantic seacoast with pipeline, then concentrated his refining at Bayonne, New Jersey. From there it was shipped, first to Europe (especially Germany and Great Britain into the 1880s), then increasingly to Asia. Petroleum products were the fourth largest U.S. export in value. William Herbert Libby, who after 1878 was Standard's top foreign agent, bragged that petroleum "forced its way into more nooks and corners of civilized and uncivilized countries than any other product in business history emanating from a

29 Allan Nevins, *John D. Rockefeller* (New York, 1959), 197–203.

single source." By the 1890s the refined liquid went to towns and villages from Siam to Sumatra to Borneo to all parts of Latin America and Canada, as well as to Europe, parts of Africa, Japan, and China.[30]

In the 1880s, however, oil began streaming from the Caucasus until by 1891 Russian gushers produced nearly 38 percent of world petroleum. The Nobels of Sweden first organized Russian kerosene production, then the powerful Rothschilds moved in. A fierce battle for the domination of world markets broke out between the French-Russian group and Standard Oil. Rockefeller formed his own marketing companies (instead of depending on independent foreign oil buyers) and tightly run distribution points that spread over Canada, Great Britain, the West Indies, and Germany, among other locales. A huge fleet of tankers was built to speed the product out of Bayonne. In the United States, new, cheaper oil was found and more cheaply refined. By the mid-1890s Standard lost markets in Austria-Hungary, Spain, Turkey, and, of course, Russia, but more than held its own elsewhere.[31]

In the western Pacific theater between 1884 and 1894, U.S. petroleum shipments to Hong Kong and to Australia and New Zealand tripled, and those to Japan rose 50 percent. The fight was difficult, but Standard's Asian operations always made profit, despite the Rothschilds and the Royal Dutch powerhouse that was developing in the East Indies. Americans even profitably bought and sold some Russian kerosene through their marketing arrangements. Libby spent years in China opening up interior markets and combating native vegetable and peanut oil competitors. He was helped by U.S. consuls and other diplomats who were under State Department instruction to clear paths for petroleum sales, especially by getting restrictive ordinances and regulations rescinded. Standard's approach meant that it would use its own worldwide network of company agents to find new markets. Of special importance were

30 R. W. Hidy and M. E. Hidy, *Pioneering in Big Business, 1882–1911* (New York, 1955), 122–4.

31 Worthington C. Ford, "Commerce and Industry Under Depression," *Banker's Magazine and Statistical Register* 50 (March 1895): 481; Hidy and Hidy, *Pioneering*, 130–1, 236–7.

to be the British, French, and Argentine markets. By 1914 Henry Ford had already set up a Model-T assembly plant in Argentina. Standard also used its political network in Washington to help protect these present and potential markets. By 1900, Rockefeller could use his own private diplomatic service, as well as his country's, as he fueled the world's internal combustion engines and lighted the lamps of China.[32]

Disorder and Darwinism

In late 1897, the influential New York *Journal of Commerce* reviewed the decade, noted the enormous growth of the nation's overseas trade, and listed three major causes for that growth: the post-1893 collapse of the home market; the drastic reductions in cost, especially in raw materials and from volume manufacturing rather than using increased labor; and the rapid rise of the manufacturing sector's competitiveness. In 1895, the *Journal of Commerce* had preached that the new industrial revolution made Americans "a part of 'abroad.'" No one could any longer "imagine that we can maintain ourselves in isolation from the rest of the commercial world."[33] Nor could Americans at home remain isolated. Many of the firms that used railways to invade towns with the products of the new technology were also the firms that were carrying out a commercial invasion as well in towns and cities globally.

The era's capitalism built a new world order, but it was in reality horrifying, disordered, wasteful, and destructive. Sir Lowthian Bill, a British steelmaker, could not believe his eyes when he saw the Pittsburgh furnaces: the "recklessly rapid rate of driving" them so their interiors were wrecked about every three years; workers, few of whom lasted beyond their fortieth birthday, who were similarly driven and burned out.[34] In its way, the destruction in the roaringly successful steel industry was the counterpart of the destruction suf-

32 *Bradstreet's*, February 24, 1893, 116; Hidy and Hidy, *Pioneering*, 137, 153, 267–8; Bruchey, *Enterprise*, 385.
33 *Journal of Commerce*, December 11, 1897, 6; ibid., January 22, 1895, 4.
34 Wall, *Carnegie*, 638–40.

fered by tens of thousands of farmers in the South and the Plains states whose soil eroded, markets disappeared, and banks foreclosed in the 1880s and 1890s.

The capitalism that shaped late nineteenth- and early twentieth-century America cared much less about order than it did profit and market share. As Homestead's bloodshed demonstrated, "the law of surplus" and "running hard" at the cheapest cost proved of greater importance to Frick and Carnegie than order and labor peace. To survive the economic depression that haunted the post-1873 years, and to survive the kind of cutthroat competition in the international marketplace that was waged by Carnegie against British steel, Rockefeller against Russian oil, and southern textile owners against New England manufacturers required not order, but cheap labor, cheap capital, and hard-driving managers. The United States produced all three in abundance; it thus became the world's leading economic power while enduring two decades of labor riots and massive dislocations.

Such an understanding of this generation's priorities helps explain as well two myths that shaped the thought of the era, but not the actual politics, economics, or diplomacy: the myth of laissez-faireism and the myth of social Darwinism. Nowhere, not even in Carnegie's Scottish castle, was the laissez-faire myth stronger than in the South. As C. Vann Woodward wrote of the era, "Laissez faire became almost a test of Southern patriotism." Given the South's bitter experience with the Washington-imposed Reconstruction measures, the feeling was understandable. But the same belief permeated the North's views as well, as illustrated by the group of business people and educators who in 1880 organized the Society of Political Education to fight "the growing tendency of government to enlarge its sphere."[35] Carnegie and Rockefeller doubtless added "amen" to such sentiments. The reality, however, was subtler. The largest and best capitalized industrialists could set up their own assured capital supply, create their own foreign service corps to seek out markets and remove political obstacles, and even hire their own

---

35 Woodward, *Origins of New South*, 65–6; Edward C. Kirkland, *Dream and Thought in the Business Community, 1860–1900* (Ithaca, 1956), 132–3.

riot forces. Even Carnegie, however, had to manipulate the tariff for his own interest. So did Standard Oil. In 1894 and 1897 tariff legislation, Congress added provisions that retaliated against nations that discriminated against U.S. petroleum exports.[36]

Earlier, the Interstate Commerce Commission, as well as the Sherman Anti-Trust Act and Sherman Silver Purchase Act, had carefully written loopholes; all three had been formulated by officials who had listened closely to industrial representatives. This primitive form of interest-group politics demonstrated how even the most powerful corporations had to deal with government.

Often they directly demanded that the government come in, not stay out. The smaller firms required, and usually asked for, extensive government intervention. The National Association of Manufacturers (NAM) was organized in 1894–5 to advance American exports, especially to Latin America. It became a major lobbyist for its hundreds of small firms who banded together for collective clout in Washington. Even the giants, however, needed direct government intervention, as Standard illustrated when it used U.S. consuls to spy on Russian oil production. And both the small and large firms increasingly demanded that the government settle the money question, build an isthmian canal, upgrade the diplomatic service, and, in some instances, use the fleet or annex outlying bases to protect economic interests. When the NAM was accused of depending on the government, the organization responded that the government was, after all, "the servant of the people."[37]

An effective foreign policy requires centralization. The apparent paradox of the late nineteenth century was that as American society became more disorderly, the federal government became more orderly and centralized. The paradox is only apparent. As disorder spread after 1873, corporate leaders urged stronger action, especially at the executive level, to arrest troublemakers at home, and to help remove the riots' causes by helping business find markets abroad. The changing interrelationships of business and foreign policy began to

36 Hidy and Hidy, *Pioneering*, 235.
37 Albert K. Steigerwalt, "The National Association of Manufacturers: Organization and Policies, 1895–1914" (Ph.D., University of Michigan, 1953), 24, 32–7, 41–2, 51–3.

change as well the balance of power within the U.S. governmental system. Young Henry Adams had accurately forecast the changes as he looked about the United States in 1870: "Under the conditions of 50 years, when the United States was a mere child among nations, and even before railways and telegraphs had concentrated the social and economic forces of the country into a power never imagined by past generations, a loose and separately responsible division of government suited the stage of national growth. . . . All indications now point to the conclusion that this system is outgrown."[38]

The ideology tried to keep up with these changes. The 1865 to 1900 era, bound at one end by Karl Marx's *Das Kapital* and Charles Darwin's *Descent of Man,* and at the other by the writings of James and Freud, had an intellectual ferment unsurpassed by other 35-year periods. American "manifest destiny" remained a ringing cry, but now it was proclaimed by the *Age of Steel* journal in regard to export trade rather than, as in the 1840s, by "Young America" expansionists who demanded taking all of Mexico. Even President Ulysses S. Grant no doubt stunned French officials in 1870 when he congratulated them on establishing the Third Republic, then added, "We cannot be indifferent to the spread of American political ideas in a great and highly civilized country like France."[39] Others, including some Populists and Socialists and individuals such as Mark Twain and Theodore Dreiser, were not as certain about those ideas.

One set of ideas, however, engaged many Americans. Social Darwinism was the loose application of Charles Darwin's theories to the socioeconomic world. Herbert Spencer helped popularize this deviant Darwinism in his British homeland. From the 1880s to World War I, frequent travel by the American social and intellectual elite, and intermarriage between U.S. and British families, created networks for the transmission of ideas such as Spencer's. Social Darwinism and its belief in evolutionary social-economic progress took hold in the United States far more than elsewhere. After all, Americans were more successful economically than those who lived elsewhere

38 Henry Adams, "The Session," *North American Review* 41 (July 1870): 60–2.
39 *Age of Steel,* August 25, 1888, 6; Gordon Wood, "Americans and Revolutionaries," *New York Review of Books,* September 27, 1990, 35.

on the globe, and to have this success explained by such terms as "survival of the fittest" seemed to provide evidence of the blessings of nature and the goddess of inevitability.

Carnegie was among the many who liked social Darwinism. It reinforced his belief in progress and reaffirmed that his capitalist order was a natural improvement over the past. It also neatly protected property by urging a reliance on evolution rather than revolution. In his powerful, highly influential paper "The Significance of the American Frontier," presented at the Chicago World's Fair amid the 1893 economic downturn, Frederick Jackson Turner of the University of Wisconsin explained four hundred years of American success by arguing that "in this progress from savage conditions [on the frontier] lie topics for the evolutionist." The best-known American popularizer of Darwin and Spencer was John Fiske, a first-rate lecturer who traveled across the country preaching the third-rate history that he had written. In such essays as "Manifest Destiny" (1885), Fiske directly linked U.S. commercial success overseas to the spread of American ideology and, thus, the triumph of peace, especially in Europe: "The victory of the industrial over the military type of civilization will at last become complete." Evolutionary progress, which to Fiske was much the same thing as U.S. economic supremacy, required such a victory.[40]

When the historian tries to use social Darwinism as an analytical tool, however, it disintegrates. Captain Alfred Thayer Mahan, the most noted U.S. naval strategist and historian of the era, also, like Fiske, used social Darwinian terms and pondered the meanings of U.S. economic prowess abroad. But he came to the opposite conclusion: Economic expansion led to conflict, which led to war (and, not surprisingly, in Mahan's formulation the need for a large navy). Other social Darwinians, such as William Graham Sumner, were more rigorous in their thinking than either Fiske or Mahan; they disliked any manifest destiny appeals because they produced war, which in turn produced territorial annexation, large navies, and big

40 Robert McCloskey, *American Conservatism in the Age of Enterprise* (Cambridge, Mass., 1951), 159–60; Frederick Jackson Turner, *The Frontier in American History* (New York, 1947); John Fiske, *American Political Ideas Viewed from the Standpoint of Universal History* (New York, 1885), 148–51.

government – all of which they deplored. Even those who liked to think of themselves as social Darwinians often deviated from the amorphous faith. Carnegie, for example, and Rockefeller believed too much in free will and individual initiative to wait for, or necessarily trust, evolution. When they, Fiske, and others such as Mahan and Josiah Strong appealed to social Darwinism, they often used it as a cover for appealing to race. The popularizers especially found elite audiences, already attached by blood or tradition to Great Britain, willing to agree with generalizations about an Anglo-Saxon–determined future. And there were few recorded appeals to other races or ethnic groups. Fiske even advertised himself as the direct descendant of King Alfred.[41]

Racism and a belief in progress had deep roots in U.S. history, not least in its foreign policy. Social Darwinism gave the patina of science and modernity to feelings that were unscientific and ahistorical. Those who professed this useful form of sociopolitical rationalization found it useful precisely because, by supposedly explaining Anglo-Saxon dominance in terms of specific, historic evolutionary stages, it imposed order on disorderly racism. These leaders of the era from 1865 to 1912 searched for some rationale to justify the disorder they were causing, and the argument that they were raising society to a new and better stage seemed to be about as good a rationale as they could find.[42] Fiske ended one popular lecture with the inevitable U.S. ideological triumph, "a world covered with cheerful homesteads, blessed with a sabbath of perpetual peace."[43] It was his popular version of the end of history. Unfortunately, the future of American foreign policy was to have more to do with its past roots than with Fiske's illusions.

41 A.T. Mahan, "The United States Looking Outward," in *The Interest of America in Sea Power, Present and Future* (Boston, 1897), 18; John Higham, *Strangers in the Land* (New Brunswick, N.J., 1955), 32–3.

42 This draws from Robert Hannigan's unpublished paper "Race, Gender, and Social Class in the Ideology of American Foreign Policy, 1898 to World War I" (1991), in author's possession.

43 Fiske, *American Political Ideas,* 151–2.

3. Race for Empire

The American population is a mosaic, a people whose makeup can resemble the world with which it deals in foreign policy. Between the Civil War and World War I the mosaic became so pronounced, and the number of immigrants so enormous, that a historic turn was reached in the 1880s when, for the first time in the nation's life, legislation excluded certain immigrants (in this case, Chinese). The exclusionary act was shaped by the economic downturn, but also by a deep-seated racism that, while it excluded some Asians, led to the lynching of numbers of Asians and African Americans in the 1880s and 1890s. It also melded with chaotic and tragic economic conditions in the West to produce a series of wars waged by the U.S. Army against Indians. With the ending of those wars, force had succeeded in consolidating non-Indian control of the continent.[1] Militant laborers and angry farmers only remained to pose a domestic threat to order after 1890. This consolidation of the continent, training of military force, contradictory feelings about immigrants, and, above all, racism not only characterized these late nineteenth-century decades but were central in shaping U.S. foreign policy then and in the new century.

"Give Me Your . . . Huddled Masses Yearning to Breathe Free"

With their Civil War triumph, Union supporters believed the immigrant was to confirm the American future. "Europe will open her gates like a conquered city," the *Chicago Tribune* announced at the end of the war. "Her people will come forth to us subdued by

1 Nell Irvin Painter, *Standing at Armageddon: The United States 1877–1919* (New York, 1987), 162.

admiration of our glory and envy of our perfect peace." Recent expansionism was also to be confirmed. At the same time Europe was to be drained of many of its people, "on to the Rocky Mountains and still over to the Pacific our mighty populations will spread. . . . Our thirty millions will be tripled in thirty years."[2]

Between 1870 and 1910, indeed, nearly 20 million foreigners came to the United States. Europeans did predominate (it is notable that the *Tribune* did not say Asia or Africa "will open her gates"), especially eastern Europeans, Germans, Irish, and British. Canadians (particularly in 1880–3) and Chinese (in the 1873–82 years) also entered in large numbers. The road was not one-way. Between 1898 and 1914, about 1 million Americans left the Plains states for wheat-growing western Canada in order to escape the collapse in the United States of both agricultural prices and radical agrarian political movements in which many of the emigrants believed. Such emigration formed part of an enormous movement of people out of economically depressed areas of the Western world. In the 1880s alone, 5 million Europeans went to the United States, 900,000 to Canada, and 500,000 to Brazil. Restrictions and travel costs were seldom again to be as low, and these, plus economic dislocations, began to change the complexion of the United States.[3]

At first the incoming masses seemed to reaffirm the manifest destiny of the future United States empire. "We are the Romans of the modern world," Oliver Wendell Holmes declared, "the great assimilating people." Expansionists of the social Darwinian persuasion were pleased to hear Herbert Spencer reassure them that "biological truths" assured Americans a great race because of their attraction to immigrants. Some skeptics on both sides of the Atlantic were less sure. In mid-1898, Andrew Carnegie strongly urged President William McKinley to read an editorial by the British periodical, the *Spectator.*

---

2 John Higham, *Strangers in the Land* (New Brunswick, N.J., 1955), 14.
3 Gabriel Kolko, *Main Currents in Modern American History* (New York, 1976), 28–9; Walter Nugent, "Frontiers and Empires in the Late Nineteenth Century," *Western Historical Quarterly* 20 (November 1989): 396.

The future of the world [the editorial began] will depend greatly upon the political character of Americans. When in 1950 they are two hundred millions, and have absorbed as they will absorb the swarms of immigrants whose presence now makes Continentals doubt – except just after a great sea fight – whether Americans are Englishmen, their purposes . . . will be to all mankind matter of the gravest moment. They will be able if much stirred to crush any single people, except perhaps the Slavs.

The problem was how to get from 1898 to 1950 without having "difficulties," including "dependencies."[4] Absorption of immigrants seemed difficult enough, the journal inferred; multiracial dependencies might be too much.

As for the "Slavs," even they were flooding out of the Tsar's empire to the United States, especially after Alexander II's reforms ended with his assassination in 1881, and a terrible backlash, including pogroms, began to sweep across Russia. Between 1880 and 1914 more than 3 million Russian citizens came to the United States. Most, especially Jews and Roman Catholics, belonged to ethnic and religious minorities. One such minority was the Mennonites, superb farmers who left the Ukraine, after turning it into the breadbasket of Russia, because the tsar insisted in 1871 that they join the military. Nearly 20,000 of this pacifist sect settled in the American Great Plains, sowed seeds they had brought with them from the old country, and so began the winter wheat crop that made the region, especially Kansas, prosperous.[5]

By the later 1880s not all Americans saw the bright side of such migration. More than one-quarter of the population had now been born in foreign nations, and increasingly those nations were not Great Britain or Scotland. The American Protective Association organized to advance the argument that it was time, if not past time, for immigration restriction because racially Americans could no longer be improved upon. There was also growing concern that

4 Higham, *Strangers in the Land,* 19–23; Carnegie to McKinley, July 27, 1898, Papers of George Cortelyou, Library of Congress, Washington, D.C.
5 Robert V. Daniels, *Russia: The Roots of Confrontation* (Cambridge, Mass., 1985), chaps. 1–2. Henry Graff, *America: The Glorious Republic* (Boston, 1985), 437.

the newcomers could be less easily absorbed than the old mainline Protestant emigrants, and that they held communal beliefs suspiciously resembling the growing European socialist movements'. As the American Federation of Labor formed in the mid-1880s, it included many immigrants, but it and other unions were concluding logically that if many more like them swarmed into the labor market, higher wages and better conditions would not result.

Voices of the nation's newer, highly successful industries agreed with the unions, although for different reasons. As a congressional report concluded in 1886, the last acre on the frontier "worth taking for a home by a farmer" will soon be "disposed of." Amid the depression-caused general strikes and riots, moreover, it was difficult enough to keep the present number employed and law-abiding, let alone millions of newcomers who understood neither the criminal law nor Carnegie's "law of surplus." The *Age of Steel* believed that it spoke for its booming sector in a column that argued the European "penitentiary and the poor house . . . were vomiting their surplus bile into the Atlantic basin; and Sandy Hook [at the entrance to New York City's harbor] was becoming the slop pail of the globe."[6]

Few of these antiimmigrant sentiments meant that Americans were becoming isolationist. To the contrary, ardent expansionists believed a more homogeneous, Protestant, and Anglo-Saxon America could best fulfill its global manifest destiny. Josiah Strong's *Our Country* (1885), combined nativist beliefs with overseas economic and cultural expansionism to become a best seller and a reference point for later Americans. James G. Blaine, the leading Republican of the 1880s and an ardent expansionist, especially in the realm of international trade, worked vigorously against allowing in any more "cheap labor," especially from Asia, even as he planned U.S. economic domination of the entire hemisphere through a Pan-American movement. Within fifteen years, Seward's antinativist belief that the nation's development, and ideals, required easy entry of all peoples,

6 Morrell Heald, "Business Attitudes Toward European Immigration, 1880–1900," *Journal of Economic History* 13 (Summer, 1953): 291–304; *Congressional Record*, 49th Cong., 1st Sess. (July 31, 1886), 7830–1.

including Asians, suddenly belonged to the past, not the present or the future.[7]

The era had begun with the *Chicago Tribune* opening gates, and the era, as well as the gates, began to close in 1886 when, ironically, the Statue of Liberty was dedicated in ceremonies that had not one reference to Emma Lazarus's poem of 1883: "Give me your tired, your poor, Your huddled masses yearning to breathe free." The speakers instead discussed the glories of American liberty spreading throughout the rest of the world.[8]

"The Right of Character, Intelligence . . . to Rule"

The Statue of Liberty's dedication began the most violent peacetime decade in American history to that point. The violence was especially generated by racism and centered on African Americans who were fully segregated, with the Supreme Court's agreement, by 1896. Segregation, however, did not save thousands who were lynched during this era. In the 1890s, white Americans lynched an average of one African American every two and a half days. The 162 lynchings of 1892 marked the historic high. (Sixty-two whites were also lynched by mobs.) Some 8 million blacks were systematically excluded from voting and holding office; George White's (R.-N.C.) departure in 1901 marked the last time a southern African American would sit in Congress until the arrival of Andrew Young (D.-Ga.) in 1967. The great abolitionist and journalist, Frederick Douglass, had been honored by four Republican presidents for his work among his fellow blacks, but as minister to Haiti in 1891 he was fired by President Benjamin Harrison for not showing sufficient enthusiasm for U.S. imperialistic ventures in the black Caribbean nation. The debates over the rise of the post-1890 American century were virtually empty of black people's voices.[9]

7 James G. Blaine, *Political Discussions, Legislative, Diplomatic, and Popular, 1856–1886* (Norwich, Conn., 1887), 216–35.

8 Higham, *Strangers in the Land*, 14, 63.

9 Howard Smead, "The Mysterious 1890s," *Washington Post*, November 1, 1987, C5; Albert T. Volwiler, ed., *The Correspondence Between Benjamin Harrison and James G. Blaine, 1882–1893* (Philadelphia, 1940), 81.

It had not begun this way in the 1860s, when Radical Republicans tried to ensure the rights of African Americans, as well as Republican power, in the South. The end of Reconstruction and the return of the South's conservative "Redeemers" to power in the late 1870s marked a turn. Paternalism over African-American rights flourished for a while in the 1880s, but as the Reverend Henry M. Field argued in 1890 after a long trip through the South, paternalism was doomed in a society so full of faith in laissez-faire individualism. As economic depression, racism, and the pressures of white politics drove the section (and nation) to segregation, a social Darwinian argument reinforced the injustice. The census of 1880 seemed to show that southern blacks were increasing in number more rapidly than whites. If, as the social Darwinians argued, high birth rates were the key to deciding which races were to survive, whites were in trouble. They began to demand more segregation and, most notably, shipping blacks to overseas colonies – a solution to the race problem seriously advanced by earlier Americans from James Madison through Abraham Lincoln. Because these colonialists usually eyed Central America and West Africa, the effects on foreign relations could have been profound. In 1890 and 1900, however, the censuses concluded the numbers of blacks were decreasing, not increasing, proportionally to whites. Walter F. Wilcox, who directed the 1900 census, drew the conclusions: African Americans were to follow the fate of Indians because the effects of "disease, vice, and profound discouragement" on these "lower people" condemned them to have ever smaller numbers in the United States.[10] This view, resting racial superiority on social Darwinian categories and doubtful statistics, also influenced U.S. foreign policy, not least in Hawaii, the Philippines, and the Caribbean.

After eleven Italian immigrants were lynched in New Orleans in 1891 and the Italian government bitterly protested, legislation was introduced in Congress outlawing lynching – of aliens. Except for some northern Republicans, few others were as concerned about African Americans. Racial problems were not limited to the South

10 George Fredrickson, *The Black Image in the White Mind, 1817–1914* (New York, 1971), 208–10, 238–40, 245–6, 251–2, 263–4, 323–4.

or, of course, to lynchings. Even as lynchings decreased to around eighty in 1905, race riots occurred in New York as well as North Carolina; Springfield, Illinois (Lincoln's home); and Atlanta (the seat of the so-called New South). Against this background, an idea of "the white men's burden" shaping U.S. foreign policy took on a particular connotation of white paternalism, which, if rejected, or unsuccessful, led easily to the use of force. Theodore Roosevelt believed at times that he was a benevolent imperialist. Just as he liked the accommodationist racial programs at home of Booker T. Washington and Edgar Gardner Murphy, Roosevelt liked to think that, given time and guidance, the Caribbean and Filipino peoples (at least those he saw as the better middle-class, urban residents) could also begin to rise through the stages to civilization. If such improvement did not occur, especially if not rapidly enough to suit Roosevelt's hyperactive temperament, he espoused the use of force. [11]

The rubbery qualities of racism and social Darwinism were remarkable. A leading spokesman of the "New South," Henry Grady of Atlanta, declared that white supremacy was merely the "right of character, intelligence, and property to rule." His definition neatly placed many poor whites, as well as blacks, among the ruled rather than the rulers. [12] Grady's phrase also anticipated some of the arguments Americans later used to justify their new foreign policies, much as they had used similar phrases in defining their manifest destiny to exterminate Indians and Mexicans before 1860. In pivotal areas of foreign policy, the "New South" sounded like the old America. The overlays of social Darwinianism and an industrializing South (and North) did not hide the traditional racism (and, as Grady indicated, the class discrimination) that lay beneath.

Along with the African Americans and Indians, Chinese immigrants were given a close-up look at this racism. Some 63,000 Chinese were in the United States, with 50,000 concentrated in California, even before the 1868 treaty allowed unrestricted numbers of Chinese laborers to enter the country. Episodes of beatings, even of Chinese being stoned to death by whites in California, were

11 Ibid., 273–5, 309.
12 Ibid., 203.

already known. As tens of thousands more entered to work, especially on railroads, the depression struck and railroad building slowed. When violence and anti-Chinese feelings grew, the Grant administration did little, but in 1879 Congress moved to reduce Chinese immigration. President Rutherford B. Hayes vetoed the bill because it was inconsistent with the 1868 treaty. An 1880 Sino-American treaty allowed the reduction, but not the prohibition, of the immigration. In the Exclusion Act of 1882, Congress suspended all immigrant labor, skilled and unskilled, entering from China for ten years. It was not enough, amid the economic bad times and growing labor union movement, to protect the Chinese. Twenty-eight Chinese miners were murdered in Wyoming in 1885, and California politicians especially coined votes from anti-Oriental feelings. In the 1888 Scott Act, Congress unilaterally not only excluded all Chinese laborers but refused reentry to any who had temporarily left to visit families in Asia. When the Chinese minister sent a string of bitter protests that the act violated earlier treaties, the State Department refused to answer. The Geary Act of 1892 finally indefinitely prohibited Chinese laborers' immigration. One irony was telling. Americans had for a half century and more demanded rights in China and had obtained them. The Chinese demanded rights in the United States and were refused. The difference was that Americans had not only racial and political rationales but also the gunboats to enforce them.[13]

Some Americans did protest this historic reversal in immigration policies and its support by superior force. Voices from the South's cotton mill areas opposed both the 1882 act and the 1892 extension. As Senator John T. Morgan (D.-Ala.) declared in 1892, it would be "a very unwise step to put China into an attitude where she would break up commercial relations with us." He and the millowners, however, were henceforth going to have to trust to diplomacy and force, not commonly agreed upon interests, to keep Chinese markets open. Mark Twain's large public learned that he not only condemned

13 Warren Cohen, *America's Response to China*, 2d ed. (New York, 1980), 35–8; Chester L. Barrows, *William M. Evarts* (Chapel Hill, 1941), 380-1; Alice Tyler, *The Foreign Policy of James G. Blaine* (Minneapolis, 1927), chap. 10.

the treatment of African Americans (his wife said Twain might get along better if he would "consider everybody colored till he is proved white,") but also defended Chinese rights in California. Twain was increasingly isolated and embittered in the 1890s as the United States rolled on toward becoming one of the great world powers by subjugating nonwhite peoples. Twain had brought in the post-1882 era with his bittersweet classic, *Huckleberry Finn*, in which Huck finds freedom, and escapes the clutches of civilization, when he decides to "light out for the territory ahead of the rest." By the end of the 1880s, after the slaughter of Chinese in Wyoming and labor protesters and Chicago police in the 1886 Haymarket Riot, Twain published *A Connecticut Yankee in King Arthur's Court*. The Yankee inventor, whom Twain privately said was a fool even if a genius with technology, discovers there is no more open "territory" and ends up using his skill with machinery to kill 25,000 people. The Second Industrial Revolution, Twain seemed to be saying, only had limited means for restoring order amid the chaos and opposition it had created.[14]

"The Spread of the English-speaking People over the . . . Waste Spaces"

American military technology created chaos and then imposed the orderliness of death over much of the West between 1865 and 1890. The relationship between this death and the death of Philippine and Cuban independence movements in 1899–1902 may have been accidental. Or the relationship may have been merely ironic or perhaps even one of those rarely glimpsed historical causes. However one characterizes the relationship, U.S. military forces consolidated white power over the entire country by destroying the last major Indian opposition in the late 1880s, and in the late 1890s white Americans were using this continental empire as a base from which

14 Patrick J. Hearden, *Independence and Empire* (DeKalb, Ill., 1982), 57-8; Mark Twain, *A Connecticut Yankee in King Arthur's Court* (1889; reprint, New York, 1960), 302; R. E. Spiller et al., eds., *Literary History of the United States* (New York, 1948), 932.

to create a new empire of commerce and insular possessions in the Caribbean and across the Pacific Ocean. The apparent triumph in one empire led to the attempt almost immediately to create another.

In this sense, of course, Seward, Greeley, Blaine, and other post–Civil War leaders misled when they claimed that they wanted no more land. Throughout the 1860s to 1880s they ordered their military forces to fight a series of wars to conquer lands west of the Missouri-Arkansas frontier claimed by the Indians. Reluctant Mexicans and Canadians were spared the fate of post-1865 landed manifest destiny, but not native Americans. Some 360,000 of these people lived beyond the Mississippi River in 1850 while about 1.4 million white Americans lived there on the eve of the Civil War. Thirty years later, the number of the latter had soared nearly six times to 8.5 million (some Indians admitted they had not known so many whites existed); in the first decade of the twentieth century, all the Indians in the United States numbered only 265,000. [15]

Patricia Nelson Limerick has argued that the word frontier, in this context, is an "Anglo-centered concept." Such "Turnerian history" led to "flattening and distorting the complexity" of the American West and pushed "minority people . . . to the edge of significance." It can be further argued that to study this West in the post-1865 years without tying it to post-1890s foreign policy – and vice versa – is also flattening and distorting the era. The relationships are many. Constitutionally, for example, early U.S. treaties defined the Indian tribes as nations, but by 1835 these people were considered "subject" to Washington's "dominion and control," and by 1871 the Supreme Court took the final step by declaring that Congress could override the old treaties by passing new laws. In the decade after the 1898 war, the Court, in the Insular Cases, similarly gave Congress virtually a blank check to pass laws governing the new colonial possessions. As Protestant missionaries intended to "civilize" the Indians by converting them from native religions to Christianity, so missionaries intended to "civilize" native Hawaiians

---

15 U.S. Department of Commerce, *Historical Statistics of the United States* (Washington, D.C., 1961), 9; Painter, *Standing at Armageddon,* 163; Robert M. Utley, *The Indian Frontier of the American West, 1846–1890* (Albuquerque, 1984), 1, 4.

or even Filipinos (many of whom were Roman Catholic). And as officials discovered that with the Dawes Severalty Act of 1887 they could force the Indians to switch from communal ownership to individual ownership and thus enable whites to buy thousands of acres of lands from puzzled or bankrupt Indians, so land policies in Hawaii, the Philippines, and the Caribbean gave white Americans and their political allies both land and leverage. This post–Civil War generation understood the power created by redistributing, or not redistributing, property. For example, while breaking up Indian lands for the benefit of white settlers, U.S. officials destroyed the hope of freedmen and yeomen farmers in the South to be more self-sufficient by not redistributing plantation lands. Americans' acute sensitivity to enormous power inherent in land redistribution, whether in the South, the Philippines, Cuba, or Central America in the late twentieth century, is a story needing to be told.[16]

Of special importance, the final post-1860 wars waged against the Indians removed, in white Americans' eyes, an internal enemy. Washington meanwhile maintained the small U.S. Army as one of the world's most experienced and efficient. Technology played an important role. Using the railroads and modern rifles, sharpshooters, or just sportsmen who killed for the supposed thrill, methodically destroyed the buffalo herds on which nomadic Plains Indians depended.[17]

The one stunning detour in this path to continental empire occurred during the nation's centennial celebration. General George Armstrong Custer's Seventh Cavalry of 260 men had been stationed in the upper Plains to prevent Indians from harassing the railroad builders. On June 25, 1876, Custer and his men were surrounded and exterminated at Little Bighorn in southern Montana by 2,000 Sioux and Cheyenne warriors who had better technology. The Indians used forty-one different kinds of firearms including sixteen-shot

16 Patricia Nelson Limerick, "A Panel of Appraisal," *Western Historical Quarterly* 20 (August 1989): 317; Walter L. Williams, "United States Indian Policy and the Debate over Philippine Annexation . . .," *Journal of American History* 66 (March 1980): 810–31.
17 William T. Hagan, *The Indian in American History* (Washington, D.C., 1971), 15–17.

repeating rifles. Whites, who thought the tribes had accepted the orders of "civilization," returned to an earlier view of the race. The *Chicago Tribune* headlined, "HORRIBLE! THE AMERICAN INDIAN EXALTS HIS REPUTATION FOR SATANIC FEROCITY." The army killed, or forced into reservations, or – as in the case of one of Custer's conquerors, Crazy Horse – allowed popular Wild West shows to exploit the Indians. Every significant war during the era was caused by Indians rebelling against being forced into controlled reservations.

In 1886 the Apache leader, Geronimo, was forced to surrender. The next year Indians still held 187 million acres of land. Then came the Dawes Act and, in 1889, the opening of 3 million acres of their land in the present state of Oklahoma. By 1900, all the Indians controlled only 78 million acres. The last major killing had occurred ten years before when President Benjamin Harrison broke the nation's treaties and opened Sioux territory in South Dakota to settlement. The tribes, devastated by illness and starvation, had turned to mystical religions, including a "Ghost Dance" that promised freedom from the white man. In January 1890, U.S. Army units surrounded the Wounded Knee settlement, and when guns were accidentally fired, the troops poured shot into the encampment. One hundred forty-six men, women, and children of the Sioux were killed.[18]

Colonel Nelson A. Miles had led the U.S. Army in the West after Custer's defeat, and he commanded the troops who dealt with the "Ghost Dance" tragedy in 1890. In the 1898 war, this most successful of Indian fighters led the triumphant U.S. Army against Spain. Three times in American history, a major U.S. military force had been wiped out, each time by Sioux. But the military learned. In the late 1880s the 25,000 soldiers and 2,000 officers were called, man for man, the best in the world by Lord Wolseley, the commander in

18 Robert M. Utley, *Cavalier in Buckskin* (Norman, Okla. 1988), 111–14, 171–92; Robert A. Trennert, "Populist Imagery and the American Indian: A Centennial View," *New Mexico Historical Review* 51 (July 1976): 215–29; *Washington Post*, December 29, 1986, A3.

chief of the British army. The force had been disciplined by decades of fierce Indian fighting.[19]

The chaos and bloodshed of these wars belied eastern propaganda about the West in the 1880s — "the garden of the world," as one publication had it. Certainly it was no garden to the one-half of western Kansas's population forced off the land by weather and low prices in the late 1880s. One Indian fighter, General George Crook, tried to describe what occurred, and explain especially the bloodshed, unrest, and disorder that plagued the West in the late nineteenth century, when he declared that "greed and avarice on the part of the whites — in other words the almighty dollar — is at the bottom of nine-tenths of all our Indian troubles."[20]

The newly consolidated West became a cockpit of post-1890s expansionism. Its most famous historian, Frederick Jackson Turner, believed that the "stronghold of these demands" to extend "American influence to outlying islands and adjoining countries" was "west of the Alleghenies." Especially strong support for the 1898 war came from the western regions of Populist radicalism and free-silver demands, where, historians have suggested, the rebellion that shaped these movements was transferred with little difficulty to opposing Spanish colonialism. The link between that political discontent in a closed West and the demand for overseas expansion had actually been made as early as 1881 when diplomatic troubleshooter and trade expert John Kasson wrote publicly, "We are utilizing the whole of our continental territory. We must turn our eyes abroad, or they will soon look inward upon discontent."[21]

No one better exemplified the link between the West and post-1890s expansionism than Theodore Roosevelt. His well-known

19 Utley, *Indian Frontier*, 186; Stanley Vestal, *Warpath and Council Fire* (New York, 1948), xi.
20 Henry Nash Smith, *Virgin Land* (New York, 1959), 215–16; Wilbur R. Jacobs, "Native American History: How It Illuminates Our Past," *American Historical Review* 80 (June 1975): 599.
21 Frederick Jackson Turner, "The Problem of the West," *Atlantic Monthly* 88 (September 1896): 289; Edward Younger, *John A. Kasson* (Iowa City, 1955), 295.

multivolume history, *The Winning of the West* (1889–96), explained landed manifest destiny and anticipated the arguments he and others used to justify overseas conquests. "The Indians never had any real title to the soil; . . . this great continent could not have been kept as nothing but a game preserve for squalid savages. . . . The man who puts the soil to use must of right dispossess the man who does not, or the world will come to a standstill." Elihu Root, perhaps the nation's leading corporate lawyer and later Roosevelt's secretary of state, justified in 1902 why Americans had a right to rule people in the Caribbean and the Pacific. The Declaration of Independence, Root argued, was for a "highly civilized, self-governing people," not the barbarians and semi-civilized. "Without the consent of hundreds of thousands of Indians whom our fathers found in possession of this land," Root continued, "we have assumed and exercised sovereignty over them." The same principle applied to "the ignorant and credulous Filipinos."[22]

Dissenters to this argument were, like the African, Chinese, and native Americans, in the minority. Senator George F. Hoar (R.-Mass.), who had led the fight against annexing the Philippines, wrote in his memoirs:

The Indian problem is not chiefly how to teach the Indian to be less savage in his treatment of the Saxon, but the Saxon to be less savage in his treatment of the Indian. The Chinese problem is not how to keep Chinese laborers out of California, but how to keep Chinese policies out of Congress. The negro question will be settled when the education of the white man is complete.

Roosevelt, however, had the last word:

During the past three centuries the spread of the English-speaking people over the world's waste spaces has been not only the most striking feature in the world's history, but also the event of all others most far-reaching in its effects and importance.[23]

22 Williams, "U.S. Indian Policy," 816; I am indebted to Robert Hannigan for Root's "American Policies in the Philippines," Sept. 24, 1902.
23 Robert L. Beisner, *Twelve Against Empire* (New York, 1968), 160; Theodore Roosevelt, *The Winning of the West*, 3 vols. (New York, 1897), 1:1.

With his interesting view of former Indian lands as waste space, Roosevelt brought together in one sentence his generation's view of race, Anglo-Saxon destiny, and the goodness of expansionism. His *Winning of the West* was a prologue to the post-1898 attempt to spread across the Pacific to the prizes of the more distant West.

4. "America Will Take This Continent
in Hand Alone"

The 1865–1912 era in U.S.–Latin American relations began with Secretary of State William Seward forswearing landed conquest in Mexico and the Congress rejecting footholds in the Caribbean–Central American region, even when tempted by the centuries-old dream of exclusive rights to an isthmian canal. The era ended with the United States exclusively owning and fortifying the canal, militarily and economically dominating the Caribbean through a network of bases, occupying Nicaragua with U.S. Marines, and verging on an invasion of Mexico. Clearly these years are pivotal in understanding how the Monroe Doctrine of 1823, which ruled out foreign interference in Latin American affairs, became the Monroe Doctrine of 1912, which justified unilateral U.S. intervention in those affairs.

It is equally clear, given the prominence of U.S. military forces in the region after the 1880s, that the nation's foreign policies did not primarily seek order and stability in Latin America. They instead placed the greatest emphasis on obtaining economic opportunity and strategic footholds from which they could move to obtain further opportunities. These policies, even by the early 1890s, led to disorder and clashes that, in turn, helped pressure U.S. officials to build the naval forces necessary to maintain their new interpretations of the Monroe Doctrine.

Settling with the British – and Canada

Until the final decade of the nineteenth century, the British were the other major power in the Western Hemisphere. Their relationship with Canada, even after 1867 when Canada received dominion status and became self-governing, and their navy, indisputably the world's most powerful, made them one of the two major obstacles to

U.S. expansionism. The other major obstacle turned out to be the nationalisms of Latin American nations themselves.

Washington-London relations had reached crisis proportions during the Civil War. The British had not only recognized the Confederacy's belligerency status; they allowed their shipyards to build vessels (notably the *Alabama*) for the South that extensively damaged Union shipping. By 1869, when President Ulysses S. Grant and Secretary of State Hamilton Fish began shaping foreign policy, the *Alabama* claims threatened a new crisis in Anglo-American relations. Grant deeply mistrusted the British, especially given his green memories of their siding with the South. He declared that if a U.S. general could not conquer Canada in thirty days, he deserved a dishonorable discharge. Fish had a less visceral response than the president, but his pre–Civil War Whig colleagues, Seward and John Quincy Adams, had also been his foreign policy mentors, and all agreed that the United States could look forward to a happy future as such states as Canada, Cuba, Mexico, and perhaps others voluntarily came into the Union – like "ripe apples" falling into a lap, as Adams memorably phrased it. Powerful Republican Senator Charles Sumner of Massachusetts, however, took a hatchet to the tree when he proposed in 1869–70 that the British could recompense the United States for their Civil War mistakes by handing over Canada immediately.[1]

In his classic autobiography, *The Education of Henry Adams,* the author recalls that this demand of Sumner's "opened the gravest doubts of Sumner's sanity." Such was not Adams's actual response nearly forty years earlier. In a widely noted essay of 1870, Adams disagreed only over tactics. Because Great Britain's interests lie in Asia, he wrote, and because "her American possessions are a source of weakness," Adams concluded that conciliation, not confrontation, would most quickly tie Canada to the United States. His article exemplified an upswing in expansionist sentiment during 1869–70. Southerners urged action in Cuba and Santo Domingo, as did many in the North. Radical Republicans besides Sumner led the successful repeal of the 1854 reciprocity trade treaty with Canada on the theory

1 Allan Nevins, *Hamilton Fish* (New York, 1936), 216–20.

that with their trade jeopardized, Canadians would seek annexation. The chair of the House Foreign Affairs Committee, Nathaniel Banks (R.-Mass.), thought, as usual, in large terms. He introduced a joint resolution declaring that an independent Canada was an "implied infraction" of the Monroe Doctrine. Such anti-British feelings were helped along by the raids of the Irish Fenian Brotherhood into Canada between 1866 and 1870. Both President Johnson and President Grant tried to stop them by enforcing U.S. neutrality laws, and thus the wonderful opportunity opened to politicians to defend the Fenians, court the Irish vote, and woo the many others who disliked the British.[2]

A fresh opportunity for expansion northward suddenly appeared in 1869–70. The Red River area of present Manitoba moved into rebellion when Canada tried to rule it. The so-called rebellion, led by Louis Riel, received warm encouragement from U.S. senators in Minnesota and Michigan, as well as from Grant and Fish. Banker, speculator, and railroad magnate Jay Cooke invested in the rebellion in the hope that annexation of the region to the United States would remove the possibility of a Canadian transcontinental rail system that would compete with his Northern Pacific Railroad in the United States. As usual, that catalyst of the West, the land speculator, encouraged the rebellion. The annexation drive failed, however, as the many Roman Catholics in the Red River country disliked the idea of joining the Protestants to the south, and Fish rejected proposals that he slip large bribes to rebel leaders to help overcome such religious feelings. Canadian officials dispatched troops, then patiently offered more local autonomy and the promise of railroads. In late 1870 Grant instructed Fish to forget about using the talks with the British to annex Canada. That decision marked a crucial turn, and, with that problem removed, the *Alabama* claims were settled.[3]

In the Washington Treaty of 1871, the British paid $15.5 million

2 Henry Adams, *The Education of Henry Adams* (Boston, 1930), 274; Henry Adams, "The Session," *North American Review* 40 (July 1869): 639–40; Fred Harvey Harrington, *Fighting Politician: Major General N. P. Banks* (Philadelphia, 1948), 177–81.

3 D.W. Warner, *The Idea of Continental Union* (Lexington, Ky., 1960), 110–27; William S. McFeeley, *Grant: A Biography* (New York, 1981), 347–8.

for the damage inflicted by the *Alabama*. Arbitration procedures were also established that led to both a settlement of outstanding boundary disputes (the San Juan Islands, south of Vancouver, became U.S. territory), and the United States received fishing privileges close to Canadian shores in return for $5.5 million. The idea of a U.S.-Canadian continental union never disappeared. Each nation suffered economic disasters in the 1870s and 1880s that led it to look to the other for relief. In the 1880s, 1.4 million Canadians, especially from the West, moved to the United States to find jobs. About the same number of discouraged U.S. citizens moved north during the next decade. In the late 1880s a bitter argument over Canadian and U.S. rights to kill seals in the Bering Sea led some to urge the use of force, until the British Navy intervened and persuaded the United States to scale back demands.[4] As late as 1911, U.S. congressional leaders reverted to the idea of a half century earlier that a reciprocity trade treaty would inevitably pull Canada into their political as well as economic orbit. Nor did the Washington Treaty end U.S.-British confrontations (as the seal controversy and the 1895 Venezuelan boundary crisis demonstrated). Sumner, Banks, and their expansionist colleagues were nevertheless silenced. For reasons of personality and patronage, Sumner had even broken bitterly with Grant who, in turn, worked to remove the senator as chair of the Foreign Relations Committee. Free of a possible clash with Great Britain and the possible forced annexation of a fragmented, newly independent Canada, the expansionists could again look southward.

Race and Revolution

Not all liked what they saw. The opportunities for expansionism seemed plentiful, but two problems – race and revolution – that did not slow down U.S. plans for annexing Anglo-Saxons to the north brought to a stop the plans of Grant to annex the races to the south.

Until 1865, southern planters and Cuba's Creole sugar barons had

4 Robert Craig Brown, *Canada's National Policy, 1883–1900* (Princeton, 1964), 125–33.

hoped that the island's annexation to the United States would preserve the slave institutions in both countries. But as slavery ended in the South, the institution began to weaken in Cuba, although Spain would not finally destroy it until 1886. Cuban rebels who declared war against Spain in 1868 freed slaves and destroyed the Creoles' sugarcane fields. Race and revolution formed a highly combustible mixture. Some Creoles moved to escape the fire by seeking U.S. annexation. A Cuban Junta, with headquarters in lower Manhattan, collected over a million dollars in 1868–9 to push annexation forward. If there was to be a revolution, conservatives in both countries planned to control and benefit from it. And if Cuba was to break loose from Spain, President Grant and Secretary of War John B. Rawlings headed the large group who wanted to annex the island.[5]

Secretary of State Fish's position was subtler. After an 1855 visit to Cuba, he concluded the United States should keep its distance politically; the problem in his mind went well beyond that of slavery: "I can see no means of getting rid of a population of some 450,000 called whites but really of every shade and mixture of color, who own *all* the land on the island." By 1869 Congress was urging a highly receptive Grant to recognize Cuban belligerency. Fish blocked this move by arguing that belligerency would relieve Spain of property damages caused by the conflict, and that Spain was a more acceptable ruler than the multiracial revolutionaries. At one point the secretary of state only stopped Grant and his congressional allies by threatening to resign. Fish would like to have controlled Cuba; he differed little from Seward and Adams in this regard. But he preferred helping Cuba purchase its independence, getting rid of slavery, then using U.S. financial leverage to protect property interests, control any new government, and ensure that other and more threatening powers (such as Great Britain) would not replace the rapidly declining Spanish. Fish wanted control of, but not day-to-day responsibility for, the island. As historian William S. McFeeley has noted, "Fish did not want a portion of America governed by landowners with whom he would be uncomfortable dining, and this

5 Jules R. Benjamin, *The United States and the Origins of the Cuban Revolution* (Princeton, 1990), 12–15; Nevins, *Fish*, 179–82.

went not only for Cuba but for [African Americans] in Mississippi." Fish received support from members of Congress who agreed with him about the racial problem, and who also fought annexation because it would threaten U.S. beet-sugar growers. By late 1869, Grant publicly announced that he would not recognize rebel belligerency (although he might in the future), and that European colonializers should now recognize facts and free their colonies.[6]

The revolution raged on, although in early 1873 hope rose when a republic replaced Spain's monarchy. The hope was short-lived. Throughout the post-1868 rebellion, U.S. filibusterers, seeking thrills, glory, and opportunities, had aided the rebels with weapons and men. In November 1873 Spain captured the *Virginius,* a U.S. filibustering ship, and quickly executed fifty-three of the American mercenaries. Loud demands for war immediately sounded in Washington, but not from Grant and Fish. The secretary of state's policy remained consistent. He wanted no quick annexation, he wrote Madrid, but desired Cuba's "elevation into an independent republic of freemen." Fish clearly thought that such an elevation would require considerable time. Most newspapers and political leaders seemed to support him. The economic panic that had suddenly struck, the hope (unrealized) that the new Spanish republic could begin liberal reforms, the *Virginius*'s shadowy mission, and the reluctance to go to war just to endure more racial problems – all advised abstention. At a pivotal moment, the British, who wanted no U.S. control of Cuba, helped work out a peaceful settlement. Spain apologized and paid an indemnity. The crisis passed, but not the revolution. It continued until 1878 when the rebels dissolved, in part because of their own internal class, racial, and geographic differences.[7]

Peace, however, was delicate. During the 1880s, and as the island's slavery formally ended, U.S. interests in Cuba rose rapidly. Many Americans bought out plantations ruined by the war. Some

---

6 Benjamin, *U.S. and Origins,* 17–18; McFeeley, *Grant,* 297–8; I am indebted to James Chapin for cabinet meeting documents.

7 Richard H. Bradford, *The Virginius Affair* (Boulder, Colo., 1980), esp. 129–39; Nevins, *Fish,* 615–37, 673.

Spaniards and Cubans sought the protection given by U.S. citizenship. In 1885 Secretary of State Thomas F. Bayard pointedly warned an interested Germany that "the condition" of Cuba is "an especially American question." When the U.S. Congress passed the 1890 reciprocity bill that gave preference to Cuban sugar, the stage had been set for a new attempt to break Spain's faltering hold.[8] After 1868 Washington officials cared less about order in Cuba than about holding Spain responsible for ruling the island, while keeping it open to U.S. investments. Not surprisingly, by 1895 U.S. officials faced another Cuban revolution.

Race also helped spur, and finally kill, another Grant adventure. Since 1865 Santo Domingo had been unsuccessfully targeted by Seward, but New York bankers and various investors, some of them heavily involved with the corrupt dictatorship that ruled the Caribbean nation, had found highly profitable land, forests, and mines. In 1869 these Americans persuaded Grant to allow his sometime private secretary, Orville Babcock, to negotiate a treaty of annexation and another pact giving the United States a lease on the superb harbor of Samana Bay. President Buenaventura Baez happily signed to ensure Washington's support of his rule and received $150,000 with a promise of more for his government. Grant sent the annexation treaty to the Senate, partly in the hope that African Americans might want to leave for the new possession, partly in the hope of helping his friends acquire a prized naval base. The president, moreover, had concluded from a personal conversation with Senator Sumner that the Massachusetts Republican would support the agreement. Fish was highly unenthusiastic, but he went along, perhaps because he thought the Senate would not ratify it anyway and in the meantime the debate would deflect attention from the more explosive Cuban problem. Grant was humiliated when Sumner fought the treaty and the 28–28 vote fell far short of the two-thirds required. Grant never forgave Sumner, but the president himself never escaped the odor he acquired by supporting his corrupt friends. Oppo-

8 Benjamin, *U.S. and Origins*, 14; Charles C. Tansill, *The Foreign Policy of Thomas F. Bayard, 1885–1897* (New York, 1940); Francisco Lopez Segrera, *Cuba: capitalismo dependiente, y subdesarrollo (1519–1959)* (Havana, 1972), 189–200.

nents had warned that annexation, or even the lease, would compound racial problems that already plagued the United States. These warnings took on urgency when it was learned that Grant's busy agents had also contacted Santo Domingo's neighbor, the black republic of Haiti, for negotiations. African-American leaders such as Frederick Douglass and Senator Hiram Revels worked for the treaty in the hope that annexation would lift the economic and political conditions of the impoverished Santo Domingans.[9]

The reverberations from Grant's defeat were many. Maria Child, well known for her pre–Civil War children's books and outspoken opposition to slavery's expansion, attacked what she termed the president's "twin brother to our taking Texas from the poor Mexicans. This Republic will sink rapidly . . . to ruin, if we go on thus seizing territory of our neighbors by fraud or force." Others also opposed Grant, but unlike Child, they feared dealing with "people of the Latin race mixed with the Indian and African blood" who have neither "institutions nor morals in common with us." At one point during the debate, Haiti and Santo Domingo fired on each other. Without consulting Congress, Grant ordered the U.S. Navy to protect Baez. A highly jealous Senate condemned the president's order as "a usurpation" of Congress's power to declare war. Grant retreated, thereafter deferred to the Senate's prerogatives, and set a precedent for presidential accountability until it was undermined thirty years later by William McKinley and Theodore Roosevelt. The reaction against Grant's Santo Domingo initiative even helped split his party and led to a Liberal Republican opposition ticket led by Horace Greeley in 1872. Grant and Fish nevertheless did manage a historic achievement: If the United States could not have Santo Domingo, the president announced in May 1870, neither could anyone else. Reiterating the Monroe Doctrine, Grant, in words written by Fish, added that it was an "equally important principle that hereafter no territory on this continent shall be regarded as subject of transfer to a European power." He had integrated an

9 McFeeley, *Grant*, 337–53; Eric Foner, *Reconstruction* (New York, 1988), 337–53; Nevins, *Fish*, 250–62; Charles Callan Tansill, *The United States and Santo Domingo* (Baltimore, 1938), esp. 362–407.

unqualified no-transfer principle for the first time into the sacred principles of Monroe. [10] It was a warning especially to the European imperialists who hovered over the slowly dying Spanish empire.

Saturating Mexico "with Americanism"

In 1860, U.S. trade with Mexico amounted to $7 million. By 1890 it had quadrupled and in 1900 it reached $64 million. Such results had been accomplished without benefit of a reciprocity treaty negotiated in 1883 by none other than the recently retired president, Ulysses S. Grant. In Congress the treaty had gone down before a coalition of Republican protectionists and Democrat low-tariff advocates, although they seemed careful to administer the final blow only in 1887 after Grant had died. The treaty's defeat obviously did not much retard the threading of the trade that was interweaving the two economies. [11]

Investments in Mexico grew even more remarkably. In the early 1870s the Mexicans, still angry over being relieved of one-third of their country by the United States in 1848, and having just expelled the French invaders of the 1860s, opposed having U.S. investors building their railroads or buying their lands. By 1910, as the Mexican Revolution was about to erupt, U.S. citizens owned 43 percent of the country's property, or more than did Mexicans. The relationship between the flood of post-1880 investment and the outbreak of revolution was direct.

As the French exited in 1866, Seward predicted an onslaught of U.S. capital and population into Mexico. The problems were Mexican political instability and fear of U.S. influences. In 1876, stability arrived when Porfirio Díaz seized power in a coup d' état and began a 35-year rule. Fish and his successor, William M. Evarts, secretary of state under Rutherford B. Hayes (1877–81), refused at first to recognize Díaz because he seemed to be unable to pay Mexi-

10 Edward P. Crapol, "Lydia Maria Child," in Edward P. Crapol, ed., *Women and American Foreign Policy* (Westport, Conn., 1987), 1–18; Dexter Perkins, *The Monroe Doctrine, 1867–1907* (Baltimore, 1937), 16, 26.
11 J. Fred Rippy, *The United States and Mexico*, rev. ed. (New York, 1931), 319; McFeeley, *Grant*, 486–92.

co's financial obligations or stop bandit raids across the U.S. border.
Evarts finally granted recognition in 1878, and in 1880 Díaz destroyed his opposition. Evarts was well prepared to realize Seward's
prophecy. A graduate of elite schools and with a powerful political
and legal mind, Evarts had helped lead the effort to make Seward
president in 1860 and remained close to his fellow New Yorker as
Andrew Johnson's attorney general. Believing that "the vast resources of our country need an outlet," Evarts stressed that "it is for
us to enter into the harvest-field and reap it." During posh dinners
at New York City's Delmonico's and elsewhere, he stressed that an
improved U.S. consular service was necessary to point investors and
traders toward those harvest fields. He understood, he declared, that
"the leading commercial communities of the United States" wanted,
among other help, consuls who regularly reported on foreign labor
conditions, wages, and business customs. In 1878, Evarts instructed
the consuls to issue such regular reports.[12]

Díaz meanwhile had sent his own agents to drum up investors'
interest. They were highly successful. Evarts's State Department
successor, James G. Blaine (1881), pushed cooperation along by
taking another leaf from Seward's book and assuring Mexico that the
United States no longer wanted land, only full and unfettered access
so that North Americans, with their "large accumulation of capital,
for which [their] own vast resources fail to give full scope for the
untiring energy of its citizens," could develop Mexico's "scarcely
developed resources." Mexico, Blaine stressed, could then "still further develop into a well ordered and prosperous state." Peace and
stability for investors and traders meant peace and stability for Mexico. By 1883 the *Chicago Tribune* termed Mexico an "almost virgin
outlet for the extension of the market of our overproducing civilization."[13]

Railroad builders in the United States were among the pioneers.
They had tried to lay track in the 1860s to link up with their own

12 Edward Crapol, *America for Americans* (Westport, Conn., 1973), 55–7; Chester
L. Barrows, *William M. Evarts* (Chapel Hill, 1941), 351–62, 375–78.
13 Blaine is quoted in James Morton Callahan, *American Foreign Policy in Mexican
Relations* (New York, 1932), 494–7; Milton Plesur, "Looking Outward . . .,"
(Ph.D. diss., University of Rochester, 1954), 63–4.

transcontinental system, but the plan fell to anti-Americanism. Between 1880 and 1883, however, U.S. investors, including Grant and Jay Gould, received concessions for 2,500 miles of track over five railway systems. Grant's and Gould's projects fell victim to the former president's bankruptcy in 1884 and Gould's disinterest, but such leading builders as the heads of the Pennsylvania Railroad and the Sante Fe Railroad did begin to construct a transportation system in Mexico. They were soon followed by an American invasion, as Europeans a generation later called the sudden appearance of many U.S. businesses: agricultural implements, weapons, sewing machines, life insurance, furniture, even two North American newspapers. Of special importance, investments in Mexico's rich mineral wealth soared. In the late 1880s the first small oil companies appeared. By 1888, $30 million was invested in mining (including investments by a group led by Senator Henry Teller [R.-Col.]) Two years later Solomon Guggenheim began his highly profitable silver-lead smelting operation.[14]

As early as 1885, George B. McClellan, the old Civil War general, declared that these multiplying investments in Mexico required that the U.S. Army be rebuilt to protect them. In 1888, Secretary of State Thomas F. Bayard (1885–9) wrote: "The overflow of our population and capital into . . . Mexico, must . . . saturate those regions with Americanism, and control their political action," but "we do not want them" until "they are fit." In 1895, Americans in Mexico City were so pleased with Díaz that they petitioned him to continue his dictatorial rule for another presidential term. The U.S. chargé was about to sign the petition until Alvey A. Adee, the all-wise and all-watchful second assistant secretary of state, told the chargé such involvement in the politics of other nations was forbidden. That same year, amid the depths of economic depression, *Bradstreet's* reported that "there are fully three times as many Americans in Mexico this winter looking up lands as were there last winter." Historian David Pletcher has well linked this early U.S. diplomatic initiative with the investment flood by examining the career

14 Rippy, *U.S. and Mexico,* 312; Callahan, *American Foreign Policy,* 475–507, 516–17.

of Warner Perrin Sutton, the U.S. consul at Matamoros, near the Rio Grande's mouth, who obeyed Evarts's instructions by flooding Washington and the business community with helpful reports and shepherding investors around Mexico:

When Sutton came to Matamoros in 1878, cumbersome bales of goods were customarily ferried across the river's mouth . . ., then moved slowly inland on mule-drawn wagons. When he left Nuevo Laredo in 1893, through trains ran between St. Louis [Missouri] and Mexico City, and the Mexican river towns were losing their economic predominance to Monterrey, the industrial hub of the future. [15]

Pletcher's emphasis on economic (and social) displacement is especially important. At the same time Sutton departed, the first significant protests were made by Mexican peasants who had been forced off their land because of the growing haciendas and mining empires. The initial steps of the Mexican Revolution had been taken.

The investment rush did not stop at Mexico's southern boundary. In Costa Rica's promising banana- and coffee-growing regions, U.S. investors clashed head-on with dominant British finance. Americans were led by Minor Keith, who had left Brooklyn in 1871 to help his uncle lay rails linking the interior with the Atlantic coast. Keith succeeded despite the death of five thousand laborers who fell victim to disease and accidents. Keith made money quickly by exporting bananas along these tracks to Atlantic ports. He had also married the daughter of a former Costa Rican president. In 1883, he took over British concessions and, in turn, received 800,000 acres, or about 7 percent of Costa Rican territory. Keith's holdings became the basis for the United Fruit Company. United Fruit and its subsidiaries soon owned mines, ranches, banana plantations, railways, ports, and – at critical moments – governments, especially in Costa Rica, Honduras, and Guatemala. Resembling Mexico, Central America was also entering into a turbulent era of war, if not yet revolution. Already in the 1880s, secretaries of state Blaine and Bayard used direct threats, and in Bayard's case the dispatch of a

15 David M. Pletcher, "Consul Warner P. Sutton and American-Mexican Border Trade During the Early Díaz Period," *Southwestern Historical Quarterly* 79 (April 1976): 373–99; Plesur, "Looking Outward," 61.

warship (commanded by Captain Alfred Thayer Mahan), to protect U.S. property threatened by the wars between Central Americans and by anti-Yankee feelings in the region.[16]

A third party, the Europeans, also shaped the area's development. The British had long been a force in El Salvador, Nicaragua, and Costa Rica. By the 1880s Germans were second to the British in Costa Rica's coffee export industry and were becoming a dominant force in Guatemala, Nicaragua, and El Salvador. German interests developed so rapidly that in the 1870s Berlin sent a six-ship war fleet to Nicaragua to protect German investors and collect an indemnity. In the early 1880s, the German minister to the region assumed the political coloration of his surroundings and accused the United States of harboring imperial designs on the region. The remark was premeditated. Otto von Bismarck, the "Iron Chancellor" whose policies created modern Germany, began in the 1880s to reach for naval bases and colonies in the region. The U.S. response was so negative that Bismarck pulled back. The retreat, however, was tactical. In the 1890s the German economic and strategic interests grew, especially along the Atlantic coasts where they built transportation networks to carry their growing exports to world markets. When Washington officials, led by Blaine, pushed for a Pan-American movement in the 1880s, they were responding to these challenges to U.S. leadership in Latin America as well as to the market and raw material needs of their industrializing economy.[17]

Quest for a Canal

In 1870, at Fish's request, all U.S. consuls and ministers in Latin America submitted detailed reports on U.S. trade in the hemisphere. The first such systematic attempt to analyze the trade, the final set of reports stressed the advantages of European competitors and, among other conclusions, noted the need for an isthmian canal

16 "Editor's Introduction," in Marc Edelman and Joanne Kenen, eds., *The Costa Rica Reader* (New York, 1989), 55; Thomas P. McCann, *An American Company* (New York, 1976), 15–30.

17 Thomas Schoonover, *The United States in Central America, 1860–1911* (Durham, N.C., 1991), 4–9, 43–5, 61, 79–93, 105–51, 168–70.

that would help loosen the hold of British trade on Latin America's Pacific Coast.[18] Seward had unsuccessfully tried to maneuver a treaty for a U.S.-controlled passageway. Over the next two decades, Washington officials, led by Evarts and Blaine, established the record and precedents that finally broke the 1850 Clayton-Bulwer Treaty and led to the Hay-Pauncefote Pact, which gave North Americans control of a canal.

Evarts had worked with Seward in the 1860s to entice investors into a canal project, and as secretary of state in 1878 warned Europeans against intervening in Central America to collect debts – a key precedent for the 1904 Roosevelt Corollary to the Monroe Doctrine that led the United States to be the policeman of the hemisphere. The quest became a crisis, however, in 1879 when Ferdinand de Lesseps, who had built the Suez Canal, announced that his French firm would build a Panamanian route. Evarts and Hayes warned, in the president's words, that "the United States should control this great highway." Not only the Monroe Doctrine but "our prosperity and safety" required, as Hayes put it, that "either an American canal or no canal must be our motto." To underline his point in 1880, he sent two warships along the coasts of Nicaragua and Panama.[19]

Blaine then took the major step of telling the British in 1881 that the 1850 treaty had to be changed to American specifications. He argued that the United States now had paramount interests in the area, especially because of the growth of the U.S. Pacific Coast states, that were "imperial in extent" and required easy transit for the growing export trade. Blaine also informed the British government that "England as against the United States was always wrong." Such sentiments, along with his continual twisting of the Lion's tail in campaigns to obtain the Irish vote, finally made him persona non grata in the British prime minister's office. Shorn of the campaign rhetoric, Blaine had nevertheless predicted the outcome. His successor in the State Department, Frederick T. Frelinghuysen, simply

18 David M. Pletcher, "Inter-American Trade in the Early 1870s: A State Department Survey," *Americas* 33 (April 1977): 607.

19 Rutherford B. Hayes, *Diary and Letters . . .,* ed. Charles Richard Williams, 5 vols. (Columbus, Ohio, 1924), 3:583–9.

ignored the 1850 agreement and in 1884 signed the Frelinghuysen-Zavala Treaty with Nicaragua that gave the United States exclusive canal rights. The Senate voted 32–23 to ratify the treaty, short of the necessary two-thirds required. The majority, however, plus the strict party-line vote (the Republicans enthusiastically for the treaty), indicated that the 1850 commitment's days were numbered. Or, as Andrew Carnegie wrote Blaine in 1882, "You are exactly right. America is going to control anything and everything on this Continent. That's settled. . . . No *joint* arrangements, no entangling alliances with monarchical, war-like Europe. America will take this Continent in hand alone."[20]

De Lesseps went bankrupt in the 1880s, victimized by tropical diseases and by technology inadequate to cut cheaply enough through Panama. United States officials never let up their pressure. Presidents and Congress, led by Alabama's Senator John T. Morgan, continued to warn, as President Benjamin Harrison put it in 1891, that "the canal is the most important subject now connected with the commercial growth and progress of the United States." The U.S. Navy, moreover, intervened in Panama on at least seven occasions between 1846 and 1903 to protect U.S. interests. In 1886, these warships stopped a revolution and thus protected American goods that were constantly in transit across the isthmus.[21] Seventeen years later the United States helped trigger a revolt and used the resulting disorder to obtain land for the canal.

Reciprocity to Revolution

Besides Colombia's province of Panama, other parts of Latin America were also in upheaval. The so-called Pacific War that broke out in 1879 and lasted until 1883 between Chile and Peru especially dis-

---

20 Alice Tyler, *The Foreign Policy of James G. Blaine* (Minneapolis, 1927), 32–45; Carnegie to Blaine, January 14, 1882, Papers of James G. Blaine, Library of Congress, Washington, D.C.; David Pletcher, *The Awkward Years* (Columbia, Mo., 1962), 1–4.

21 Pletcher, *Awkward Years,* 105; James D. Richardson, *A Compilation of the Messages and Papers of the Presidents, 1789–1897,* 10 vols. (Washington, D.C., 1900), 9:188–9.

tressed U.S. officials. The war was caused by ancient rivalries, fights over Pacific Coast outlets, and contested guano beds. To Blaine, however, the higher stakes included Great Britain's trade advantages in, and strong support for, Chile. Above all, he and Frelinghuysen wanted to keep European powers as uninvolved as possible. To accomplish this, Blaine decided in 1881 that U.S. commercial dominance in the hemisphere required stopping wars that Europeans could exploit.[22] Peace, he argued, was a prerequisite for American commerce, at least until the United States had enough power itself to determine, and take advantage of, the outbreaks.

Blaine therefore issued invitations to the Latin American states to discuss these subjects at a historic conference in Washington. He left the department after President James Garfield's death in 1881, and the conference did not convene. But others, including Bayard and members of both parties in Congress, as well as powerful members of the business community including Carnegie, maintained interest in such a meeting. Bayard issued fresh invitations just before Blaine returned to the State Department in 1889. The first Pan-American conference indeed marked a turning point in hemispheric relationships, even if it did not achieve all that Blaine had hoped. In the 1820s Henry Clay had coined the term "good neighbor" to describe the correct approach to the Americas, and one of Blaine's friends learned that "he regarded Henry Clay as the originator of the ideas relating to the subject" of Latin American policy. The Good Neighbor approach in the 1889–90 conference produced an arbitration convention to help settle disputes, a recommendation to build a railroad uniting North and South America, and the establishment of the Commercial Bureau of American Republics (or the Pan American Union as it became known later). The conference rejected the idea of a common silver coin. Most notably, the Latin Americans turned down Blaine's idea of a customs union. The tariff policy of the United States and their historic economic ties to Europe, the

22 Henry O'Connor, "Blaine's Nine Months as Secretary of State" (1888), Henry O'Connor Papers, Notre Dame University, South Bend, Ind.; James G. Blaine, *Political Discussions, Legislative, Diplomatic, and Popular, 1856–1886* (Norwich, Conn., 1887), 411–19, 425–6.

southern delegates argued, made a hemispheric common market impossible. [23]

Above all, Blaine emerged from the fight over the customs union determined to bring the high post-1861 tariffs into accord with the economic realities of the 1890s. The realities were that the United States was producing a huge glut of industrial goods that had natural markets to the south; the Europeans, led by the British and Germans, were instead grabbing those markets; and the United States consequently had an unfavorable balance of trade (and an outflow of money to pay for it), because of its economic dependence on Latin American raw materials. Blaine did not think small. A consummate backroom wheeler-dealer and stump orator, "the Plumed Knight from Maine," like Seward, developed a systematic worldview. (He even liked to amuse himself in his study by spinning a world globe and contemplating its future.) Having taught Virgil, Cicero, and mathematics at Western Military Institute at age eighteen, he served in Congress seventeen years, including seven as the powerful speaker of the House. Republican nominee for the presidency in 1884, he understood the Second Industrial Revolution and seemed to be the front-runner for the nomination in 1888 until Civil War hero Benjamin Harrison, aided by Blaine's growing number of enemies and by his ill health, won the nomination and the office. The two men mistrusted each other, but Harrison respected Blaine's power and vision. When he invited the Plumed Knight to become secretary of state, the president-elect wrote, "I am especially interested in the improvement of our relations with the Central and South American states." In 1886, Blaine had outlined his view of those relations:

What we want, then, are the markets of these neighbors of ours that lie to the south of us. We want the $400,000,000 annually which to-day go to England, France, Germany and other countries. With these markets secured new life would be given to our manufactories, the product of the

23 Achille Viallate, "Les États-Unis et le Pan-Américanísme," *Revue des Deux Mondes* 51 (1909): 420–2; Crawford to Barker, February 2, 1893, Papers of Wharton Barker, Library of Congress, Washington, D.C.

Western farmer would be in demand, the reasons for and inducements to strikers, with all their attendant evils, would cease.[24]

Reciprocity became a focal point for both men.

Blaine had little patience for laissez-faire illusions. He knew that trade moved not because "of a mere ability to produce as cheaply as another nation," but because of "special trade relations by treaty." Politics (including tariffs and the Civil War mercantilist acts that accelerated industrialization), not an imaginary open marketplace, determined power. As one journalist observed, "It was Blaine who had the big idea that water could be made to run uphill; or, what was the same thing, that trade currents could be diverted from their natural courses." A half-dozen treaties with reciprocity clauses had been made with Latin American nations in the early 1880s; the argument went on as well about whether to renew the 1854 reciprocity pact with Canada. But the 1890 McKinley Tariff that contained the Blaine-Harrison reciprocity provisions was different.[25]

It anticipated the key principle of U.S. trade policy in most of the twentieth century by enabling the president to reduce tariffs on foreign goods (especially raw materials), when other nations reduced their tariffs for U.S. products (especially industrial and staple agricultural goods). The act was constructed as a blunt weapon: The five key articles of sugar, molasses, coffee, tea, and hides were to be allowed in duty-free, but if a country producing those goods did not reciprocate by allowing in U.S. goods at preferential rates, Harrison could slap heavy duties on the five articles exported by the recalcitrant country. Harrison did the major political work during the hot Washington summer of 1890 in pushing the legislation through a protectionist Republican Congress, while the ailing Blaine took in the sea breezes at Bar Harbor.[26]

24 The 1886 quotation is in Crapol, *America for Americans*, 166–7; Tom E. Terrill, *The Tariff, Politics, and American Foreign Policy, 1874–1901* (Westport, Conn., 1973), 42–9; Otto zu Stolberg-Wernigerode, *Germany and the United States During the Era of Bismarck* (Reading, Pa., 1937), 169–70.

25 Arthur Wallace Dunn, *Harrison to Harding* (New York, 1922), 45.

26 Homer E. Socolofsky and Allan B. Spetter, *The Presidency of Benjamin Harrison* (Lawrence, Kan., 1987), 113–20.

Economic historians have judged the act a failure because treaties with only eleven nations were concluded, and the Democrats repealed the reciprocity provisions in favor of an across-the-board freer trade measure in 1894. That judgment, however, is myopic. As Blaine and Harrison hoped, the treaties created important new trade with Spanish and British colonial holdings in the New World (how better to wean Cuba, Puerto Rico, Jamaica, and other colonial possessions from their parents?), with all five Central American nations, and with Brazil. Of special note, Harrison used the treaty as a club to coerce Germany. The Germans had begun in 1879 to protect their farmers by prohibiting U.S. pork imports on the grounds the pork was contaminated with trichinosis. Berlin then pressured other Europeans to follow its lead. Some 1.2 billion pounds of U.S. pork exports were suddenly jeopardized. Washington's protests went largely unheeded until 1891 when Harrison threatened to impose prohibitive tariffs on large beet-sugar imports from Germany. Berlin then responded more agreeably. Harrison improved U.S. inspections of meat exports and, at the president's demand, Germany reduced its tariff on U.S. exports other than pork. When Colombia, Haiti, and Venezuela refused to be as cooperative, Harrison penalized their exports to the United States.[27]

Blaine had begun by talking about the need for peace and order. Harrison was completing Blaine's Good Neighbor approach by threatening to declare economic war on the uncooperative, or using economic war to obtain long-sought prizes. Canada, in the view of Blaine and Harrison, was one of the greatest prizes. They wanted to annex it, but to do so only after the Canadians voluntarily asked to join the Union. Reciprocity seemed to offer a no-lose policy: If Canada signed such a trade treaty, it would slowly be integrated into the United States. If it did not, the many Canadians who depended on the U.S. market (both Blaine and Harrison kept in close touch with such people) would demand either a treaty on Washington's terms or annexation. Sir Alexander Galt, Canada's leading financial expert, declared the 1890 tariff act was aimed at forcing Canada to

27 Ibid., 131–5; James L. Laughlin and H. Parker Willis, *Reciprocity* (New York, 1903), 212–15, chap. 7.

break its "Colonial connection" with Great Britain, and further claimed it was "a hostile measure – an act of commercial war." Galt was correct. Blaine urged Harrison not even to approach Canada for a reciprocity treaty because it could not be worked out to U.S. satisfaction. Canada, he added, will then "find that she has a hard row to hoe and will ultimately . . . seek admission to the Union." Blaine was wrong. After a bitter political battle, Canadian Conservatives triumphed over Liberal continentalists in 1892 and turned toward Great Britain. United States officials had lost this battle.[28]

They succeeded spectacularly, however, in their war for Hawaii and, ultimately, Cuba. When Harrison signed a reciprocity treaty with Spain to give free access for Cuban sugar, the result quickly cut lethally in two directions. One was sketched out by Carnegie as he gloried in the disorder that would afflict Cuba. Noting that "all classes" on the island were in an "uproar" to sell to the United States, the steelmaker concluded the Cuba "will become the source of serious trouble and danger to Spain." Indeed, when the 1894 tariff ended reciprocity and removed Cuban sugar's favored access to U.S. markets, the island spun into revolution. Hawaii's revolt occurred in 1893 precisely because Cuban sugar had replaced its own in U.S. markets as a result of the 1890 act. The white planters, with the help of U.S. sailors, deposed the Hawaiian king and asked for annexation and assumed access to the continent's markets.[29] The Americans' search for disorder had paid off handsomely.

Contrary to Blaine's assertions in 1881, the first principle of U.S. policy in the hemisphere (and Hawaii) was not peace and stability, but the creation of policies and institutions that gave the United States new markets, economic advantages, and – if it all worked out – Cuba, Hawaii, and Canada. A revolution was not necessarily a bad result. Order was not necessarily to be preferred.

28 E. Farrer to J. W. Foster, April 14, 1892, Papers of Benjamin Harrison, Library of Congress, Washington, D.C.; Tyler, *Blaine*, 347; A. T. Volwiler, *The Correspondence Between Benjamin Harrison and James G. Blaine, 1882–1893* (Philadelphia, 1940), 193–4.
29 Socolofsky and Spetter, *Presidency of Harrison*, 121; Blaine to Harrison, January 1891, Harrison Papers.

Chile, Haiti, and the Need for a Navy

During the same year it passed the McKinley Tariff, Congress also appropriated funds to build the first three modern U.S. battleships. Growing demands in the Caribbean, the Pacific, and even Africa, as well as from the professional military, finally floated these ships into service. A crisis in Chile during 1891 confirmed the need for a new fleet, and for the bases that could be used as refueling and rest stops.

Animosity arose between Chile and the United States in the early 1880s when, during the so-called Pacific War against Peru, Chile tried to seize disputed territory and Washington, trying to be a mediator, favored Peru. In 1886, the Chilean government of José Manuel Balmaceda moved closer to Washington, and farther from dominant British influences, especially in the economic realm. Trade improved, and U.S. investors moved into the nitrate and shipping businesses. When a revolt erupted against Balmaceda in early 1891, Blaine supported the government, not least because the rebels were painted as pro-British by U.S. Minister Patrick Egan. One of the "Blaine Irishmen," Egan knew American politics but not Latin American diplomacy, other than that he could clearly see British plots, sometimes when they did not even exist. In May–June 1891, the United States tried to seize a rebel ship, the *Itata,* that was carrying arms from California to Chile, but the seizure backfired when the Balmaceda regime was toppled from power and a U.S. court ruled the ship had not broken international law. The United States, much to Harrison's disgust, had to pay costs for the ship seizure. Anti-Yankee feelings spread in Chile until October 1891, when two U.S. sailors were killed and seventeen seriously wounded in a Santiago barroom brawl. War threatened as Harrison became more demanding and the new Chilean regime grew sensitive to its nation's anti-U.S. feelings. Blaine finally moderated Harrison's position. So did the realization that when the president ordered the navy ready for action, the fleet was weaker than Chile's. In 1892, fortunately, Chile apologized and the crisis passed.[30]

---

30 Joyce S. Goldberg, *The Baltimore Affair* (Lincoln, Neb., 1986), 1–19, 43–8; Crapol, *America for Americans,* 180–3; Board of Investigation Report to Schley,

The ever louder demands for a new navy and shipping bases, growing out of these crises and the burgeoning U.S. commerce, had been noted by Harrison as well as Blaine. In his inaugural, the president observed that U.S. interests were no longer "exclusively American" – U.S. interests and citizens abroad were to be protected. "The necessities of our navy require convenient coaling stations and dock and harbor privileges." In 1891 he told a friend that bases in Europe and Africa were not needed, but it was "very important that in the West Indies, in the Pacific islands, South America we should have such stations."[31]

An opportunity arose in Haiti when a revolution split the country between a northern pro-U.S. group and a southern faction supported by European interests. The northern group, led by Hyppolite, won, and Harrison instructed U.S. Minister Frederick Douglass to ask the new government to show its appreciation by leasing the fine harbor of Môle St. Nicholas to Washington. At the same time, the U.S.-owned Clyde Steamship Line asked Haiti for choice shipping routes and a $480,000 subsidy. The Haitians, Douglass reported, refused to lease their territory or submit to Clyde's demands. Blaine dispatched Rear Admiral Bancroft Gherardi to apply pressure. The admiral complained that Douglass was too sensitive to Haitian concerns; the talks needed an "able, vigorous, aggressive white man." Douglass was recalled in 1891, but Haiti refused to change its position, even for such an aggressive white man as Gherardi.[32]

Harrison and Blaine, resembling Seward before them, did not obtain the Caribbean bases they sought. They did, however, pass a reciprocity bill and a battleship measure that helped obtain the empire that was acquired after 1897. They also gave glimmerings of the post-1898 executive power that was to transform the Constitution's checks and balances, by cutting drastically the congressional

October 19, 1891, Area 9 file, box 16, National Archives, Naval Records, Record Group 45, Washington, D.C.

31 Richardson, *A Compilation,* 9:10; Harrison to Reid, October 21, 1891, Harrison Papers.

32 Rayford W. Logan, *The Diplomatic Relations of the United States with Haiti, 1776–1891* (Chapel Hill, 1941), 427–57; Socolofsky and Spetter, *Presidency of Harrison,* 126–8.

domination of foreign policy between 1865 and the 1890s. Harrison's authority to negotiate reciprocity treaties was one indication. The Chilean crisis revealed how the executive could seize upon an incident and take the country toward war with little congressional consultation. In the 1880s, moreover, the modern intelligence services, operating under the president's direction, began when the Military Information Division appeared, and the navy named four officers to the Office of Intelligence to oversee global affairs. In 1889, Congress created the army and navy attaché system to staff diplomatic outposts. The Supreme Court, meanwhile, declared in *In re Neagle* (a case that had nothing directly to do with foreign affairs) that the president's power was not limited to carrying out Congress's wishes but extended to enforcing "the rights, duties, and obligations growing out of the Constitution itself, our international relations, and all the protection implied by the nature of the government under the Constitution."[33] These words of 1890 anticipated the nearly open-ended power of the post-1898 presidency, much as U.S. policies in Mexico, the Caribbean, and Central America between 1865 and 1893 anticipated, and helped cause, post-1898 instability and even revolution.

33 Lyman B. Kirkpatrick, Jr., "Intelligence and Counterintelligence," in Alexander DeConde, ed., *Encyclopedia of American Foreign Policy*, 3 vols. (New York, 1978), 2:418–19; implications are noted in Walter LaFeber, "Lion in the Path," *Constitution Magazine* 3 (Spring–Summer 1991): 14–23.

5. Crossing the Oceans

Almost from their beginnings as an independent people, Americans used the oceans not as a moat to protect themselves against the corruptions and armies of Europe but as a highway to reach the markets of Europe and Asia as well as the colonial settlements of West Africa. In the 1780s, as a century later, merchants were driven abroad by the exigencies of economic depression at home, as well as by the attraction of profits (and settlements) overseas. By the 1830s, colonizers of both the white and black races had, with the help of several presidential administrations, established an American settlement for freed African-American slaves in Liberia. A decade later, driven again in part by the economic bad times of 1837 to 1841, U.S. officials signed their first treaty with China. In the next decade of the 1850s they sent Matthew Perry to open Japan to U.S. interests, both secular and religious. After 1865, the United States rapidly became one of the six great powers fighting over the remains of China's Manchu dynasty and, for a time, even was an unlikely participant in the great colonial struggle over Africa's riches.

Africa, Kasson, and African Americans

Africa burst into American (and much of the world's) attention in 1870 when the *New York Herald* sent Henry M. Stanley to find the supposedly lost missionary David Livingstone in the interior of Africa. Stanley's alleged greeting, "Dr. Livingstone, I presume," became famous, but Stanley's discovery of the Congo's rich mineral wealth received more attention at the time. In 1878 one of the great U.S. explorers, Rear Admiral Robert Shufeldt, sailed along the West African coast and into several of its rivers. Convinced that the region was to be the "great commercial prize of the world," he renewed ties with Liberia; gained rights to a coaling station on the other side of the continent, at Madagascar, where U.S. merchants for a time dominated the island's profitable trade; and signed trade treaties with African leaders. In his reports home, Shufeldt told Secretary of State William Evarts that U.S. consular services (a topic close to Evarts's heart) should be established along the coasts, especially since "we must bear in mind that with the old markets overstocked with goods," it was necessary to take "time by the forelock" and gain a share of "the only remaining unoccupied mart in the old world, . . . the virgin soil of Africa with its teeming population."[1]

Until the late 1870s, U.S. officials, distracted by Reconstruction and labor upheavals, had shown little interest in African affairs. In 1874, the U.S. minister to Turkey, George H. Boker, urged Secretary of State Hamilton Fish to annex Bab-al-Mandeb Cape, which controlled the strategic entrance to the Red Sea between the Suez Canal and the Indian Ocean. If Fish had done so, the U.S. military position in the Middle East during the post-1945 era would have been impressive. He instead responded that purchasing the area had to be delayed until a more important purchase was completed: "the site for an observatory on the reverse side of the moon." Such sarcasm was less likely in response to Shufeldt's trip. A New York business group approached Washington officials for help on a possible trans-African railroad. In his annual message of 1883, President Chester A. Arthur declared that the United States should cooperate in opening the Congo economically but should keep clear of political entanglements. In 1884, on State Department orders, a special agent, Willard P. Tisdel, began bringing U.S. goods into the Congo and scouted out business opportunities. In the Senate, John T. Morgan (D.-Ala.) led the fight to guarantee both freedom of access and protection for Americans who moved into the Congo Basin. By 1884, Belgian King Leopold II's African International Association was starting one of history's most reactionary and brutal colonial rules in the Congo. Morgan pushed to have the United States support Leopold. The Alabama senator eyed Africa's millions not only

1 Robert L. Beisner, *From the Old Diplomacy to the New,* 2d ed., (Arlington Heights, Ill., 1986), 64; David Pletcher, *The Awkward Years* (Columbia, Mo., 1962), chap. 7.

as a gigantic export market for depressed southern textile firms but also as an area to which his section's freed African Americans could be exported. With one commitment to the Congo, Morgan hoped to solve domestic racial problems and – working through the exiled African Americans – domestic economic upheavals as well.[2]

Morgan and Arthur received key support from John Kasson, the U.S. minister to Austria-Hungary. Kasson had a close-up view as the European powers struggled with each other for control of potential colonial areas. In the early 1890s alone, the British were fighting in Afghanistan, occupying Egypt and the Sudan, and establishing protectorates throughout sub-Saharan Africa. The French took Tahiti and extended their domination in parts of Southeast Asia. Germany took over Togo and Southwest Africa, then moved toward Zanzibar, Tanganyika, and Samoa. The powers were well on their way to controlling more than 150 million people and 10 million square miles of territory (about one-fifth of the world's land) that they conquered between 1870 and 1900.

Kasson was one of many influential Americans who used their Old World vantage point to keep people back home informed about European affairs. Some of them were widely read novelists. The international novel developed with the books of Henry James and Edith Wharton. Even Bret Harte, famous for his California frontier stories, moved to Europe in 1878, became a U.S. consul, settled in London, and never returned to the United States. Ties of literature were reinforced with transatlantic marriages and increased travel by young people with names such as Roosevelt, Lodge, Adams, and Hay. Travel books, not least those by James and Mark Twain, were highly popular. Kasson, who had traveled widely in the 1860s on international business, became one of many who acted as conduits in the growing exchange of views and biases between Americans and Europeans that marked the era.[3]

2 Robert L. Beisner, "Who Lost Babelmandeb?" *Washington Post,* Outlook section, March 4, 1979; Joseph A. Fry, "John Tyler Morgan's Southern Expansionism," *Diplomatic History* 9 (Fall 1985): 329–46; Otto zu Stolberg-Wernigerode, *Germany and the United States During the Era of Bismarck* (Reading, Pa., 1937), 204.
3 Milton Plesur, "Looking Outward . . ." (Ph.D. diss., University of Rochester, 1954), chap. 10.

Kasson, however, was in a position to change views into policy. Convinced that the United States, whether it wished to be or not, was caught up in a vital struggle for world markets, the minister moved to open the Balkans and Eastern Europe to American goods through treaties with the Rumanians and Serbs. He then focused on the Congo's wealth. Kasson fully agreed with the *New York Herald*'s suggested slogan: "Let the Congo be opened to the trade of the world. That is all we demand." The minister believed this could be achieved by going along with King Leopold's request for an international conference that would certify Belgium's hold on the rich area and, Kasson hoped, would guarantee that the Congo be opened to all investors and traders on an equal basis. Kasson and Senator Morgan found an influential supporter in Colonel Henry S. Sanford, once a diplomat of Lincoln's, now a Florida real-estate speculator living well in Belgium. Sanford pushed the line of Leopold, his close friend, on the State Department: It is to the "vast" Congo "that we are to look for relief from the overproduction which now threatens us in some of our manufactories."[4]

In 1884, Chancellor Otto von Bismarck moved to stop a growing struggle over the Congo by calling a conference in Berlin. Arthur and Secretary of State Frederick Frelinghuysen broke the historic U.S. policy of not becoming involved in European conferences and sent Kasson as Washington's delegate. The U.S. position was to support Leopold's claims against opposition from the French and Portuguese and, above all, to parlay the Belgian king's promises into a guaranteed Open Door for U.S. interests in the Congo. (Kasson also wanted a U.S. base on the Congolese coast, but Frelinghuysen thought that went too far, although he did order a U.S. naval commander to search out a spot for "a commercial resort.") The U.S. position, which was virtually identical with Leopold's thanks to Thatcher, Kasson, and Morgan, was written into the treaty. Kasson was elated. The Senate was not. Despite Morgan's pleading, the body disliked what it saw as an entangling alliance. James G. Blaine, the Republican presidential nominee, criticized the outgoing Republican administration for signing a treaty that obliterated

4 Pletcher, *Awkward Years*, chap. 17; Plesur, "Looking Outward," 115.

the separation of the Old and New Worlds, and consequently destroyed a key assumption, he claimed, of the Monroe Doctrine. In 1885, the new Democratic president, Grover Cleveland, withdrew the treaty.[5]

The Congo problem, however, did not disappear as a political and even religious concern. Nor, by any means, did Leopold's promises and the Open Door principle bring order and hope to West Africa. The Belgians' brutality was first revealed by George Washington Williams in his "Open Letter" of 1890. An editor, pastor, and appointee as U.S. minister to Haiti (although he never served), Williams was the first African American elected to the Ohio legislature and the first scholarly black historian. Williams's "Open Letter" scandalized Europe and enlightened Americans by making dozens of well-substantiated charges against Leopold, who had unjustly seized the Congolese land, "burned their towns, stolen their property, enslaved their women and children," but had done nothing to educate or improve their lives economically. Williams's spectacular charges forced even the president, the glacial Benjamin Harrison, to come out against Leopold's depredations. Williams unfortunately died in 1891, and American concern turned away from the king's atrocities and back to the Congo as a marketplace.[6]

Other African Americans became quite differently involved. Missionary publications had long been taking credit for bringing their light to the so-called dark continent. The *New York Herald,* with its highly sensitive nose for profitable imperialism, bragged that in Africa the missionary and merchants worked as teams to destroy Islamic beliefs. One missionary took a different tack. William Henry Sheppard had graduated from Stillman College, in Tuscaloosa, Alabama, which the Southern Presbyterian Church had built to train African-American missionaries. From a middle-class Virginia family, Sheppard worked easily with whites and joined Samuel Lapsley on a missionary trip to the Congo in 1890. Sheppard worked

5 Edward Younger, *John A. Kasson* (Iowa City, 1955), 280–7; Pletcher, *Awkward Years,* chap. 17.
6 John Hope Franklin, *George Washington Williams: A Biography* (Chicago, 1985), xv–xxiv, 234–41.

with African leaders, Lapsley with the white officials, to produce a flourishing mission. Sheppard became highly knowledgeable about, and sensitive to, the Africans' customs. He returned to the United States to recruit more missionaries, including African Americans, to work in the Congo. By 1899 the missionaries were educating U.S. churches about the Belgian practice of taking a "goodly number" of the "people around us here" for forced, state labor. They also revealed how Leopold used the feared Zappo-Zap tribe to collect taxes, while the Zappo-Zaps used Leopold's relationship as a cover for their own slave raids. The resulting uproar finally forced the State Department to protest to the king. In 1909, the Belgian company sued Sheppard for libel. In an internationally watched trial, the missionary was exonerated. As trade developed between white Americans and the Congo, so, for quite different reasons, did links between Africans and African Americans.[7]

Crossing the Pacific: Samoa

In Samoa as in West Africa, ambitious naval officers made the initial important American claims. And as in Africa, so the hope evolved that as a strategic base Samoa would help relieve the growing glut of U.S. goods. In the southern Pacific, however, few missionaries or publicists appeared to act as conscience, as had Williams in the Congo debate. The struggle over Samoa was a straight-out battle of three imperial powers. Nor did the U.S. government formally withdraw, as it had after the 1884 Berlin conference; it instead remained and nearly went to war against Europeans.

In 1872, Navy Commander Richard W. Meade signed the first U.S. treaty with Samoan native chieftains. American firms and land speculators had arrived earlier, but Meade was primarily interested in the fine, protected harbor of Pago Pago, for which he received a lease in return for a protectorate. The Samoans, rightly fearing British and German attention, were playing off foreigner against foreigner. The Senate accepted the harbor but rejected the respon-

7 Walter L. Williams, "William Henry Sheppard, Afro-American Missionary in the Congo, 1890–1910," in Sylvia M. Jacobs, ed., *Black Americans and the Missionary Movement in Africa* (Westport, Conn., 1982), 135–49.

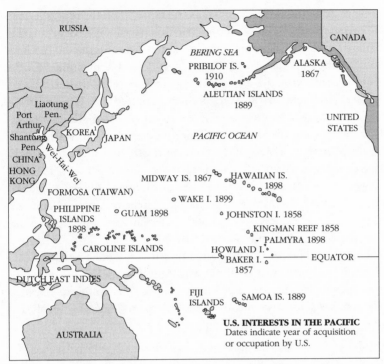

RUSSIA

CANADA

BERING SEA

PRIBILOF IS.
1910

ALASKA
1867

ALEUTIAN ISLANDS
1889

Liaotung
Port Pen.
Arthur
Shantung
Pen.
CHINA²
HONG
KONG

KOREA¹ JAPAN

Wei-Hai-Wei

UNITED
STATES

PACIFIC OCEAN

FORMOSA (TAIWAN)

MIDWAY IS. 1867

HAWAIIAN IS.
1898

WAKE I. 1899

PHILIPPINE
ISLANDS
1898

GUAM 1898

JOHNSTON I. 1858

KINGMAN REEF 1858
PALMYRA 1898

CAROLINE ISLANDS

HOWLAND I.
BAKER I.
1857

EQUATOR

DUTCH EAST INDIES

FIJI
ISLANDS

SAMOA IS. 1889

AUSTRALIA

U.S. INTERESTS IN THE PACIFIC
Dates indicate year of acquisition
or occupation by U.S.

¹Korea: 1st U.S. treaty, 1882
²China: U.S. intervenes with other Powers, 1900-1901

sibility of a protectorate. A modified pact offered simply U.S. good offices in return for Pago Pago, and this proved more acceptable. In reality, the U.S., British, and German consuls worked out a tripartite agreement in 1879 that Secretary of State Evarts did not bother to place at the Senate's mercy. The arrangement existed for the next eight years, although not without growing conflict between U.S. and German claims. In 1885, Secretary of State Thomas F. Bayard warned Berlin that he would "not allow any one power to have a commercial preference," and, somewhat contradictorily, demanded independence for Samoans. In 1886, Great Britain secretly supported German claims in return for Bismarck's supporting London's position in Egypt.[8] The United States was becoming enmeshed in those European quarrels about which Washington and Jefferson had warned.

8 Charles Callan Tansill, *The Foreign Policy of Thomas F. Bayard* (New York, 1940), 30–1.

This generation of U.S. officials, however, thought it was necessary to stand and fight. With the British in Germany's pocket on the Samoan question, the three powers met at Washington in 1887 to sort out the imperial claims. Bayard beat down German plans for de facto control with the argument that in U.S. eyes, Samoan ports were a vital link in the system that connected the U.S. railroad network to Asia – especially if an isthmian canal was built. In part because of the daily hundred-plus degrees of a Washington summer, mostly because of the growing rivalry, nothing came out of the conference. In 1888 Germany moved more directly to seize power. Samoans captured a number of German soldiers (and beheaded some), but Bismarck's grip had tightened. American opinion flared, led by business groups such as the San Francisco Chamber of Commerce, which darkly warned that if Samoa fell to the Germans, Hawaii would be next. Washington prepared to send a warship. The Iron Chancellor wondered aloud why Americans were so concerned about these "remote, inconsiderable islands." In a note to Bayard, Second Assistant Secretary of State Alvey A. Adee outlined the geopolitics of a rising Pacific empire:

They may be remote and inconsiderable for Germany, but to us they are proximate and considerable, for in the hands of a naval Power they threaten our Pacific flank, and indeed they threaten all the Pacific Coast of South America too, and Hawaii besides. Samoa offsets Pearl Harbor, and Bismarck so intends it.[9]

President Grover Cleveland, often incorrectly viewed by historians as an antiexpansionist, picked up on Adee's ideas and sent a ringing message to Congress upholding U.S. rights. Congress began to consider military appropriations.

Bismarck now asked for a conference in Berlin. Before it could convene, the three nations' warships, whose men had been staring each other down in Apia harbor, were struck by a mighty hurricane. Of the thirteen warships, only one British vessel escaped to open water and survived. Properly chastened by near war and nature, the three nations worked out a three-power protectorate at Berlin. The

9 Ibid., 81, 100–1; "Protocol of Second Samoan Conference," July 2, 1887, Box
    162, Papers of John Bassett Moore, Library of Congress, Washington, D.C.

United States received its main demand, its own protectorate over Pago Pago harbor. The crisis calmed until after the 1898 war when the powers' struggle over China again drew attention to Samoa. In 1899, the British, preoccupied with the Boer War in South Africa, pulled out. The United States and Germany divided the islands, with the Americans obtaining Pago Pago. American Samoa resulted from the clear U.S. choice of standing firm — for commercial and strategic reasons — regardless of instability, civil conflict, near war, and the danger of becoming embroiled in European colonial quarrels. Assistant Secretary of State John Bassett Moore later placed the episode in perspective: "No incident in the history of the United States . . . better prepares us to understand the acquisition of the Philippines" than U.S. policy in Samoa.[10]

Bringing Revolution to Hawaii

American missionaries arrived in Hawaii after 1819 to find the land owned in a type of feudal system with the king as feudal lord. The missionaries converted Hawaiian rulers to Christianity, became their translators and advisers, and by 1849 had the power to destroy the traditional land system and kin-based production. In their place appeared, by missionary-inspired law, yeomen farmers, wage laborers, and, most notably, vast opportunities for buying up the land. By the 1850s sixteen Congregationalist missionaries held land titles that averaged 493 acres per person. By 1892, Americans and Europeans owned two-thirds of Hawaii. The U.S. consul called the missionaries the "bloodsuckers of the community," living "like lords" and "disturbing the minds of these children of Nature." Seward had failed to lock up Washington's control of the islands with a reciprocity treaty in 1867, but the U.S. consul nevertheless reported in 1871 that the most-heard songs on Hawaiian streets were "Marching Through Georgia," and "John Brown's Body." Hawaiian control of Hawaii was fast slipping away. In 1876, Secretary of State Hamilton Fish finally pushed a reciprocity treaty through the Senate. Fish emphasized not the economic benefits, but the

10 "Autobiography," Envelope II, Folder C, Box 207, Moore Papers.

warning that if the United States did not tighten its grip on the islands, Great Britain and Canada would do so.[11] The treaty's effects were electric.

Between 1876 and 1885 annual sugar production soared from 26 million pounds and $1.3 million in value, to 171 million pounds and $8.4 million. Plantations tripled in number during the four years after 1876, and two-thirds of all sugar property was held by Americans. Hawaiian sugar moved so quickly into the U.S. market that American beet-sugar producers and East Coast refiners formed a phalanx with protectionists to kill renewal of the treaty in 1883. They failed. As usual, James G. Blaine had well explained the course of the nation's empire and why the opponents' efforts were doomed: The 1876 treaty, the Secretary of State said in 1881, makes Hawaiians "practically members of an American Zollverein in an outlying district of the state of California." It was time, Blaine added, to quit evading responsibility and annex the islands before native rulers caused problems. Then U.S. capital and "intelligent workers" could develop Hawaii in "a purely American form of colonization." Blaine believed the United States had no use for bases in Africa, the Indian Ocean, or the Danish West Indies, but three places should be taken – Hawaii, Cuba, and Puerto Rico. The last two would not be ripe "for a generation," but Hawaii "may come up for decisions at any unexpected hour."[12]

When the renewal struggle began in 1886, President Grover Cleveland and Secretary of State Thomas Bayard, not usually known for jingoistic foreign policies, fought and won an all-out battle against opponents led by well-heeled domestic sugar interests. Cleveland further sweetened the treaty by obtaining an exclusive right to Pearl Harbor, an undeveloped but (as many observers pointed out) magnificent protected port on Oahu Island. The Hawaiians, helped

---

11 Gary Y. Okihiro, *Cane Fires: The Anti-Japanese Movement in Hawaii, 1865–1945* (Philadelphia, 1991), 5–7; Tansill, *Bayard,* 361; William A. Russ, Jr., *The Hawaiian Revolution, 1893–1894* (Selinsgrove, Pa., 1959), 6–7, 30–2.

12 Alice F. Tyler, *The Foreign Policy of James G. Blaine* (Minneapolis, 1927), 200; Blaine to Harrison, August 10, 1891, in Albert T. Volwiler, *The Correspondence Between Benjamin Harrison and James G. Blaine, 1882–1893* (Philadelphia, 1940), 173–4.

along by British and Canadian officials, had opposed renewal because their sovereignty was disappearing, but the foreign planters
and their political allies pressured the king to offer Pearl Harbor and
then agree to a new treaty. Cleveland knew what was at stake in
Hawaii: "Our close and manifest interest in the commerce of the
Pacific Ocean upon which we hold the most important seaboard,
renders the Hawaiian group of essential importance to us on every
score." Bayard added the usual argument that if the United States
rejected the islands, the powers would gladly step in to take them.[13]

In 1887, the planters struck. In what they termed a "revolution,"
they demanded that a weak king, Kalakaua, sign a new constitution
turning de facto control over to whites who had sufficient property
qualifications. Bayard helped. He gave the U.S. minister a blank
check to aid the white planters fully, including, by inference, the
landing of American troops if necessary. They were not needed in
1887, but landed two years later during an outbreak. In 1890 the
annexationists lost control of the government; led by Lorrin A.
Thurston, who had masterminded the 1887 takeover, they now
secretly prepared a second "revolution." Meanwhile, Canadian Pacific Railroad and British interests became more prominent. The British minister to the United States, Julian Pauncefote, suggested to
Secretary of State Blaine in 1890 that both nations pledge to ensure
Hawaiian independence. "Mr. Blaine," Pauncefote recalled, "in a
very emphatic way said the United States would do nothing of the
kind."[14]

Then the hammer blow fell. The reciprocity provision of the 1890
McKinley Tariff not only put sugar on the free list, and ultimately
through a treaty gave Cuban sugar preferential entry, but bought off
domestic sugar producers by giving them a subsidy of two cents per
pound. The Hawaiian economy went into a tailspin. Perhaps Harrison, Blaine, and McKinley had foreseen this result; certainly they
were ready with a measure declaring that the new tariff in no way
affected the 1887 treaty or the lease on Pearl Harbor. The anti-

13 Tansill, *Bayard,* 373-4.
14 Pauncefote to Salisbury, January 10, 1890, Papers of Lord Salisbury, Oxford,
   England; "Memo of Conversations," Great Britain, National Archives, Department of State, Record Group 59, Washington, D.C. (hereafter NA, RG).

American group seized the offensive in 1891 by putting in power Queen Liliuokalani, who, U.S. Minister John Stevens warned Blaine, had "extreme notions of sovereign authority." Stevens also sent so many messages to Washington claiming that the British and Canadians were poised to strike that Harrison started to mention his fears of the threat in private correspondence. The smaller planters who were most damaged by the tariff meanwhile prepared to seize power. A U.S. Navy official reported to Washington that if a revolt erupted, "it would simply be the old struggle of the Anglo Saxon race against the weaker element." Just in case he had miscalculated, however, U.S. forces remained close by.[15]

The 1890 tariff triggered political war in Hawaii. The white planters and the queen maneuvered for power, with the queen gaining the upper hand until January 1893 when she issued a constitution giving herself greatly enlarged power. She overreached. When she tried to pull back her constitutional claims, it was too late. The annexationists, with encouragement from Blaine, prepared to move. American sailors landed on January 16, 1893, to protect American property. The annexationists seized power without significant opposition. In his last days as president, Harrison sent a treaty of annexation to the Senate. A national debate erupted. The *Review of Reviews* argued that Hawaii was essential to Americans because of "its central position in the commerce of the Pacific Ocean" and linked the islands directly to the importance of the China market. Opponents, however, argued in the words of the independent *Boston Herald*, "In a trade way we could not gain by annexation of anything we do not now possess, while politically the union would bring with it new problems of difference in race and conditions to add to those which we now have." The new Democratic president, Grover Cleveland, and his secretary of state, Walter Quintin Gresham, agreed with the opposition. Cleveland withdrew the annexation treaty. Gresham especially feared the consequences of a colonial policy that stretched the Constitution so far over water. He nevertheless took pains to

---

15 Sylvester K. Stevens, *American Expansion in Hawaii, 1852–1898* (Harrisburg, Pa., 1945), 187–203; Commander Felix McCurley to Tracy, August 29, 1890, Area 9 file, box 14, Naval Records, NA, RG 45.

inform foreign powers that annexation or no, for them Hawaii remained off limits. Gresham, like the *Boston Herald*, believed the
United States possessed the benefits and did not need the political
responsibilities. [16] Four more years of economic disorder followed in
the United States before McKinley returned, this time as president,
to annex Hawaii and complete the process that his 1890 tariff bill
had accelerated.

Asia: Goods, God, and Gunboats

In the post-1865 era, U.S. foreign policy was consistently shaped by
choosing opportunity, both secular and religious, over stability. The
series of Hawaiian upheavals after the 1870s was one example. Nowhere, however, was this choice more obvious, and the consequences
more enormous, than in Asia. Traders and diplomats, propelled by
the economic crises after 1873, helped push an already fragile Asian
balance of power into a series of wars. Missionaries, moved by
threats of science and secularism that confronted their faith at home,
determined to prove the worth of themselves and their religious
beliefs by proselytizing in what they considered to be the world's
richest market for evangelicalism; they too thus contributed to the
destabilization of an already tottering Korea and Manchu dynasty.

Seward had placed U.S. policy in Asia on two principles: the use
of force and cooperation with other powers. In policy toward China,
those principles remained in place for most of the following three-
quarters of a century. In regard to Japan, however, they were broken
within a decade. In the 1870s, in a historic turn that revealed much
about the future of Washington's approach to the Far East, U.S.
officials departed from their European colleagues and unilaterally
helped Japan, which beginning in 1868 had transformed its government in a spectacularly successful commitment to modernize the
country along Western industrial lines. The U.S. minister to Japan
in the mid-1870s, Judge John A. Bingham, started the process by

16 Homer E. Socolofsky and Allen B. Spetter, *The Presidency of Benjamin Harrison*
(Lawrence, Kan., 1987), 200–6; *Public Opinion*, February 4, 1893, 415–17;
ibid., February 18, 1893, 464–5.

showing sympathy to Japanese demands for tariff autonomy, and by understanding that U.S.-Japan cooperation could undercut the powerful British position in the Japanese market. Bingham's view of a rising Japan was reinforced in 1876 when Tokyo signed a pact directly with Korea. The treaty for the first time split Korea apart from its tributary relationship with China and signaled that a dramatic rearrangement of power relationships was beginning in the region, with Japan doing much of the rearranging. In an 1878 treaty, the United States, to the displeasure of Europeans, granted Tokyo large measures of tariff autonomy. The British were able to kill this concession, but the United States (again over British objections) had taken an interest in removing extraterritorial rights in the 1880s. Washington signaled that it was betting on Japan's future, rather than China's or Korea's, in Asia. [17]

The United States then followed through by copying the Japanese example and opening Korea to Western interests. Some Americans, especially those from California, had been calling for access to Korea in the 1870s. Japan's treaty, recognizing Korean separateness from China, provided leverage. Secretary of State James G. Blaine and Rear Admiral Robert Shufeldt provided the initiative. Blaine's interest in Asia was distinctly secondary to his involvement with Latin American affairs, but in November 1881 he instructed Shufeldt to make a treaty with Korea because its ports, "so near to Japan and China," should "be opened to our trade and to the convenience of . . . vessels of our navy." Shufeldt needed no urging. He had extensively worked with the Chinese to improve their navy, and he understood the opportunity that was, in his view, nothing less than civilizing Asia. As he told a Stamford, Connecticut, audience:

As everything that is bright comes from the East – even as the sun rises in the East and as still the Star of Empire westward takes its way – so China must look to the shores of America for a new Civilization and a more vigorous regeneration. This is the natural course of events, the true march of human progress, the irresistible flow of the human tide.

17 W. G. Beasley, *The Rise of Modern Japan* (London, 1990), 142–4; Payson Treat, *Diplomatic Relations Between the United States and Japan*, 2 vols. (Stanford, 1932), 2:2–7, 48–55.

A civilization will come from California, more rough and uncouth, but with kindly sympathies; it may kick and cuff and curse and swear, but it will shake the hand and if need be lend a hand to their pig-tailed friends. . . .

The Pacific is the ocean bride of America – China, Japan and Corea – and their innumerable islands, hanging like necklaces about them, are the bridesmaids. California is the nuptial couch, the bridal chamber, where all the wealth of the Orient will be brought to celebrate the wedding. Let us as Americans . . ., determine while yet in our power, that no commercial rival or hostile flag can float with impunity over the long swell of the Pacific sea. [18]

Shufeldt's 1882 treaty with Korea gave Americans the right to live in port cities, a role in setting tariff rates, the privilege of extraterritoriality protection, and the power to end the opium trade. The pact further weakened the power of the Chinese empire, which had considered Korea a tributary state. Blaine, Bayard, and other U.S. officials believed the United States could profit from this weakness and by the late 1880s Bayard was telling the pivotal U.S. diplomat in Korea, Horace Allen, where to go for loans in California if New York City bankers could not help. Allen needed little encouragement. A devout Presbyterian, Allen became one of the first Protestant missionaries to enter a country that had been violently anti-Christian. (No more had he gotten into Korea than he tried to exclude Roman Catholics.) By the mid-1880s, Allen cared less about saving souls than making money for Americans, including himself, and collecting valuable Korean art. He worked closely with the progressive, pro-Japanese party that wanted to break Korea cleanly from China and modernize it, especially through concessions to Allen and his friends. As early as 1884 such changes had exploded in a bloody, anti-Japanese war in Korea. But Allen scarcely missed a beat. By 1889–90, he worked with Blaine and Vice-President Levi P. Morton's Wall Street firm of Morton, Bliss to obtain a range of Korean property, including rights to perhaps the richest gold mines in Asia. Allen was weakening China (and Korea) and playing into Japan's hands. The Japanese were not yet ready for war during

18 F. C. Drake, *The Empire of the Seas: A Biography of Rear-Admiral Robert Nelson Shufeldt* (Honolulu, 1984), chap. 5, esp. 116; Tyler, *Blaine*, chap. 10, esp. 269.

the 1884 outbreak. A decade later they were, and Asia's balance of power was transformed.[19]

Even as the United States helped separate Korea from China, and in 1882 broke an 1880 pact by prohibiting Chinese laborers from entering the United States, Americans worked to develop their economic and political ties with China. In the Seward-Burlingame Treaty, Washington had pledged to follow a noninterventionist policy in China's internal development. Through the 1880s, U.S. officials said they wanted to protect the status quo; while they wanted no Chinese territory, they did not want other powers to obtain any either. But there were the usual contradictions. Shufeldt's mission to Korea had broken up the status quo, and as U.S. Minister to China John Russell Young declared in the 1880s, his first duty was to protect U.S. claims in China.[20]

The U.S. claims and involvement picked up after 1885 when Charles Denby became the U.S. minister. A railroad entrepreneur, Denby was close to other railway builders, especially James Harrison Wilson, of Secretary of State Bayard's hometown of Wilmington, Delaware. Wilson had visions of linking China and Korea into one huge market for U.S. goods. Bayard reassured a New York businessman that Denby understood he was to help U.S. firms, and that the ambitious Wilson also was ready "to rattle all the china in the National Cupboard." Such reassurances were welcome, especially to southern textile interests and to journals of the iron and steel industry that urged immediate and full entry into the race for the China market. Working closely with Li Hong-zhang, who led the drive for Chinese development in the 1870s and 1880s, a Philadelphia syndicate tried to set up a bank to finance railroad construction, but internal Chinese politics killed the project.[21]

The enthusiasm generated for the China market by the business community was at least matched by the go-for-broke determination

19 Fred Harvey Harrington, *God, Mammon, and the Japanese* (Madison, 1944), 1–17, 52–3, 134–45.
20 Warren Cohen, *America's Response to China,* 2d ed. (New York, 1980), 34–5; Plesur, "Looking Outward," chap. 7.
21 Tansill, *Bayard,* 422–31; Tyler Dennett, *Americans in Eastern Asia* (New York, 1922), 579–80.

of American missionaries. The 1880s to 1920s era marked the golden age of missionary enterprise, most notably in the Near East, where they were deeply involved in Turkey and North Africa, and in the Far East. At a Protestant meeting in China during 1890, the call went out for 1,000 more evangelists to enter in the next five years; more than 1,100 appeared, with Americans predominating, despite the upheaval of the 1894 Sino-Japanese War.

The causes of this invasion were many. Back home, churches were challenged by the new Darwinian science, and the church's social status came under siege by the secular demands (and profits) of the industrial transformation. Fundamentalist leaders, such as the charismatic Dwight L. Moody, met Darwinism with an emphatic reiteration of the old-time religion and the command that believers were to show their worth by bringing into the fold more believers. Expansion was as much a requirement for religion as it was for Carnegie's steel mills; or as one missionary phrased it, "Christianity is a religion that will not keep." Others dealt with Darwinism by trying to coopt its social-Darwinian variant. Perhaps the leader here was Josiah Strong, a Congregationalist minister whose book *Our Country* sold 175,000 copies in the 1880s and was translated into Asian and European languages. His lectures were nearly as much in demand as his books. Strong's message was a paean to Anglo-Saxon expansionism; it outlined the usual Darwinian stages to justify the conclusion that historically empire had moved west from Persia and Greece to reach its peak in "our mighty West, there to remain, for there is no further West; beyond is the Orient." Strong followed the logic of his argument and, by 1902, headed an international gospel movement. By 1913 he had begun writing four volumes entitled *Our World.* Two decades earlier, however, another Congregationalist minister had exhibited the influences that Strong exemplified with an article entitled "The Anglo-Saxon and the World's Redemption."[22]

Such contagious enthusiasm easily found its way into women's clubs, which proliferated after 1870 and became highly important sponsors of missions both at home and abroad. The enthusiasm

22 Josiah Strong, *Our Country* (New York, 1885), 29.

especially struck colleges. The Student Volunteers for Foreign Missions became part of the booming YMCA and YWCA movements in the post-1887 years, and soon had chapters on nearly every American college campus. By 1914 the Student Volunteers had nearly six thousand missionaries stationed abroad. Nowhere was passion higher than at Yale, which produced three of the loudest voices for redeeming China — Horace Pitkin (who was beheaded by the Chinese during the Boxer Rebellion), Sherwood Eddy, and Henry Luce (father of the founder of *Time, Fortune,* and *Life* magazines). All three men practiced in China the motto of the Student Volunteers: "The Evangelization of the World in this Generation." Prohibited in China before the 1850s, and encountering bitter opposition afterward from Chinese authorities, Christian missionaries by 1898 had infiltrated every Chinese province plus Manchuria. They also followed Horace Allen's lead in Korea and worked to separate that country so they would not have to put up with Chinese anti-Christianity.[23]

As their view of Korea illustrates, the missionaries were not political amateurs. They well understood the growing contradiction between U.S. public support for Chinese territorial integrity and autonomy on the one hand and, on the other, U.S. private and public demands for concessions and the full rights and protection of American citizens. "The indications of Providence all point westward," one missionary voice argued in 1890, and "China is open to the Gospel now" although "it may not be so when she becomes strong enough to dictate the terms of her treaties. . . . It is the full hour of opportunity." The matter was of the utmost urgency; as a Congregationalist leader argued, missionaries "are laying the foundations of empires, and we are shaping the future of great populations and mighty states." A great part of that future was built around prosperity. As the *Congregationalist* phrased it, "Commerce follows the mis-

23 John K. Fairbank, "Introduction," and Clifton J. Phillips, "The Student Volunteer Movement and Its Role in China Missions, 1886–1920," in John K. Fairbank, ed., *The Missionary Enterprise in China and America* (Cambridge, Mass., 1974), 1–19, 91–109; Paul Varg, "Missionaries," in Alexander DeConde, ed., *Encyclopedia of American Foreign Policy*, 3 vols. (New York, 1978), 2:567–71.

sionary."[24] No missionary expressed this idea more plainly than Isaac Taylor Headland, who had begun his service in 1893. In a 1912 memoir he recalled:

If I were asked to state what would be the best form of advertising for the great American Steel Trust or Standard Oil or the Baldwin Locomotive Works . . . or the Singer sewing machine, or any one of a dozen great business concerns, I should say, take up the support of one or two or a dozen mission stations, an educational institution, a hospital, a dispensary, or a hundred native preachers or teachers. Everyone thus helped would be, consciously or unconsciously, a drummer for your goods, and the great church they represent at home would be your advertising agents.[25]

Not everyone agreed. E. L. Godkin, the editor of *The Nation,* noted that when a missionary was expelled from a country, "he gives the impression of a furious animal robbed of his prey." Godkin, doubtless noting the dispatch of U.S. warships to China and the Near East in 1893–4 to protect the missions and other American interests from war, sarcastically added that the missionary expected the U.S. military to "stand by with fixed bayonets while he preaches peace on earth good will to men." Godkin's words were not hyperbole. The commander of a U.S. gunboat on the Yangtse River reported home in 1891 "that the Missionary cause has made most extraordinary progress. . . . Their number is constantly increasing and there seems to be no limit to the money that is behind them." He also noted, however, that the reason the region was quiet was "entirely . . . the presence of gunboats."[26]

"We, more than any other Power, are to have the Pacific trade – the trade with China and Japan," a New York business newspaper announced in 1894. But the Americans were also guaranteeing the blessings of the West with gunboats, and proclaiming that an Open Door for China was so important that not even the Chinese could

24 *Public Opinion,* February 8, 1890, 432; Ralph Dewar Bald, Jr., "The Development of Expansionist Sentiment in the United States, 1885–1895, as Reflected in Periodical Literature," (Ph.D. diss., University of Pittsburgh, 1953), 92–9.
25 Isaac Taylor Headland, *Some By-Products of Missions* (Cincinnati, 1921), 33–4.
26 Bald, "Development of Expansionist Sentiment," 106–9, has the Godkin quotation; Commander Barber to Belknap, December 1, 1891, Area 10 file, box 8, December folder, Naval Records, NA, RG 45.

close it. As Korea moved out of control, China became more difficult to govern, the great powers began to circle, and Japan poised to strike, all the assumptions of U.S. policy came into question. Indeed, as John K. Fairbank has argued, when Chinese authority crumbled, the privileged and protected missionaries became highly influential with certain Chinese audiences, and "through this interaction, the Protestant missions began to make their contribution to the Chinese revolutionary process."[27]

Washington would not back off. Opportunities for missionaries and concessions in the greatest of all potential markets took precedent over order and, consequently, over Chinese self-rule, which became more difficult to realize as the country became more destabilized. Nor did the Japanese offer as much hope anymore. The commander of the U.S. Asiatic squadron reported to Washington in 1893 that "Japan is likely to add to the complications at Hawaii" and "was anxious to enlarge her possessions" in Asia. He quoted a Japanese naval officer as saying, "We aim to make Japan the England of the Pacific." The U.S. commander also quoted a former Japanese minister of foreign affairs declaring that building an isthmian canal would be fine because it would stimulate "Japanese emigration to Central America [and] even to Mexico."[28]

The United States and Japan had traveled far since 1868. Each hoped now to impose its own order on large parts of Asia. Instead, each nation's quest for opportunity helped trigger one of the twentieth-century's great revolutions.

27 Fairbank, "Introduction," and Arthur Schlesinger, Jr., "The Missionary Enterprise and Theories of Imperialism," in Fairbank, *The Missionary Enterprise*, 10, 371–3.
28 Belknap to Herbert, Area 10 file, box 9, January–June 1893 folder, Naval Records, NA, RG 45.

6. 1893–1896: Chaos and Crises

The United States drive to become the world's most powerful nation climaxed successfully in the generation that came to power during and immediately after the Spanish-American War of 1898. The success had been long in forming, but the catalyst was the 1873–97 depression and, especially, the economic crisis of 1893–7 that transformed a long era of deflation into a full-blown economic depression. The post-1898 American empire was a product of the pre-1897 chaos at home. As we have seen, the crisis was triggered by the technological and managerial advances of the Second Industrial Revolution, advances that were exemplified by Carnegie's policy of "running hard" to compete and indeed dominate market share. By the 1890s the Second Industrial Revolution, by all odds the most important event in American history between 1865 and 1914, had already begun spinning off a new, extracontinental foreign policy whose voices were Seward's and Blaine's especially. Culture (as manifested in the missionary movement), ideas (as seen in social Darwinism), and politics (as exemplified by an evolving Republican party and its fresh-found interest in reciprocity), as well as foreign policy had to adapt to the industrial changes.

American and Roman Empires

By 1893 the social trauma was becoming pronounced. Even the 1877 general strike and the 1886 Haymarket Riot paled in comparison. The percentage of unemployed in the total labor force of the manufacturing and transportation sectors has been estimated at about 4 percent in 1892, doubling to 9.6 percent in a year, and nearly doubling again to 16.7 percent in 1894. It remained between nearly 12 percent and 14 percent through 1898 and then, finally, dropped to 7.7 percent in 1899.[1] Those were only stark figures. More real were the general strike called by 160,000 miners in the soft-coal fields; a strike that paralyzed the Great Northern Railway; the massive march of the unemployed eastward toward Washington in the Coxey and Hogan "armies"; the near capture of the American Federation of Labor (AFL) by its socialist wing; the Pullman strike in Chicago that President Grover Cleveland put down with federal troops, and which one historian called "almost a reign of terror"; and the claim by *The Nation* that California was "in the hands of mobs at Oakland, Sacramento, and Los Angeles, and when the militia are called out to enforce the law, they side with the rioters and throw down their arms." All that (and more) occurred only in 1894. If any intelligent observer had doubts about the class warfare inherent in these crises, they were removed in 1895 when a highly conservative Supreme Court struck down income tax legislation, and when the Cleveland administration had to turn to J. P. Morgan to save the near-bankrupt U.S. Treasury by floating bonds to wealthy American and British investors. As one businessman wrote his good friend, the president of the United States, in mid-1894, "My thoughts have been a good deal with you of late. The crisis, long approaching, is now upon us."[2]

Cleveland's attorney general (and later U.S. secretary of state) Richard Olney placed the American crisis within a larger, indeed global, crisis of capitalism. He told a Brown University audience that the causes were not "temporary, accidental, superficial, and isolated." but "lie deeper [and] are of no recent origin." Olney continued, "All over the civilized world the working man is in a state of unrest." Such laborers believe they "are preparing a revolution which shall do for the emancipation of labor what Luther and the Reformation did for freedom of conscience, and what [1776] did for political liberty." In his memoirs, AFL leader Samuel Gompers phrased the problem more simply: "The period of depression was often called a period of so-called overproduction, which was really a

---

1 Paul H. Douglas, *Real Wages in the United States, 1890–1926* (Boston, 1930), 440.
2 *Nation,* July 12, 1894, 20; A. B. Farquhar to Cleveland, June 1, 1894, Papers of Grover Cleveland, Library of Congress, Washington, D.C.

period of under-consumption for the people I knew, a period of hard times."[3]

No government official agonized over the deeper historical meaning of these "hard times" more than Cleveland's first secretary of state, Walter Quintin Gresham, who served from March 1893 until his sudden death two years later. Gresham had been the judge who handled the 1877 general strike. Resembling Olney (and many others), Gresham defined the problem not as temporary or limited to the United States, but as a long-term crisis of global capitalism. Its effects, and the social and political ills that accumulated in the 1880s, finally drove Gresham to leave the Republican party and join the Democrats. He left even after having served as President Chester Arthur's postmaster general and secretary of the treasury during 1882 and 1884. After a brief flirtation with the Populists, he tied the crisis to the Second Industrial Revolution. In 1892, he wrote that the "labor question" emerged from "new conditions utterly unlike anything in the past. Labor-saving machinery has given capital an advantage that it never possessed before. What is an equitable division of the joint product of capital and labor, and who is to decide the question" — settling that issue would produce "serious consequences." Gresham and British Ambassador Julian Pauncefote discussed "the greatest question of the age . . . that of capital and labor," as Mrs. Gresham recalled their definition of the problem. "The labor-saving machine had satisfied him as a patent judge that the productive power of the world would be increased, had increased beyond the capacity of the world to consume. [How] to keep the people of the various countries employed, prosperous, and happy at home, were the great questions to be met." In 1893, Secretary of State Gresham told a U.S. consul that the repeal of the 1890 Sherman Silver Purchase Act would be useful in that it might help restore faith in American money, but the economic problems' causes lay far deeper. Gresham had little belief in American exceptionalism. "The danger that menaces society in this country is like the menace in Europe. . . . Honest laboring men will not quietly see

3 Clipping of June 20, 1894, Papers of Richard B. Olney, Library of Congress; Samuel Gompers, *Seventy Years . . .*, 2 vols. (London, 1925), 2:3.

their families starve," he wrote a friend on May 2, 1894. Freer raw materials could, however, help in the United States because "this would lower the cost of the manufacturing article and enable our people to compete in foreign markets with Great Britain." Five days later, in a "personal and confidential" letter to a close friend, Gresham declared: "The present condition of things was brought about largely by our high tariff legislation. . . . What is transpiring in Pennsylvania, Ohio, Indiana, and Illinois, and in regions west of there, may fairly be viewed as symptoms of revolution." He then added the non sequitur that "those troubles will pass by, and like you, I regard them as the dark hour just before dawn." But nine days after that he seemed to wonder when, or if, the dawn would appear. He told the distinguished international lawyer John Bassett Moore that the "outlook" now seemed to "portend revolution." Gresham passed on the evaluation of a close friend and former senator: "There probably would be a revolution in the U.S., with a great leader emerging and then there would be a quest for empire."[4]

Influential *Banker's Magazine* did not want to touch the growing class problem, or confront it as had Gresham. It instead argued that the country had become sectionalized "on business and economic questions." Americans had become too pluralistic: They "will scarcely admit that we have grown too great, to hold our wide Empire intact, by the bond of common weal." But "it was this . . . that disintegrated the Roman Empire." Either more local autonomy was required, or centralization until "the majority may govern without obstacle, somewhat along the lines of those existing between England and her semi-independent colonies." James Madison's *Federalist* 10 seemed to have reached its limit as a usable theory of constitutional government; Madison's belief that bad "factions" could be controlled by a policy of "extend the sphere" of government had finally hit its boundary. The sphere was too large in the widely

4 Gresham to Morris Ross, August 1, 1892, Papers of Walter Quintin Gresham, Library of Congress, Washington, D.C.; Gresham to Wayne MacVeagh, May 7, 1894, Letterbook, ibid.; Gresham to Judge Dyer, May 2, 1894, Letterbook, ibid.; Matilda Gresham, *The Life of Walter Quintin Gresham, 1832–1895*, 2 vols. (Chicago, 1919), 2:802–3; Diary, Memoranda, 1894, Papers of John Bassett Moore, Library of Congress, Washington, D.C.

settled continent. *Banker's Magazine* paraphrased, apparently unknowingly, Madison's great theory, and – certainly unknowingly – laid out the evidence to support Madison's belief in 1829–30 that the constitutional system he had helped create would probably not last more than another century before it would have to be fundamentally reevaluated. *Banker's Magazine* then watched President Cleveland send troops to smash the Pullman strike. A sectional analysis leading to more centralized authority suddenly became a class analysis that feared centralization. Cleveland's use of force to put down a local uprising was "a very dangerous precedent," because if the government fell under "the control either of corporate combinations or of the new Populist party," such a class-dominated government could use Cleveland's precedent as a rationale to employ military force against its enemies. Class conflict seemed to be imminent.[5]

The Implications: Sacrificing Farmers, Shunning Colonies

The industrial changes forced the most fundamental questioning of the political order that had occurred since 1787. (Even in 1861–5 only the South actually questioned that order.) The results, however, were broad rather than deep. The constitutional system and the property relationships changed little in the post-1893 generation. Other parts of the society did change, however. Americans seemed to try to escape the crises by being constantly in motion, or becoming attracted to those who were. Professional baseball, heavyweight boxing, basketball (invented in 1891), and bicycle riding became the preoccupations of the 1890s. At the renewal of the Olympic Games in Athens in 1896, the peripatetic Americans won nine of fourteen gold medals, then took fourteen of twenty in Paris four years later. Frederick Jackson Turner's famous 1893 essay on "The Significance of the Frontier" analyzed the importance of space in forming American character and its political system over four hundred years of history. He left open at the end of his paper how that character and system were endangered now that the 1890 census

5 *Banker's Magazine* 48 (February 1894): 563–5; ibid., 49 (August 1894): 85–6.

officially declared the frontier closed. Frank Lloyd Wright employed the concept of open space in designing a new architecture; Mark Twain's, Brooks Adams's, Hamlin Garland's, and William Dean Howells's writings (and the rediscovery of Walt Whitman's after his death in 1892) explored the meaning of frontier space and, more particularly, the implications of its closing.[6]

The Second Industrial Revolution struck at the moment when space, especially the existence of a supposed frontier, seemed to be closing. As Twain described graphically in *A Connecticut Yankee,* technology had left no place to hide. President Cleveland noted the meaning of the frontier's closing in less apocalyptic terms in his 1893 annual message. Winslow Homer similarly redirected the observer's attention in his magnificent 1890s seascapes. These were not the soft sea scenes of the impressionists in Europe, nor were they the westward-looking paintings of the Hudson River School and later influential American artists. Homer instead turned one's attention to the new U.S. frontier, now that the supposed old one was closing – that is, to the merciless and unpredictable ocean. If Americans sought escape from the growing political and economic crisis that now filled their closing land, Homer seemed to be warning that to try to escape through the greatest of all frontiers held equal, if not greater, dangers.[7]

The majority of Americans, those who lived on farms, did not have to be told about the dangers of western settlement. By the 1890s they had been bludgeoned by falling crop prices, harsh winters, too little credit, expensive transportation, and massive foreclosures. Many debtors in both the country and the city turned to silver as a panacea. They were met head-on by creditors and Washington officials who had little sympathy for the silverites. Historians have argued that Presidents Benjamin Harrison and Grover Cleveland represented a Presbyterian type that insisted on probity, hard work, and paying off, rather than discounting, debt. Harrison

6 John Higham, "The Reorientation of American Culture in the 1890s," in John Weiss, ed., *The Origins of Modern Consciousness* (Detroit, 1965), 25–48.

7 James D. Richardson, *A Compilation of the Messages and Papers of the Presidents, 1789–1897,* 10 vols. (Washington, D.C., 1900), 9:454; Michael Brenson, "Homer's Epic," *New York Times,* March 31, 1991, H29.

blunted the attempt to coin large amounts of silver in the 1890 compromise, and Cleveland killed the compromise outright in 1893. Their morality received impressive support from their economic beliefs. Cleveland's secretary of the treasury, John G. Carlisle, argued vigorously in his annual reports that too large an infusion of silver could ruin U.S. currency by destroying its credibility in world markets. By 1892 the United States was second only to Great Britain on the list of the world's largest international traders. "Gold is the only international money, and all trade balances are settled in gold," Carlisle lectured. American farmers were in a poor position to argue the point. For more than a century these producers of grain, cotton, tobacco, and other staples had depended on prices set abroad.[8]

Leading, well-connected economists provided intellectual support for the Cleveland-Carlisle argument. Few were more prominent or better connected than David Ames Wells, a Republican whose reports as commissioner of revenue in the mid-1860s launched him as a pivotal voice of low-tariff advocates. He was joined by other leading economists, publicists such as E. L. Godkin of *The Nation,* and important newspaper editors such as Henry Watterson. In August 1893, as the economy seemed to be sliding toward oblivion, Wells declared that because U.S. manufacturers produced more than "the existing market demands," and because "foreign markets have been cut off" by high U.S. protective tariffs, it was time to slash those tariffs.[9] The 1890 Republican reciprocity act was a start, but insufficient. In 1894, Cleveland obtained repeal of the act and tried to replace it with the low-tariff Wilson-Gorman legislation that allowed the import of cheaper raw materials. The 1894 measure did not go nearly as far as Wells, Cleveland, and other low-tariff disciples wanted, but the general case had been made and accepted by a majority: The future of the U.S. economy lay increasingly in foreign markets; more silver coinage would ruin rather than help the dollar

8 Robert Kelley, *The Transatlantic Persuasion* (New York, 1969), 316–17; James A. Barnes, *John G. Carlisle* (New York, 1931), 299–302.

9 *New York World,* August 8, 1893, article by Wells, in Papers of Thomas F. Bayard, Library of Congress, Washington, D.C.

compete in those markets. Consequently, the markets had to be captured by reducing tariffs, bringing in cheaper raw materials, and thus making U.S. goods more competitive.

Henry Adams's firsthand summary of the 1893–6 debate caught it perfectly. In 1893, with the gold standard's victory,

> a capitalistic system had been adopted, and if it were to be run at all, it must be run by capital and by capitalistic methods; for nothing could surpass the nonsensity of trying to run so complex and so concentrated a machine by Southern and Western farmers in grotesque alliance with city day-laborers, as had been tried in 1800 and 1828, and had failed even under simple conditions. [10]

In Western Europe the post-1873 depression's effects, and rising industrial competition, had driven one nation after another toward protectionist policies. In Bismarck's Germany, moreover, the great industrial-capital hub of the European continent was being politically based (after the late 1870s agrarian crisis) on a conservative alliance between large landowners and major industrialists. The alliance's protectionism began to be matched by its support for Bismarck's accelerating search for formal territorial empire. [11] The United States, catching up with and then outstripping even Germany in industrial production, went in the opposite direction in its tariff and agrarian policies. Instead of moving toward more protectionism, after 1890 the Americans, slowly and with much backing and filling because of the entrenched high-tariff interests, which attached themselves to congressmen like barnacles, chipped away at those barnacles and moved toward a low-tariff policy that made food and raw material imports cheaper. As for the farmers, they were sacrificed on the altar built and sanctified by the post-1870 Industrial Revolution. Unlike Bismarck's Germany, agrarians in the United States were told to "raise less corn and more hell" in Populist Mary Elizabeth Lease's famous proclamation. But neither she nor anyone else could tell them how they could raise less corn, sell

10 Henry Adams, *The Education of Henry Adams* (Boston, 1930), 344.
11 Hans-Ulrich Wehler, "Industrial Growth and Early German Imperialism," in Roger Owen and Bob Sutcliffe, eds., *Studies in the Theory of Imperialism* (New York, 1972), 80.

more corn in world markets, and override the growing banker-industrialist power simultaneously.

The die had been cast at least since 1879–81, an economist told the British Royal Statistical Society in 1895. In New York, *Bradstreet's* devoted two full columns to this analysis by R. F. Crawford. Since the early 1880s, the opening of "fertile areas of virgin soil" in America had allowed farmers to grow more wheat for less cost. The farmers had since suffered from world-depressed prices, but much worse lay ahead. When Russia completed its Trans-Siberian Railway and opened up vast new fertile areas, its wheat would drive the U.S. crop out of world markets. Other observers noted that India and Argentina were also becoming large grain exporters. By 1894–5 a consensus was forming among economic analysts: Cheap U.S. farm staples appeared to be inevitable, so the best should be made of it and the staples should remain cheap so they could help lower labor and manufacturing costs, thus making U.S. industrial goods the world's most competitive, as well as the best. The trade figures seemed to indicate that sacrificing farmers was already working. "One of the features . . . for the fiscal year 1895 which should attract attention," the *Journal of Commerce* noted in September 1895, "is the large proportion of manufactured articles." After a three-century reign, farm products were giving way to industrial goods as the most important U.S. exports.[12]

The *Baltimore Sun* spelled out the interrelationship:

Cotton, wheat, petroleum, cattle from other countries are competing with ours in the markets which once we regarded as almost exclusively our own. The time has come when our manufacturers must help to swell the volume of our export trade, and the effect of tariff reduction, by curtailing the domestic demand for their goods and giving the American consumer the benefit, to some extent, of foreign competition, must be to compel them to seek foreign outlets for their wares.[13]

The argument had been completed by Cleveland in his 1893 annual message when he declared that laborers' true interests were not to seek help in the "narrow market" produced by high tariffs,

12 *Bradstreet's*, April 27, 1895, 259; *Public Opinion*, September 5, 1895, 315.
13 *Baltimore Sun*, May 27, 1895, in Bayard Papers.

but by low tariffs that gave them cheaper raw materials and ever greater markets that would keep them fully employed.[14] Gresham had drawn the foreign policy implications: Hawaii was neither needed nor wanted as a formal colony; not only did such a formal, annexationist, imperial policy threaten the Constitution, but America's future was to be in the open marketplace and not among those European imperialists who sought refuge from the rigors of the Second Industrial Revolution by seeking out closed, formal colonial empires. It all fit together once the farmers were in their proper place, industry was "running hard," and the tariff no longer separated efficient Americans from the world's markets.

The historic meanings of these turns became apparent as the 1890s progressed. Under strong pressure from business leaders who demanded a reform of the consular service for "extending our commerce and trade with foreign countries," Secretary of State Richard Olney worked closely with Cleveland to toughen the examinations for those agents. The U.S. diplomatic service was finally being prepared to enter the twentieth century. The National Association of Manufacturers (NAM), born in 1895, pushed for this reform, as well as demanded that the government build a great merchant fleet, an isthmian canal, and strong ties with Latin American markets. Such demands put the NAM, and many other Americans, at crosspurposes with the British. An NAM founder made the point, and several other points besides: The British "come over here every day and trade us a second-class duke or a third-class earl for a first-class American girl, and get several million dollars to boot. And the very next day the entire outfit goes back to Liverpool on a British vessel. We didn't even get the freight back to Liverpool on the earl, the girl, or the money."[15]

Americans, however, were getting their revenge. During the 1890s, foreign investment in the United States not only began to be replaced by American, but U.S. money competed for the first time with British and European investors abroad. A turn came with the

14 Richardson, *Compilation of Messages and Papers*, 9:459.
15 J. Potter to Olney, September 30, 1895, Olney Papers; Albert K. Steigerwalt, "The National Association of Manufacturers: Organization and Policies, 1895–1914" (Ph.D. diss., University of Michigan, 1952), 71–2.

failure of London's Baring Brothers in 1890; the firm had funneled much development capital into the United States throughout the nineteenth century. The 1890s depression in Europe caused other overseas investors to pull back or to turn to quick riches in Australian mines or Argentine staples. But with their incredible savings rate, and their industries "running hard," Americans were becoming capital rich. Their overseas investments jumped by an estimated $250 million during the depressed 1890s. Joseph C. Hendrix, then NAM president, succinctly marked the turn in 1898: "We have the Anglo-Saxon thirst for wide markets growing upon us. We have long been the granary of the world, we now aspire to be its workshop, then we want to be its clearing house."[16]

Ironically, the horrors of depression and the sacrificing of the farmers had in the end produced the world's next great imperial power. The post-1870 Industrial Revolution brought about the post-1873 social and political chaos, then the need for an expanding, open overseas empire. This new capitalism produced initially not a quest for stability and order but a search for an escape from the chaos through opportunities abroad.

The World's Fair, a World Navy

It was clear by 1893 that the quest for opportunities abroad could produce more, not less, disorder. The crises in Panama, Samoa, Chile, and Hawaii, among others, had vividly illustrated, moreover, that in each instance the U.S. Navy was involved, and naval power was required to protect American interests.

The great Columbian Exposition, the Chicago World's Fair of 1893, was a case study of how the new U.S. industrial power and the young navy had become wedded. The industrial exhibitions were breathtaking, not least the demonstration of the new dynamo machine that indeed rocked Henry Adams, because it seemed to defy the laws of both physics and history on which he had based his

16 Charles Hoffmann, "The Depression of the Nineties," *Journal of Economic History* 16 (June 1956): 156–7; Thomas McCormick, *China Market* (Chicago, 1967), 35.

nineteenth-century world. The scientific (and social) shocks caused by such exhibitions were carefully encased, as if in lead, by the neoclassical architecture of the exposition's halls. It was as if the unknown but certain chaotic consequences of the scientific and industrial exhibitions required the reassurance and controls suggested by the neoclassical architecture. The real control, however, occupied thirty acres of space and became one of the most popular displays: the U.S. Navy's exhibition of the new "Great White Fleet," including full-sized and perfect models of the first American battleships that had been authorized three years earlier. [17]

The fleet was the fitting centerpiece of the World's Fair for at least two reasons. First, it represented national achievement and honor, and in this sense well symbolized the amazing growth in recent years of patriotic organizations (such as the Daughters of the American Revolution, the Naval Order of the United States, and the U.S. Daughters of 1812). These groups represented the "grand wave of patriotism," as one observer called it, that washed over Americans in the post-1880 years as they sought a historical refuge amid the unpredictability of the Second Industrial Revolution. The growing U.S. military, led by the glamour and technological breakthroughs of the Great White Fleet, represented the perfect object for such patriotism – a patriotism caught in 1897 by the Marine Corps Band Director, John Phillip Sousa, when he penned the new national march, "The Stars and Stripes Forever." Second, the fleet exhibition also was the appropriate centerpiece because it necessarily complemented the vast industrial and scientific displays. As major U.S. economic interests led the world, and spread to its four corners, they also helped cause the disruptions that inevitably occurred when economic development clashed with political and social tradition (and when foreign intrusion conflicted with nationalism). The navy then had to be present, prepared, and superior.

The new fleet had grown even more rapidly than the Carnegie and Rockefeller industrial complexes. In the 1880s the British Navy numbered 367 modern warships while the American could total up

17 Robert W. Rydell, *All the World's a Fair* (Chicago, 1984), esp. 40–8; James Marston Finch, *American Building* (New York, 1973), 207–12.

almost 90 ships, 48 of which were capable of firing a gun, and 38 of which were made of wood. The Civil War fleet had nearly disintegrated, but not its personnel, at least numerically: There was approximately one officer for each enlisted man. This underequipped and top-heavy fleet nevertheless seemed to be constantly engaged in protecting the spreading U.S. interests abroad, from Admiral Robert Shufeldt's historic journeys to the abortive Hawaiian revolution in 1893. The near war with Germany in Samoa during 1889 especially focused the nation's attention on the jarring statistic that the U.S. Navy ranked twelfth in the world, below Turkey's, China's, and Austria-Hungary's. Already the naval officers were lobbying Congress about the necessary interrelationships between economic interests and military power. They found support from iron- and steelmakers, as well as shipbuilders, whose successful attempts to find relief from the economic depression in government appropriations for warships made these "the formative years of America's Military-Industrial Complex," to use Benjamin Franklin Cooling's phrase. Consequently, in 1882, contracts for the first four modern U.S. warships were let to shipbuilder John Roach. He anticipated later chapters of the military-industrial complex by having huge cost overruns, production breakdowns, and a failure to keep up with shifting navy standards. In 1885 Roach went bankrupt and died from the strain two years later. Bethlehem Steel and Andrew Carnegie then stepped in to develop the complex more systematically and profitably. [18]

At another level, two other figures appeared to provide the strategic and political rationale for the new navy. The first was Benjamin Harrison's secretary of the navy, Benjamin Tracy. A strong imperialist, successful New York lawyer, and able politician, Tracy's annual reports of 1889 and 1890 successfully demanded appropriations for the first three modern, armored battleships. Tracy wove together the lessons of the Samoa crisis with the radical thinking emerging from

---

18 Kenneth J. Hagan, *American Gunboat Diplomacy and the Old Navy, 1877–1889* (Westport, Conn., 1973), 188; Benjamin Franklin Cooling, *Gray Steel and Blue Water Navy: The Formative Years of America's Military-Industrial Complex, 1881–1917* (Hamden, Conn., 1979).

the new Naval War College at Newport, Rhode Island. He also took advantage of the Republicans' having gained control of both houses of Congress for the first time since 1875 and pushed a series of naval measures through Congress along largely partisan lines.[19]

The other figure who appeared at the same time was Captain Alfred Thayer Mahan. A Democrat, antiimperialist, middle-aged naval officer until the mid-1880s, he suddenly discovered in his reading of ancient Rome the key that he and his colleagues in the dead-end officer corps had been seeking: proof, as he read the history, that it was control of the sea, not of land, that determined crucial turns in Rome's imperial development. After developing his theory at the Naval War College, Mahan published his magisterial book *The Influence of Sea Power upon History, 1660–1783* in 1890, just at the time of the Samoan crisis and Tracy's 1890 annual report. Mahan directly linked the central event of his era, the growing productivity of U.S. factories and farms, to the need for a great battleship fleet that could protect the nation's foreign commerce, destroy an opponent's commerce in battle, and annihilate the opponent's fleet in decisive combat. Such a navy required coaling bases and rest stops. Mahan thus demanded the annexation of bases in the Caribbean and the Pacific. He turned Republican in 1893 after Cleveland rejected annexation of Hawaii. Mahan's work quickly made him an intimate of the powerful who wanted a great fleet, not least young Theodore Roosevelt, who gave the 1890 book a rousing review in *Atlantic Monthly* ("our greatest need is the need of a fighting fleet," he concluded). By the mid-1890s, Mahan was lionized in London, Berlin, and Tokyo as well as Washington. "The London Times has been calling me Copernicus again," he proudly wrote home in 1894. "Copernicus taught that the sun was the center of the system . . . and I have been the first to show that sea power is the centre around which other events move, not it around them."[20]

Specifically, he and others, including Roosevelt and powerful

19 Kenneth J. Hagan, *This People's Navy: The Making of America's Sea Power* (New York, 1991), 194–7.
20 Robert Seager II and Doris D. Maguire, eds., *Letters and Papers of Alfred Thayer Mahan*, 3 vols. (Annapolis, 1975), 2:342, 361; *Atlantic Monthly* 66 (October 1890): 567.

members of Congress, were concluding that, in Mahan's words, the nation's growing productivity demanded that either the surplus of goods be consumed at home through "socialistic" measures that Mahan bitterly detested, or else the goods find markets across the new "frontier" – the seas.[21] Moving into foreign markets, however, raised the probability of conflict that could escalate to war. In Mahan's view, such war was a natural and inevitable result of industrial success in an increasingly closed world. Competition led not to order but to instability, clashes, and the need for a battleship fleet. That fleet's purpose was less to impose order than to create and protect vitally needed opportunities for business. It must be emphasized that in this search for markets neither Mahan nor his fellow naval officers lobbied for specific economic interests. They indeed looked down on many business people as selfish, narrow, and insensitive to the risks the navy had to take on their behalf. Mahan and other officers disliked missionaries even more, and for the same reasons. These naval leaders, however, were committed to the national interest as they saw it, and Mahan saw it as revolving around an expansionist economic policy that was a prerequisite to preserving the system and stopping any socialistic practices at home.

Mahan understood other implications of his reading of history. He preached that the new United States needed a new presidency that could act quickly and decisively abroad, instead of being tied down by outdated political tenets and an eighteenth-century constitution. Mahan provided the rationale for the twentieth-century presidency, created by foreign policy crises and unfettered by congressional checks and balances, that was first represented by William McKinley and Theodore Roosevelt. Mahan's theory also explained why the U.S. merchant marine, which had rapidly disappeared since its historic high point in 1860, was not really needed. Anyone could carry the goods; capital should go into more efficient production or into battleship fleets to protect the commerce. In all, he underlined the need for growing foreign markets and, hence, the need for a navy. Squadron maneuvers were impossible to practice, Mahan ob-

---

21 Alfred Thayer Mahan, *The Influence of Sea Power upon History, 1660–1783* (Boston, 1890), 35, 39.

served in late 1895: "Just as we expect them to begin, a bobbery starts up in Central or South America, or Hayti, or elsewhere, and away go one or two ships."[22]

The Sino-Japanese War

Such "bobberys" appeared with increasing frequency in the 1890s. A pivotal outbreak, much more than a bobbery, occurred during 1894–5 in Asia, a theater that had come to fascinate Mahan as it had Seward a generation earlier. By early 1895, Asia was also fascinating the Cleveland administration and business leaders. Until 1894 a delicate balance of power had been maintained by the British presence and China's presumed ability to defend itself. In reality the balance had been undermined by the Japanese, then American, opening of Korea between 1876 and 1882. Korea moved out of direct Chinese control as Japanese industrial and military power developed. Simultaneously, another piece of the Asian puzzle became eccentric as Russia, led by its visionary finance minister, Count Sergei Witte, lay its Trans-Siberian Railway toward Manchuria and regions that, in Japan's eyes, directly threatened its security. This destabilization of East Asia was helped along by the influx of foreign goods and missionaries. As U.S. Minister to China Charles Denby noted, the two were linked: "The missionary inspired by holy zeal, goes everywhere, and by degrees foreign commerce and trade follow."[23]

The tipping over of the delicate balance began when Japan seized upon an antiforeign incident in Korea to declare war against China in April 1894. As the Japanese stunned the world by scoring quick, decisive victories, European powers finally moved to block Tokyo by trying to mediate the conflict. They also asked Gresham to act with them, an offer the secretary of state refused. He was not reversing Seward's cooperative policy; indeed, U.S. warships worked with

---

22 Alfred Thayer Mahan, *The Interest of America in Sea Power, Present and Future* (Boston, 1897), 71–2; Mahan to Thursfield, November 21, 1895, Papers of Alfred Thayer Mahan, Library of Congress, Washington, D.C.
23 McCormick, *China Market*, 67–8.

European fleets in protecting China's open ports, and Gresham moved U.S. Marines into Korea to help protect foreigners and their property. But, as he had warned the Japanese, they were not to push for a total victory or Europeans would interfere to "demand a settlement not favorable to Japan's future security and well-being." Gresham finally unilaterally offered U.S. good offices to prevent such a result. In the peace talks, Japan won nearly everything it demanded: a large indemnity from China, Korea's independence, the cession of Formosa to Tokyo, and extensive new trade concessions for foreigners involved in China's trade. Above all, Japan received rights to the strategic Liaotung Peninsula, a gateway to Manchuria, and thus was suddenly in the position to block Russia and exploit some of Asia's potentially richest markets. Then, in late 1895, a Japanese-inspired coup placed a pro-Tokyo regime in charge of Korea. The most important U.S. diplomat in Seoul, Horace Allen, bitterly protested and tried to bring in a Russian presence to balance the Japanese. The State Department reprimanded him and disavowed his policy.[24]

Indeed, throughout 1894–5 Gresham, then Olney, supported the Japanese with few reservations. Washington's June 8, 1895, note to its diplomats in China demanded, in words strikingly similar to the famous Open Door notes of four years later, equal and liberal trade access in both Korea and China. Japan was seen as a strong supporter of the Open Door and as an enemy of the Russian, German, and French attempts to cordon off parts of China for their own private exploitation. Even when Japan moved to seize all Korea, the United States showed little displeasure. Not so the Europeans. As Gresham had predicted, they shocked Japan in 1895–6 by forcing Tokyo officials to surrender claims on Korea and, especially, to give up the Liaotung Peninsula's entrance into Manchuria. Witte had drawn the line: He convinced Tsar Nicholas II that Russian forces would be in no position to determine China's future until the Trans-Siberian Railway was open, probably in the early twentieth century. Until

24 Ibid., 49–50; Pauncefote to Kimberley, August 10, 1894, Confidential, FO 5/2234, Public Record Office, Kew, England; Fred Harvey Harrington, *God, Mammon, and the Japanese* (Madison, 1944), chap. 15.

then, Witte argued, St. Petersburg could not agree to any other power, especially Japan, obtaining a headstart. With French and German help, Witte forced Japan to surrender much of what it had obtained in the negotiations with China. Neither a sympathetic Washington nor London could help. The Japanese fell back and worked furiously to prepare their industry and military for the unavoidable showdown with Russia.[25]

Closely monitoring the sharpening conflict over a disintegrating China, Americans followed a two-prong policy. On one, they showed sympathy and admiration for the Japanese. As the *Philadelphia Press* wrote in late 1895, "Americans cannot but wish them success. Nippon is indeed the day-star of the East. Its future is indicated by a rising not a setting sun." The other part of the policy was to push U.S. economic interests as hard as possible in the race to exploit China through its new treaty ports and newly gained access to the interior. The object was not stability but profits. Denby stressed that U.S. concession hunters could find good game because China needed money to pay the indemnity. The U.S. minister grew furious when foreign governments helped their entrepreneurs cut deals with the vulnerable Chinese officials; he demanded that Washington allow him to do the same. In 1895–6, Olney set a precedent by instructing Denby to assist U.S. businessmen to gain access to key Chinese officials, although the minister was not to play favorites among the Americans. Intensifying competition had forced the discard of another piece of laissez-faireism.[26]

The new policy, however, was insufficient. So was the banqueting and flattering of China's foreign policy leader, Li Hong-zhang, when he visited the United States. Olney and Denby supported the American China Development Company's attempt to obtain the rich Peking-Hankow railway concession. Organized in 1895, the company's members included such powerful robber barons as James Stillman, president of National City Bank and adviser to the Rocke-

25 Dun to Gresham, May 2, 1895, Dispatches, Japan, NA, RG 45; W. G. Beasley, *The Rise of Modern Japan* (London, 1990), 147.
26 Alfred Vagts, *Deutschland und die Vereinigten Staaten in der Weltpolitik,* 2 vols. (New York, 1935), 2:960–1; *Philadelphia Press,* December 12, 1895, 6; McCormick, *China Market,* 79–82.

fellers; Jacob H. Schiff of Kuhn, Loeb, and Company; E. H. Harriman; and Carnegie. The effort, however, fell victim to quiet British opposition, Chinese demands, and, most of all, the company's own undercapitalization. In 1896, meanwhile, the Russians signed the Li-Lobanov Treaty that gave them control of the Chinese Eastern Railway as a terminal point for the Trans-Siberian. The Chinese were desperately trying to balance the Russians and the Japanese. To Americans, however, Russia had emerged as the real, and threatening, victor of the 1894–5 war. "This war," wrote the secretary of the U.S. legation, Charles Denby, Jr., "has done more to open this vast field to Western commerce and civilization than five hundred years of foreign trade and one hundred years of missionary teaching." Cramp Shipbuilding, the Union Iron Works, Bethlehem Iron, and other U.S. concession seekers had tried to enter that "vast field" after 1895, but with little success compared with Russia's achievements. In truth, Americans were discovering a less mythical, more real, Japan market. American shipbuilders obtained rich contracts for the new Japanese battleship fleet, Japan doubled its cotton imports from the United States, and, in return, Japanese manufactured goods found surprisingly good American sales. As China weakened, a new economic and political alignment was developing among the great powers, an alignment that would shape U.S. foreign policy well into the next century.[27]

American Doctrine, British Appeasement

A similar realignment occurred in the Western Hemisphere, but it was simpler. Great Britain's century-long supremacy in many New World affairs rapidly was giving way to U.S. superiority. The historic turn can be pinpointed: a series of confrontations between the two powers during 1894–6 in which London gave way on every occasion.

The first occurred in the harbor of Rio de Janeiro. In 1891, U.S.-Brazilian ties tightened when the two nations signed one of the most

27 Denby to Olney, May 25, 1896, Olney Papers; Charles Denby, Jr., "America's Opportunity in Asia," *North American Review* 66 (January 1898): 32–9.

important reciprocity treaties that emerged from the 1890 tariff bill. Those ties were further strengthened when the Brazilian republic, which had replaced the monarchy in 1889, looked to the United States as a model. In 1893, however, elements of the Brazilian Navy rebelled against the republic. The rebels were helped, carefully and quietly, by British interests who saw this as a chance to check the growing U.S. influence. The rebels announced their intention of breaking the government by sealing off trade, and hence customs collections, in Rio's harbor. The U.S. naval commander agreed to honor the blockade. He was promptly removed by Gresham and replaced by a new commander who, perhaps because of his earlier service in Asian waters, understood gunboat diplomacy.

Gresham's move was motivated both by particular U.S. economic interests (including Rockefeller's Standard Oil exporting office, which wrote Gresham directly), which demanded he protect their growing markets in Brazil, and by the secretary of state's own belief that the British were challenging the Monroe Doctrine and the U.S. right to protect its friends in the hemisphere. Julian Pauncefote, London's ambassador, admired Gresham (especially in comparison with Blaine's blatant anti-British activities), and Gresham returned the friendship. But mutual admiration did not stop the secretary of state from ordering U.S. warships to accompany American merchantmen to Rio's customshouses, and to use force if necessary. When the rebels challenged the convoy in late January 1894, the U.S. commander fired a shell across the bow of the rebel ship. The rebels backed away. The revolt ended and Rio again was open to a free flow of goods. A grateful Brazilian government erected a statue of President Monroe to celebrate his now famous Doctrine, ordered celebrations held on the Fourth of July, and had a serenade performed for the U.S. minister.[28]

28 João Pandía Calogeras, *A History of Brazil,* trans. and ed. Percy Alvin Martin (Chapel Hill, 1939), 292; "Memorandum of Conversation" between Gresham and Pauncefote, February 5, 1895, Notes from Great Britain, vol. 123, National Archives, Department of State, Record Group 59; William Rockefeller to Gresham, January 4, 1894, Area 4 file, box 23, January 1–8 folder, Naval Records, NA, RG 45; Joseph Smith, *Illusions of Conflict* (Pittsburgh, 1979), 163–84.

A second confrontation erupted at the Mosquito Indian Reservation on the Atlantic Coast enclave of Nicaragua. The English-speaking Indians and blacks were separated from the distant Managua government by language, history, impenetrable jungle, and — since 1860 — a British protectorate. London had grown fond of the Mosquito because it would be the Atlantic entrance for a Nicaraguan isthmian canal. British investors, moreover, had profited from the region's natural wealth, especially its mahogony forests. Since the mid-1880s, however, hundreds of Americans had built up $2 million in investments and $4 million in trade with the United States. The U.S. minister estimated in the mid-1890s that Americans held at least 90 percent of the reservation's wealth. In 1894, the new Nicaraguan regime of General José Santos Zelaya moved to extend Nicaragua's control over the Reservation-Bluefields region. When the British threatened to enforce its protectorate, Gresham summoned Pauncefote, told him that Nicaragua had the right to control its own country, and suggested a British retreat. London did so, only to have the foreign investors, led by Americans, demand that the British be allowed to protect them against Zelaya. Their fear was made real when Zelaya began to arrest British subjects. London threatened to protect its citizens with force. Gresham, trapped between his view of the Monroe Doctrine and the demands of American investors, reassured the Americans and the British that he would guard all their interests. The secretary of state thus replaced the British protectorate with an American in one of the most strategically important regions in the hemisphere.[29]

The third crisis threatened to become a war. In retrospect, the danger was overblown, but it became one of those transforming events that changed a fundamental diplomatic relationship of the United States and marked a recognition of U.S. power that would have been unimaginable in Seward's time. Its roots lay a half century before when London laid claim to disputed territory between British

29 David Healy, *Drive to Hegemony: The United States in the Caribbean, 1898–1917* (Madison, 1988), 32–4; "Conversation between the Secretary of State and Sir Julian Pauncefote . . . July 26th, 1894," Notes from Great Britain, vol. 124, NA, RG 59.

Guiana and Venezuela. The problem largely lay dormant until the 1890s when it appeared that Great Britain was beginning to assume it controlled the territory, and Venezuela brought the issue before the Cleveland administration – not least by hiring a lobbyist, William L. Scruggs, who effectively publicized Venezuela's view. Among other issues, Scruggs noted that the territory included the Orinoco River, and that the waterway could control commerce into vast South American markets. By now, Americans were highly sensitive to British ambitions in the hemisphere and the European imperialists' carving up of other southern continents. Senator Henry Cabot Lodge (R.-Mass.), a close friend of Roosevelt and Mahan, provided a historical context for the Venezuelan claim: "These powers have already seized the islands of the Pacific and parcelled out Africa. Great Britain cannot extend her possessions in the East. . . . She is now turning her attention to South America."[30]

The British seemed undisturbed, perhaps because in a secret letter only recently discovered, Gresham assured London on April 12, 1895, both of "the thorough friendship of the American people," and that U.S. fleet movements in the Caribbean were not meant to be hostile to British interests. This letter probably was indirectly referring to the clash over the Mosquito Reservation, but Whitehall could have been excused for reading a broader meaning into the rather obsequious message.[31] Gresham, however, died shortly after writing the note and was replaced by Olney. In July he delivered a quite different message. Demanding that the Monroe Doctrine be honored, and that the British refer the dispute to arbitration, Olney added, for London's information, that "today the United States is practically sovereign on this continent, and its fiat is law upon the subjects to which it confines its interposition." Olney explained why this was so in phrases that again would have been unheard a generation earlier: the "infinite resources" of the United States, "combined with its isolated position render it master of the situation and practically invulnerable as against any and all powers."

30 Healy, *Drive to Hegemony*, 33–4.
31 I am indebted to Michael Sewall and Warren Kimball for this reference from Gresham to Lord Rosebery, April 12, 1895, Cecil-Spring Rice Papers, 1/57, Churchill College Archive Centre, Cambridge.

The puzzled, distracted British prime minister, Lord Salisbury, delayed answering in order to deal with more pressing diplomatic matters. When he did respond, Salisbury denied Olney's argument, including the reference to the sacrosanct Monroe Doctrine. In December, President Cleveland publicly announced that the United States would carry out its own investigation of the boundary line and enforce the result. Salisbury realized he had underestimated the seriousness of the issue, the importance of the Monroe Doctrine, and the significance of the Orinoco River to the Americans. He was, moreover, confronted with serious crises involving Germany and African questions. The British watched in wonder as the Americans grew warlike. "I do hope there will not be any back down among our people," Theodore Roosevelt wrote Lodge. "I don't care whether our sea coast cities are bombarded or not; we would take Canada." Salisbury pushed the question to arbitration. Venezuela's claims were largely vindicated, especially its claim to the mouth of the Orinoco – although the United States never bothered to consult with the Venezuelans.[32]

The results of these episodes were far-reaching. The United States had stood up to the world's greatest power not once, but three times and had won three times. American diplomats defined the issues not narrowly but in large terms that were understandable in the context of the post-1873 economic crises: In Brazil the issue was preserving a major turn toward U.S. goods and ideology; in Nicaragua it was who would control great wealth and a strategic point of global importance; in Venezuela the issues were two – who would define the Monroe Doctrine and who would control one of the continent's great commercial waterways. British officials shrewdly understood that they had to come to terms with the New World's industrial tyro.

The relative decline in British industrial power, combined with the growing competition with Germany, led to Joseph Chamberlain (the former British secretary of state for the colonies), referring to

---

32 Healy, *Drive to Hegemony*, 32–5; Theodore Roosevelt, *The Letters of Theodore Roosevelt*, ed. Elting E. Morison et al., 8 vols. (Cambridge, Mass., 1951–4), 1:500–1.

this "weary Titan, staggering under the too vast orb of his own fate." One historian has concluded that the British moved to resolve this dilemma by "appeasing" the United States so they could avoid a war with Anglo-Saxon brothers and sisters. London could then be better prepared to fight elsewhere. A potential enemy was thus transformed into a needed friend. Only the Latin Americans seemed to have felt they lost. If Washington won its point with Salisbury, the Chilean minister to Washington observed, "the United States will have succeeded in establishing a protectorate over all of Latin America." Latin American editorials discussed "the suffocating pressure of the Colossus," whose Anglo-Saxon race sought to "found a single colonial state extending from the North to the South Pole." John Bassett Moore privately expressed a more modest and accurate evaluation in late 1895: "Since the [economic] panic two years ago, there has grown up quite a war party" in the United States, which "thinks that a war would be a good thing for the country."[33]

The Turn of 1896

The 1896 presidential election reflected the post-1873 changes, but not because "a war party" determined the result. As has nearly always been the case in U.S. presidential politics, those results were shaped by domestic, not foreign, issues. The importance of the 1896 election is that it was determined (like so much of the decade's foreign policy) by the long depression, especially by the 1893–6 crisis. The coming to power of a Republican party that represented a new consensus politics to deal with that crisis, and of William McKinley as the voice of that consensus, determined U.S. foreign policy for the next sixteen years.

The Democratic party's disaster began directly after the 1893 crash. In the 1894 congressional elections, Democrats, who controlled the executive and Congress when the crash occurred, lost 113

33 Paul Kennedy, *Strategy and Diplomacy, 1870–1945* (London, 1983), 23-4; Frederick B. Pike, *Chile and the United States, 1880–1962* (Notre Dame, Ind., 1963), 137; Richard Van Alstyne, "The Monroe Doctrine," in Alexander De-Conde, ed., *Encyclopedia of American Foreign Policy*, 3 vols. (New York, 1978), 2:593; Charles Callan Tansill, *The Foreign Policy of Thomas F. Bayard, 1885–1897* (New York, 1940), 714–15.

House seats. They had comprised 61 percent of Congress before the election, 29 percent after. In New England, where they had been strong for generations, they were virtually wiped out as their 8 House members were reduced to 1 ("Honey-Fitz" Fitzgerald, John F. Kennedy's grandfather). What the economy missed doing to the Democrats their choice of candidates did. Until the mid-1890s, many ethnic groups especially favored the Democracy because it believed in limited government and had left them alone. William Jennings Bryan, the Democratic presidential nominee in 1896, was, however, a midwestern pietist who believed deeply in social improvement and Protestant mission. His opponent, William McKinley, played down the Republican pietist tradition and ran a more inclusive campaign, the kind of campaign he had learned to conduct as a House member, then governor, in multiethnic Ohio politics. He consequently scored heavily among immigrant and urban groups that before 1894 had voted Democrat.[34]

Foreign policy played a minor role. The Democratic platform bowed before the Monroe Doctrine and extended "sympathy" to Cubans for their revolution that had reerupted a year earlier. The Republicans devoted more attention to overseas affairs. They asked that Hawaii be "controlled' by the United States (not directly mentioning annexation); that a Nicaraguan canal and a Danish West Indies naval base be obtained; that the Monroe Doctrine be upheld and "the eventual withdrawal of the European powers from this hemisphere" take place; and that Spain's retreat from Cuba – or the use of U.S. "good offices to restore peace and give independence to the Island" – occur. Populist party leaders endorsed Bryan and took a strong pro-Cuban stand, in part because such a stand was popular in the West where war fever was rising, in part because they hoped it would be attractive to those who disliked the Populists' pro-silver passion. McKinley emphasized a tariff policy of protectionism plus reciprocity. The British disliked McKinley until they saw that Bryan, with his silverite cry ("Gold monometallism is a British policy," the Democratic party plank blared), was infinitely worse. In

34 Joel Silbey and Samuel McSeveney, eds., *Voters, Parties, and Elections* (Lexington, Ky., 1972), 186–90; for another view: Allan J. Lichtman, "Political Realignment and 'Ethnocultural' Voting in Late 19th-Century America," *Journal of Social History* 16, no. 3 (1983): 55–82.

the end, McKinley not only ran a well-financed, highly organized campaign that appealed to populous urban areas in the midwestern and northeastern states, but he also became lucky when the favorable U.S. export balance shot up from $46 million in the last one-third of 1895 to $96 million in the comparable 1896 months. This surplus, in addition to a slowing of selling by Europeans of U.S. securities and a sudden rise in world gold production, brought the precious metal into the country in larger quantities, raised prices, lifted the economic cloud, and dimmed silver's appeal.[35]

McKinley won 271 electoral votes to Bryan's 176, but most notably he branded the 1894 election results firmly on the American body politic. Republicans became so dominant in the more populous and wealthy North, and the Democrats more fixed in power in the much poorer South, that not only was Republican ascendancy in place for all but eight of the next thirty-six years, but the resulting one-party states discouraged voter participation. The American elite – bankers, industrialists, and large commercial farmers, led by McKinley – thus became insulated against radicalism. Foreign policy could be conducted on the basis of this solid, growing consensus, with little danger of the sudden turns marked, say, by Cleveland's repudiation of Harrison's Hawaiian annexation policy in 1893. The results turned out to be every president's dream. With obvious relief, Mahan wrote a friend after the election that it had been the "most important" event of the time, and "I don't except the [Civil] War." Bryan's platform, "wrong and even revolutionary," had been repudiated.[36] Mahan and McKinley were prepared to take the leap from the chaos of the mid-1890s to an overseas empire of the new twentieth century.

35 *Official Proceedings of the Democratic National Convention, 1896* (Washington, D.C., 1896), 192; *Official Proceedings of the Eleventh Republican Convention* (St. Louis, 1896), 84; Ernest R. May, *Imperial Democracy* (New York, 1961), 75; Curtis to Charles W. Dabney, Jr., October 14, 1896, in Papers of W. E. Curtis, Library of Congress, Washington, D.C., for new gold imports' effects.

36 Walter Dean Burnham, "The Changing Shape of the American Political Universe," in Burnham, *The Current Crisis in American Politics* (New York, 1982); Mahan to Ashe, November 7, 1896, Papers of Alfred Thayer Mahan, Duke University, Durham, N.C.

7. The Empire of 1898 – and Upheaval

Simply by manipulating tariff schedules, the United States triggered two revolutions in the 1890s and accelerated a third (in the Philippines). The first, forced by the 1890 tariff, occurred in Hawaii during 1893 and led to American annexation in 1898. The second, caused by the sugar provisions of the 1894 Wilson-Gorman Tariff, created chaos in Cuba. Between 1894 and 1896, Cuba's exports to its best customer, the United States, fell 50 percent. The results were revolt, then war, then a new United States empire in the Caribbean and the Pacific and – as an integral part of these developments – a new U.S. executive that evolved precisely to try to create a modicum of efficiency and stability out of a foreign policy that gave priority to commercial opportunity, domestic politics, and strategic power and only then to a concern for order.

Cuba: The Grave Danger of "Revolution Within Revolution"

Since the outbreak of the 1868–78 revolt and the growing integration of U.S. capital with the island's rich sugar plantations, which found a huge U.S. market, Cuba's society and economy had been transformed – and made highly vulnerable. The rich Creole planters and the growing number of North American investors in sugar mills and mines found their interests at one with the U.S. market. In 1892 alone, U.S. investors put in $1.2 million. When the 1894 tariff act threatened to paralyze both the sugar and cigar-making industries, unemployment spread and revolution reerupted. The rebellion was led by José Martí, who became the most beloved and important figure in Cuban history. Born in 1853 as the son of a Spanish military officer stationed in Cuba, he was arrested as a danger to the state at the age of seventeen during the first revolt.

Martí was deported to Spain, then went to New York where he lived as a journalist during most of the 1881–95 era. Watching Americans closely, he concluded in 1889 that the republic was becoming "plutocratic and imperialistic." When Cuban cane cutters, cigar makers, and other laborers went on strike in 1895, Martí was the leader able to bridge class and racial lines to piece together a Cuban nationalist force. Declaring that "Cuba must be free from Spain and the United States," he landed in Cuba in April to lead the revolution. On May 19, 1895, he was killed by Spanish troops in an ambush.[1]

Martí's martyrdom, the crumbling economy, and Spain's gross colonial mismanagement helped the revolution spread. Even after its General Antonio Maceo was tricked into surrender and then murdered by Spain in December 1896, the revolt gained fury, not least because by then large sectors of U.S. opinion, including Congress, were demanding that Spain meet rebel demands. The Cubans split into many factions, but two were most important. One comprised Creoles and U.S. investors who now had, according to the State Department's assessment, about $50 million in the island. They initially wanted, as one of the richest U.S. planters, Edwin Atkins, put it to Secretary of State Richard Olney in 1896, "autonomy," or home rule. But as the revolt spread and became more radical in its demands, Atkins and his fellow planters began to consider outright U.S. annexation. The second group, made up of the mass of Cubans, took its lead from one of Martí's most famous statements: "Once the United States is in Cuba, who will get her out?" The rebels wanted complete independence. A much less important third group was loyalists who were so procolonial that they refused even to support the idea of autonomy within Spain's ramshackle empire. Their intransigence, and the revolutionaries' growing power, gave Madrid, Washington, and increasingly the concerned European capitals (including the Vatican, which had little enthusiasm for Americans' taking over the Catholic island) limited maneuvering room.[2]

---

1 Francisco Lopez Segrera, *Cuba: capitalismo dependiente y subdesarrollo* (1510–1959) (Havana, 1972), 199–204; Jules R. Benjamin, *The United States and the Origins of the Cuban Revolution* (Princeton, 1990), 22–6, 32–3; Raymond Carr, "A Revolutionary Hero," *New York Review of Books*, July 21, 1988, 26.

2 Robert L. Beisner, *From the Old Diplomacy to the New, 1865–1900*, 2d ed. (Ar-

Support for "Cuba Libre" appeared in the United States immediately after Martí fired up the revolt. State and national leaders
appeared at rallies to raise money. The decade-old American Federation of Labor resolved to support the revolt, but carefully avoided
favoring annexation and the waves of cheap labor and cheap products
it could bring. The pro-Cuban sentiment swept like a huge wave
over much of the Midwest and West. But support also cropped up in
New York City's posh Union League Club. Movers and shakers of
New York politics, including August Belmont and the lawyer
John J. McCook, not only gave vocal support but, through the
Cuban Junta, raised millions of dollars and bought bonds for the
revolutionary cause. As the threat of war and possible U.S. annexation neared in 1897–8, McCook and Samuel M. Janney, a Wall
Street banker, even offered to purchase Cuba's independence from a
money-starved Madrid. Spanish honor overcame Spanish needs; otherwise the investment could have paid rich dividends because the
purchase was to be secured by liens on the island's customshouses.[3]

President Grover Cleveland wanted Spain to grant autonomy; that
solution, he hoped, would appease the Cubans but hold Spain continually responsible for the protection of U.S. property. Washington-
Madrid relations were good in 1895, but in 1896 the revolt spread,
class differences widened, and the Spanish retaliated with 150,000
troops and a brutal *reconcentrado* policy of General Valeriano ("the
Butcher") Weyler, a policy that proved to be as ineffective as it was
offensive to U.S. sensibilities. Cleveland, the president who had
rejected Hawaii's annexation in 1893, wanted no part of any plan
that would bring the multiracial, class-riven island within the
Union. By 1896, however, even his patience was ending. In one
draft of his final annual message he was prepared to give the Spanish
a time limit to end the revolt or, he implied, the United States
might have to do it for them. He backed off into generalities in the
final paper, but his concern about both U.S. investments and the
growing anger and unpredictability the revolt was generating in

lington Heights, Ill., 1986), 116; Ernest May, *Imperial Democracy* (New York,
1961), 80–1; Atkins's views are in Lodge to Charles Francis Adams, January 22,
1897, Lodge Letterbooks, Papers of Henry Cabot Lodge, Boston, Mass.
3 A. G. Vansittart to Viscount Gough, September 23, 1895, FO 5/2263, Public
Record Office, Kew, England; Benjamin, *U.S. and Origins*, 44–5.

New York financial markets was pushing Cleveland toward a more active policy. "I am thinking a great deal about Cuba," the president wrote Olney on July 13, 1896, "but am as far as ever from seeing the place where we can get in."[4]

The danger as U.S. officials began to perceive it, however, was not merely that Spain's brutality could not end the conflict. The danger was that Spain would lose its place to revolutionaries who coalesced as the proautonomy and proannexation groups splintered. "There may be a revolution within a revolution," U.S. Consul Fitzhugh Lee warned the State Department in 1897. "In that case foreigners will have to look to their government for protection and the preservation of peace."[5] North Americans could have come face-to-face at this point with their first twentieth-century revolution. They instead supported William McKinley and the first twentieth-century presidency.

McKinley: The First Modern President

Born in Niles, Ohio, in 1843, McKinley had been a Civil War hero and was highly experienced militarily. Elected to Congress in 1876, he had risen to the top rank of House leadership by 1890, only to be gerrymandered out of his district. He promptly ran for governor and won two terms between 1891 and 1895, despite having to handle massive labor unrest during the economic crash. By the mid-1890s he had not only survived Ohio politics, won the support of capital, and become a trusted friend of AFL leader Samuel Gompers, but was acknowledged to be a leading expert on tariff policy and the political-economic needs of the Second Industrial Revolution. The first president whose inaugural parade was recorded by the new motion-picture camera, McKinley understood both the dangers of the long economic depression and the government's necessary role in ending it. "The restoration of confidence and the revival of busi-

4 Cleveland to Olney, July 13, 1896, Papers of Richard Olney, Library of Congress, Washington, D.C.; H. Wayne Morgan, *America's Road to Empire* (New York, 1965), 6–7.
5 Lee to Day, November 27, 1897, Consular, Cuba, National Archives, Department of State, Record Group 59 (hereafter NA, RG).

ness . . .," he declared, "depend more largely upon the prompt, energetic, and intelligent action of Congress than upon any other single agency affecting the situation." McKinley was explicit. His "greatest ambition," he told Wisconsin Governor Robert LaFollette, was to attain U.S. supremacy in world markets.[6]

To reach the pinnacle, the president demanded that Congress pass two special measures. The first was a refined version of McKinley's 1890 tariff measure. He wanted it all: "I believe in practical reciprocity," he told a friend in 1895, one that "while seeking the world's markets for our surplus products shall not destroy American wages or surrender American markets for products which can be made at home." When he used a close variation of that sentence before the National Association of Manufacturers convention in 1895, he brought the audience to its feet in applause. John Hay, whom McKinley appointed ambassador to Great Britain in 1897, accurately characterized the theme of another, similar presidential speech to the NAM in early 1898: "The greatest destiny the world ever knew is ours." The Dingley Tariff of 1897 did not give McKinley all he wanted; it nevertheless did refine and advance the reciprocity principle. John Kasson negotiated eleven such treaties, but at the time of McKinley's death in 1901, the Senate had not acted on any of them.

The second piece of legislation the president demanded was a gold standard act that would kill the silverite demands once and for all. McKinley had been a bimetallist and even wanted more silver coinage early in his career. By the 1890s he was a convinced gold advocate. A halfhearted approach to the British for a conference to discuss bimetallism had been rebuffed in late 1897, as McKinley probably knew it would. Not only the powerful banks in the City of London opposed such a proposal, but "all the American banking interest has been enlisted in opposition," Hay reported from London. The need for more money in circulation was being solved by the discovery of more gold, and a rising U.S. export table that

---

6 Tom E. Terrill, *The Tariff, Politics, and American Foreign Policy, 1874–1901* (Westport, Conn., 1973), 207; Margaret Leech, *In the Days of McKinley* (New York, 1959), 142.

reported an unfavorable balance of $18.7 million in 1893, then a favorable $286 million balance in 1897 and double that amount in 1898. Exports soared over the billion-dollar mark in 1897. By 1900, McKinley had his Gold Standard Act, which declared the gold dollar to be the only currency standard. All other forms of money were to be maintained at parity with gold. The gold standard, Secretary of the Treasury Lyman Gage explained, "enables us in our commercial affairs to measure with the same measure by which the industrial and commercial affairs of our great industrial competitors measure with." Such a "great economic value," Gage believed, "is worth very great sacrifice, if need be, to maintain it." The tariff and the gold standard, combined with the new U.S. Navy and closer government-business relations, created a "promotional state," as historian Emily Rosenberg termed it, to push and protect U.S. business abroad.[7]

The post-1873 depression had forced tremendous sacrifices from Americans, but McKinley received little blame. He instead represented, as Henry Adams observed, "the instinct of what might be named McKinleyism: the system of combinations, consolidations, trusts, realized at home, and realizable abroad." Adams, who was cynical about nearly everyone he watched from his home across Lafayette Square and the White House, called McKinley "a marvelous manager of men. McKinley found several manipulators to help him, one of whom was [John] Hay."[8]

Power was centralizing into presidential hands. This change, a transforming event in American history, preceded the foreign policy watershed of the post-1898 years, but the change was shaped by that foreign policy. As Walter Dean Burnham described the result of the "system of 1896," a "fairly democratic regime" was converted into "a

---

7 McKinley to Curtis, December 2, 1895, McKinley Letterbooks, Papers of William McKinley, Library of Congress, Washington, D.C.; Kenton J. Clymer, "Checking the Sources . . .," *Historian* 48 (November 1985): 82–7; Hay to McKinley, October 11, 1897, McKinley Papers; Gage to Burdick, August 20, 1897, Letterbooks, Lyman Gage Papers, Library of Congress, Washington, D.C.; *Journal of Commerce,* October 1, 1897, 4; Emily Rosenberg, *Spreading the American Dream* (New York, 1982), 49.

8 Henry Adams, *The Education of Henry Adams* (Boston, 1930), 373–4, 423.

rather broadly based oligarchy." McKinley manipulated this system to his advantage. In the first instance, he created a new cabinet that included fewer appointees with independent political bases, and more administrators whose political power depended on their allegiance to him. The new presidency — and the new industrializing, urbanizing, internationalizing United States — required a cabinet made up not merely of political representatives but of persons experienced in administering complex organizations in a world made smaller by communication and transportation technology. McKinley thus named as his secretary of state John Sherman, senator from Ohio, but only to create room in the Senate for the appointment of the president's campaign manager, Mark Hanna. The de facto secretary of state was McKinley's little-known longtime Ohio friend William R. Day; he was followed by Hay (1898–1905), Elihu Root (1905–9), and Philander C. Knox (1909–13). All these men were widely experienced in the ways of corporate America and, without strong political bases of their own, dependent on the president's will. In a centripetal-centrifugal effect, as U.S. foreign policy spread globally, authority over that policy centralized in the chief executive's office.

Presidential-congressional relations went through a similar transformation. Republican majorities in both the House and Senate increased steadily between 1897 and 1904; by the later date the Republicans controlled the Senate 53–29 (with 8 third-party representatives), and the House 198–151 (with 8 independents). The Senate, where the foreign policy fulcrum lay, was run as a club by a tight group of insiders who had immense power in shaping domestic affairs, but usually deferred to the president in the foreign policy realm. The factions were closely linked to the post–Civil War economic interests. In 1902 political analyst Moisei Ostrogorski believed these interests "equipped and kept up political organizations for their own use, and ran them as they pleased, like their trains." This view was only slightly exaggerated when applied to Washington decision making. The president's role, one that McKinley and Roosevelt played brilliantly, was to provide an overarching foreign policy that benefited as many of these interests as possible. As the cosmopolitan of the system, the president was to create a policy that helped those functional groups that, in turn, most enriched the national interest – even if it meant, as it sometimes did, knocking heads in Congress to have the president's program accepted. In the 1880s, recalled Massachusetts Republican Senator George F. Hoar, senators visited the White House only to give advice.[9] By 1898 they visited McKinley to receive advice as well. They then returned to a Senate where party loyalty, presidential patronage, and well-oiled caucus machinery delivered the vote for the White House. This was not always done easily. The president waged and won one of the toughest and historically significant battles in April 1898 when he took the country into war with Spain. First, however, he had to avoid an Asian crisis.

The Asian Crisis of 1897–1898: "Diplomacy Is the Management of International Business"

It was a measure of the new U.S. global power and the extent of American foreign interests that in 1897–8, McKinley was nearly drawn into a confrontation in Asia even as the nation's eyes focused on Cuba and domestic problems. American interests in Asia were not military; in the late 1890s Great Britain had more battleships stationed in Asia than McKinley had first-class ships in his entire fleet. The interests were economic and missionary, and these had to be protected by Seward's innovation of political cooperation with the powers and, if necessary, cooperative use of force. Missionaries, with help from Washington, which demanded such rights, were finally gaining permission from the Chinese government to work in some of the interior regions, not just along the seacoast. Meanwhile, the export of U.S. cotton goods to China jumped from $1.7 million in 1895 to $4 million in 1896, and $7.4 million in 1897.[10]

9 Joel Silbey and Samuel McSeveney, eds., *Voters, Parties, and Elections* (Lexington, Ky., 1972), 224; Robert A. Diamond, ed., *Origins and Development of Congress* (Washington, D.C., 1976), 224; J. D. Sundquist, *Decline and Resurgence of Congress* (Washington, D.C., 1981), 28.
10 Charles S. Campbell, Jr., *Special Business Interests and the Open Door* (New Haven, 1951), 19–20; Thomas McCormick, *China Market* (Chicago, 1967), 130–2.

This apparent realization (at last) of the fabled China market was suddenly threatened in 1896–7. The European powers, led by Russia, had begun to roll back Japan's gains from its 1894–5 war with China. In 1897–8, Germany, using as an excuse the murder of two of its missionaries, forced China to cede part of the strategic Shantung region that opened into the potentially vast markets of Manchuria. Germany received rights to build railroads and exploit mines. The Russians were already roping off parts of Manchuria for a terminal point of their Trans-Siberian Railway. McKinley could choose from two broad alternatives. One was the traditional, post-1844 Open Door policy that would lead to cooperation with Great Britain, and probably Japan, in opposing any cordoning off, or the imposition of preferential transport and tariff systems, by the Europeans. The other alternative was posed by New York lawyer John J. McCook and railway promoter James Harrison Wilson. With close ties to St. Petersburg officials, McCook and Wilson wanted to cooperate with Russia by linking U.S. steamship lines (and the American transcontinental railway system), to the Trans-Siberian for the beginning of an around-the-globe transportation system. As Wilson explained to Theodore Roosevelt, "There is a great field for American interests in both Russia and China but they are interdependent. . . . Diplomacy is the management of international business and the Russians understand this as well as any peoples in the world." To pivot U.S. policy toward Russia, McCook and Wilson sought key positions in the McKinley administration, but the president turned them down. He had already appointed too many northeasterners and, besides, he privately worried – correctly – that McCook was too closely tied to the Cuban Junta to be trusted on foreign policy questions.[11]

With McCook and Wilson outside the administration, McKinley heard mostly from those such as his assistant secretary of the navy, Theodore Roosevelt, who warned of the growing Russian threat to U.S. interests in Asia, and from Hay, his ambassador to the Court of St. James, who emphasized the need to cooperate with the British in

---

11 Wilson to McCook, December 5, 1897, Letterbooks, Papers of James Harrison Wilson, Library of Congress, Washington, D.C.

maintaining the Open Door despite Russian, German, and French colonial intentions to close it. Observers began to believe that the world's balance of power might be at stake. After all, when Count Witte pushed his railway scheme he claimed that the Trans-Siberian and its tributaries would not only open up the vast Russian East, but change the direction of world trade, replace London's Suez Canal as the key route to China, secure the Asian market for Russian goods, and dominate Chinese – if not the Pacific Ocean rim's – affairs. Germany, for its own imperial reasons, supported the precedents set by Russia's encroachments in Asia.

As the confrontation grew in early 1898, Great Britain approached McKinley for a joint British-American-Japanese response. Hay strongly advised cooperation. On January 31, 1898, U.S. Minister to China Charles Denby wired excitedly to the State Department that Germany and Russia had to be stopped: "Partition would tend to destroy our markets. The Pacific Ocean is destined to bear on its bosom a larger commerce than the Atlantic," and in a whole, noncolonized Asia, "we are destined to find our best customers." Publicly, a McKinley mouthpiece in the Northeast, the *New York Tribune,* declared in March 1898 that "Slav-Tatar-Cossack rule means tyranny, ignorance, reaction. Japanese rule means freedom, enlightenment, progress. If in a contest between the two opposite principles the latter does not win the human race will suffer a dire catastrophe."[12]

The problem, however, was that the president had a crisis on his doorstep that had to be dealt with before he could free his hands to deal with the great questions of U.S. interests in Asia. As Day explained to the British in mid-March 1898, the United States sympathized with London's (and Japan's) policy, but the Cuban crisis made immediate U.S. cooperation impossible. The delay was made more tolerable when assurances came in from reluctant Berlin and St. Petersburg officials that they would agree to keep China's ports open to world commerce. How dependable such assurances were was not clear to McKinley who, as his private secretary noted, "appeared

12 Geoffrey Barraclough, *Introduction to Contemporary History* (New York, 1964), 54; McCormick, *China Market,* 141–2; *New York Tribune,* March 18, 1898, 6.

careworn, did not look well, and his eyes had a far away, deep set expression in them."[13]

Cuba: Revolution and War

McKinley had good reason to appear careworn. He was about to lead the nation into war despite grave personal misgivings. He had little choice. The demands of the post–Civil War American system – at home, in the Caribbean, in Asia – required war. In his inaugural, McKinley had noted the delicate situation, then declared, "We want no wars of conquest; we must avoid the temptation of territorial aggression." This theme had been common to American statecraft after the Civil War as U.S. interests turned from continental to commercial. McKinley, however, meant it. His primary problem was to restore the nation's economy. Foreign policy, whether expansive or isolationist, had to fit that objective. Consequently, throughout 1897 McKinley pushed Spain to end the revolt by granting more autonomy and stopping "Butcher" Weyler's concentration camp policies. In November, Madrid recalled Weyler and outlined an autonomy plan that the rebels rejected and McKinley found disappointing.

The turn to war occurred in January and February 1898. On January 12 Spanish army officers destroyed a newspaper that had attacked Weyler. Street riots erupted in Havana. Madrid disavowed the attack and promised calm, but McKinley apparently began to assume at this point that Spain could no longer maintain order. He dispatched the *Maine* to Havana harbor, ostensibly on a goodwill visit, in reality to protect U.S. citizens and property. In late February, the president's view of Spain was reinforced by a long letter from E. A. Fuertes, a professor of engineering at Cornell University. Fuertes wrote that "Spain stands upon a volcano about to break into fearful eruption and needing only a misstep to precipitate a desolating revolution from the French frontier to the Mediterranean." Familiar with the Iberian Peninsula, Fuertes emphasized that Spain

13 Pauncefote to Salisbury, March 17, 1898, FO 5/2361, Public Record Office; Cortelyou Diary, March 20, 1898, container 52, Papers of George Cortelyou, Library of Congress, Washington, D.C.

was politically isolated in Europe. "A foreign war may tide Spain over its present crisis," but it would be a short-term fix, he implied. McKinley, who asked that this letter be made "easily accessible" for his reference, could only read it as arguing that Spain, corrupt and in irreversible decline, could not be trusted to undertake real Cuban reforms. Stunning proof for this view had emerged in early February when the Cuban Junta, perhaps masterminded by McCook, had obtained a private letter written by Dupuy deLome, Spain's minister to the United States. DeLome had attacked McKinley personally, but the letter was especially revealing in that it indicated that Spain's promised reforms were only for cosmetic and diplomatic purposes. The Spanish intended to hang on. DeLome was immediately removed as minister, but a week after his sensational letter was made public, a tremendous explosion sent the *Maine* to the bottom of Havana harbor and killed 266 Americans. McKinley quickly played for time by ordering a commission to investigate. It reported in late March that the explosion had occurred outside the ship – not, that is, in the engine room – but the commission refused to blame the Spanish directly. (Some eighty years later, another U.S. investigation concluded that the explosion had occurred accidentally inside the ship.)[14]

The ship's sinking created the battle cry of the 1898 war ("Remember the *Maine*!"), but it did not determine McKinley's diplomacy. Nor did the yellow-press journalism cry for war, generated by a circulation race between Joseph Pulitzer's *New York World* and William Randolph Hearst's *Journal,* push the president and the nation into war. McKinley refused to read sensational newspapers; in any case, the press had been demanding war since 1895 without effect. The president's policies began to move in February and March through a careful process that in the end took a united nation into battle and did so completely on his own terms.

The first step was to prepare the military. On March 9 he asked for a $50 million appropriation to ready the army and navy. By late March he continued to worry that "We are not prepared for war,"

14 E. A. Fuertes to McKinley, February 28, 1898, Cortelyou Papers; *Washington Post,* July 21, 1983, A23.

but it was clear to his military advisers that Spain was not an overpowering foe. Assistant Secretary of the Navy Roosevelt agreed. When politicians from coastal cities pleaded for protection, he sent some broken-down Civil War artifacts to stand guard in the harbors. Meanwhile he and his superior, John D. Long, prepared the fleet for the important tasks of destroying Spanish power in Cuba — and the Philippines. The Philippine plans did not come out of the blue. The war objectives of the U.S. Navy had long targeted the Philippines, in case of war with Spain, and Roosevelt had briefed McKinley during relaxing buggy rides around Washington. On January 14, 1898, Roosevelt gave Long a nine-page letter outlining war preparations. A month later, while Long was away, Roosevelt sent orders to Admiral George Dewey of the Pacific fleet to prepare to attack Manila in case of war, and he also put other units on alert. The next day the surprised Long and McKinley rescinded much of Roosevelt's handiwork, but approved the orders to Dewey. By April, war preparations were moving ahead and Dewey was prepared to seize one of the most strategic points in the Asian region. McKinley was moving the United States into position to deal simultaneously with crises in Cuba and China. [15]

The next step in the process was to reassure the skittish business community that a war, its expenses and dislocations, would not return a recovering economy back to the crises of 1893–6. The business community, as always, was divided over the possibility of war. Many midwestern voices had long supported "Cuba Libre," as had the usually expansionist westerners, who now also wanted to become more active in Asia. In the money capitals of the Northeast more pacifism appeared, although as February turned into March, the business community, carefully nurtured and comforted by McKinley and his policies, began to unite behind the realization that war would not harm the recovery and, indeed, could end the ongoing festering in Cuba; protect U.S. trade and investments in the Caribbean and the Pacific; and, perhaps, even stimulate interesting profits in iron, steel, textiles, and food processing. Certainly the

---

15 Leech, *Days of McKinley,* 176; Roosevelt to Dewey, February 25, 1898, Ciphers Sent, No. 1, 1888–98, Naval Records, NA, RG 45.

U.S. investors in Cuba, led by Atkins, wanted less dickering and quick annexation to the United States. On March 25, 1898, McKinley received a telegram from a political adviser and journalist in New York City, W. C. Reick: "Big corporations here now believe we will have war. Believe all would welcome it as relief to the suspense." Trade journals were declaring that the chance of war had "stimulated the iron trade," "been beneficial to the railroads," and could "very decidedly enlarge the business of transportation." Whitelaw Reid, the powerful publisher of the *New York Tribune,* took a cross-country trip, then assured McKinley on March 8 that "the more intelligent classes" cared little about "the sensational press" but would follow McKinley wherever he led, even if it meant war. If the leading business voices were ready for war, the key Protestant religious bodies positively embraced it. McKinley, a devout Christian who paid attention to religious leaders, and his political crony Mark Hanna were amazed at the outpouring of war spirit once Roman Catholic Cuba and the Philippines seemed to be obtainable. As one Methodist journal phrased it, "Our cause will be just. . . . Every Methodist preacher will be a recruiting officer."[16]

By April, when *Bankers Magazine* assured its readers that war was imminent and could be easily financed, McKinley had already laid down a series of ultimatums that the Spanish government could not accept in full without committing political suicide. By April 15, Madrid had agreed to arbitrate the causes of the *Maine*'s sinking, accept Cuban relief from the United States, repeal the *reconcentrado* policies, and even grant an armistice, but it refused McKinley's central demand: that Spain allow the United States to mediate the conflict, and to do so without more delays – that is, to accept the president's involvement before the rainy season began in May. That season could shut down the need for further diplomacy until the weather cleared in September. The Spanish queen regent desperately searched for an escape as McKinley tightened the noose. In March her government tried to obtain a deal: more Cuban autonomy in

16 Reick to Young, March 25, 1898, McKinley Papers; Reid to McKinley, March 8, 1898, ibid.; *Tradesman,* March 1, 1898, 58; Julius W. Pratt, *The Expansionists of 1898* (Baltimore, 1936), 282–3.

return for McKinley outlawing the Cuban Junta's operations. The United States flatly rejected the offer. She then turned to her aunt, Queen Victoria of Great Britain, for help. In the first week of April the European powers, led by Germany and France (whose bankers held large amounts of Spanish bonds), discussed the possibility of intervening to mediate and avoid war. The British government killed the effort by refusing to cooperate. The appeasement policy again won the day. As a jubilant Hay informed Washington on April 6, the British had declared they would "be guided by the wishes of the President." McKinley then politely rejected the European proposal. At the same time, a deeply worried Vatican moved to help Spain obtain a cessation of hostilities in Cuba. The pope sent word to McKinley that the granting of an armistice "would avert danger of war." The U.S. minister to Spain supported the Vatican's initiative. McKinley did not. He believed an armistice was insufficient. By demanding nothing less than U.S. involvement in Cuba, the president raised the stakes, made it impossible for Spain to accept, and undermined the Vatican's proposal.[17]

McKinley had one more battle to win. On April 11, he sent a carefully worded message to Congress that meant war. Over the next week, Congress debated not whether to declare war (the sentiment for that was overwhelming), but whether to recognize the Cuban revolutionary government. Millions of dollars of Junta bonds rode on that recognition, but so, as well, did McKinley's freedom of action and the possibility that the revolutionary regime might threaten Creole-U.S. property interests on the island. As the president told a friend, the rebels "are more difficult than Spain to deal with." In a brutal political struggle, McKinley forced the House, then the Senate, to surrender to his demand that no recognition be granted, and that he have the widest possible freedom of action. In return, he did accept the Teller Resolution: "The United States hereby disclaims any disposition or intention to exercise sovereignty, jurisdiction, or control" over Cuba, "except for the pacification

---

17 Hay to Sherman, April 6, 1898, Great Britain, Dispatches, Department of State, NA, RG 59; French Minister of Foreign Affairs to French Ambassador, April 7, 1898, McKinley Papers.

thereof." Henry Teller, Republican of Colorado, intended to protect his state's beet-sugar producers from cheap Cuban sugar, as well as take a moral antiimperialist position. As usual, American idealism and realism were two sides of the same coin. McKinley, who had no intention of trying to annex the multiracial island, had no objections. On April 29 he signed the declaration of war.[18]

It had been a remarkable display of presidential power. Midway through the battle, the *New York Post* noted on April 2 how McKinley had kept control of a militant Congress as he carefully prepared for war. The *Post* compared him with "the trapper who can lure his game with sweets," and who "brings home just as many pelts as the hunter who has his gun. . . . In some cases he undoubtedly obtains more, for he gets better acquainted with the habits of his game than [does] the hunter."[19]

In the end, McKinley sought war and domination in the Caribbean and the southern Pacific. His concern for order was strictly secondary. Indeed, if he sought stability, it was mostly at home, and for that he needed war and an extended military commitment to the two theaters. Only then, he believed, could he protect U.S. property in Cuba, stop the interminable and unsettling rebellion, and work with the British and Japanese to protect the Open Door in a crumbling China. If he had truly sought order, he had other alternatives, notably allowing Spain to crush the rebellion as it had in the 1870s, or recognizing the Cuban revolutionary government and allowing it to govern its own homeland. He did neither. As a result of McKinley's foreign policy choices in early 1898, the United States first went to war, then became responsible for a series of interventions in Cuba to protect U.S. interests, and next sank into a decade-long involvement in Asia that led to more war, conflict with Japan and Russia, and the acceleration of the Chinese revolution. The United States willingly assumed such burdens, never considered retreating from either Cuba or Asia, and accepted both war and

18 Benjamin, *U.S. and Cuban Revolution*, 50–1; Diary, March 19, 1898, Papers of Oscar Straus, Library of Congress, Washington, D.C; John L. Offner, *An Unwanted War* (Chapel Hill, 1992), 189, is key for understanding the Teller Amendment.

19 Quoted in *Philadelphia Press*, April 2, 1898, 6.

revolution not in the naïve belief that they somehow produced order, but in the confidence that if properly exploited, they could produce more American power and opportunities. For such power and opportunities, disorder was a small price to pay.

Splendid War, Splendid Islands

That "splendid little war," as Hay termed the three-month conflict, was the easiest labor any nation ever endured in giving birth to an empire. Keen observers had long assumed this would be the case. "I can hardly think there can be any serious war," James Harrison Wilson wrote John McCook as early as February. "The modern Spaniard is like the French Duellist [and] it takes but one shot to satisfy his honor." Business boomed after late April. McKinley had carefully planned to pay as fully as possible for the war and avoid debt; taxes could be imposed on the products of the Second Industrial Revolution, including a "temporary" tax of one cent on each phone call that, with several modifications, actually remained as a cash cow for the government nearly a century later. Americans flocked to enlist. Several all-male schools (notably Lafayette College) volunteered in a body. Roosevelt's famed "Rough Riders" symbolized the new nationalism. "Our men represent every phase of American life," Roosevelt's chief aide, Leonard Wood, wrote McKinley in May, ". . . ultra-fashionables from New York, men from the North, South, East, and West, ranchmen, cowboys, miners, every profession, half-breeds from the Indian territory; in fact, pretty much every variety of American manhood. They are working together most harmoniously."[20] The war was healing the Civil War wounds of race and geography, and the Gilded Age's wounds of class warfare.

McKinley and his advisers assumed the conflict would be decided on the seas. Here U.S. superiority was overwhelming. The president could order four new battleships into action. Spain had nothing remotely comparable, nor could it match the U.S. second-class battleship and several armored cruisers. The army, on the other hand,

20 Wilson to McCook, February 2, 1898, Letterbooks, Wilson Papers; Wood to McKinley, May 22, 1898, container 56, Cortelyou Papers.

was ill-prepared, due largely to Secretary of War R. A. Alger's, and his department's, slowness, corruption, and inability to change clothing and gear prepared for northern campaigns into battle equipment for a Cuban midsummer. On May 1, Admiral George Dewey, carefully installed by Roosevelt as commander of the Pacific fleet and following his orders, obliterated the Spanish ships at Manila. Some four hundred Spaniards were killed or wounded, while only one American received a scratch. On May 26, U.S. troops were ordered to leave sweltering Florida camps to take Cuba. Three weeks passed before sixteen thousand sailed on makeshift transports. The disintegrating Spanish fleet had gotten across the Atlantic, then sought cover in Santiago harbor. American troops, including African-American units, gained the heights around Santiago. The Spanish fleet attempted to escape and was destroyed by the U.S. Navy. On July 17, Spain's army in Santiago surrendered. A week later, General Nelson A. Miles's troops took Puerto Rico with few shots fired in anger; three U.S. lives were lost. Spain secretly approached Great Britain and other European powers for help, especially in the hope of holding the Philippines until Madrid could make a favorable deal with Washington. Lord Salisbury killed the plan by flatly rejecting any British involvement. Spain was left to McKinley's mercies. On July 22 peace negotiations opened and an armistice signed August 12. The war was over. Some two thousand Americans had died of disease, five times the number killed in battle.[21]

McKinley completely controlled U.S. strategy. Using three telegraph wires and twenty-five telephone lines running into the White House, he could contact U.S. commanders in Cuba within twenty minutes and follow, virtually minute by minute, military changes as shown in the war room (or map room, as it was known), next to his office. He also used the new communications to impose tough censorship on war news. The good reports from Manila were made public, but the corruption, mismanagement, and disease-laden

---

21 Salisbury to Wolff, June 13, 1898, FO 72/2067, Public Record Office; Frank Friedel, "Dissent in the Spanish-American War . . .," in Samuel Eliot Morison, Frederick Merk, and Frank Freidel, *Dissent in Three American Wars* (Cambridge, Mass., 1970).

camps in Florida and Cuba were not fully revealed. McKinley changed the White House into the nation's news center, and he manipulated his control of communications to make public the news he thought fit to print.[22]

The president used the war and his wartime powers to obtain the prize that he and his Republican party had sought since the days of Harrison, if not of Seward. In May 1898, he asked Congress to pass a joint resolution that would annex Hawaii. It was not McKinley's first try. In 1897 he used the more traditional (and constitutional) approach of trying to obtain a two-thirds vote of the Senate to ratify an annexation treaty. His arguments were strong. For one, Hawaii was dominated by white planters who used the islands as the extension of the frontier in Oregon and California: In 1890 they sent 224 million pounds of sugar to the mainland; in 1896, 352 million pounds; and by 1898, shipments would soar to a half-billion pounds. All Hawaiian sugar plantations were capitalized at $36.8 million; of this, $21.7 million was controlled by Americans, who also dominated the islands' trade. For another, Japanese population had grown to 24,000, or about one-quarter of the entire population, and was increasing rapidly. When the Japanese had arrived initially in large numbers in the mid-1880s, the Hawaiian king welcomed them as newcomers who would counterbalance the whites. Instead, the new immigrants became subjugated labor. Nevertheless, by 1890 while Hawaiians made up about 45 percent of the islands' population, Chinese and Japanese accounted for 33 percent, and whites 21 percent. When McKinley moved to annex Hawaii in 1897, the Japanese government strongly opposed him. The situation grew so tense that the president dispatched the new battleship *Oregon* to Honolulu and secretly ordered the navy to seize the islands if Japan made any attempt to use force. Despite the economic ties and Japanese threats, however, opponents stalled the annexation treaty. They argued it would require an even greater and more expensive navy to protect the territory; that it would be the first step toward colonialism and the destruction of the Constitution (which, they believed, could not easily extend across large expanses of water

22 Beisner, *Old Diplomacy to New*, 88, 138–9.

and over multiracial populations); and that the United States already effectively controlled Hawaii anyway. Opposition was especially strong from antiimmigrant groups in California, sugar-beet interests, and organized labor that feared an influx of cheap, Asian workers. Congress adjourned without acting on the pact.[23]

When McKinley resubmitted his proposal to annex the islands in 1898, conditions had transformed. The president now demanded Hawaii as a necessary military base en route to Manila and Shanghai. (Opponents argued in vain that the circle route via the Aleutians, not Hawaii, was the shortest path to Chinese ports.) Japan, moreover, was reeling from German and Russian moves in China, and now, with a new, pro-U.S. government, made overtures for cooperation to Washington by withdrawing its objection to annexation. Missionaries, who had initially led the white settlements on Hawaii, demanded annexation so the islands could become "a base of operations for the enterprise of universal evangelization." In the House, the tough, antiexpansionist speaker, Thomas B. Reed (R.-Maine), held up discussion for three weeks until McKinley threatened to use his war powers to seize Hawaii. The resolution then passed after four days of debate, 209–91. In a free-for-all secret Senate debate, Henry Cabot Lodge charged that other powers besides Japan were waiting to seize the islands. He doubtless had Germany in mind. Opponents warned that annexation would open "a second avenue of conquest" that would lead to "the Philippines next. Part of Asia next. Where will be the limits?" But McKinley had boxed them in. He privately stated his argument succinctly: "We need Hawaii just as much and a good deal more than we did California. It is manifest destiny." His resolution received a bare two-thirds vote in the Senate.[24]

23 Gary Okihiro, *Cane Fires: The Anti-Japanese Movement in Hawaii, 1865–1945* (Philadelphia, 1991), 25, 42, 57; Department of State to Sewall, July 10, 1897, Area 9 file, box 30, July 1–15 folder, Naval Records, NA, RG 45; *Public Opinion*, June 24, 1897, 771–3.

24 "Debates in Secret Legislative Session, 55th Cong., 2nd Sess.," May 31, 1898, transcript, U.S. Senate Archives, Washington, D.C., 21–2, 52–3, 145–6, 150–1; Pratt, *Expansionists of 1898*, 323–5; Diary, June 8, 1898, container 52, Cortelyou Papers; Lewis L. Gould, *The Spanish-American War and President McKinley* (Lawrence, Kan., 1982), 64–5.

On July 31, 1898, McKinley indeed prepared to take the Philippines next, or at least a strategic part of them. At this point, he seemed unclear whether he could take only the port of Manila, which he and such advisers as Mahan preferred, or whether he would have to take all the Philippines to secure Manila. What was clear was his determination to take all that his forces had conquered until he made a careful analysis of the overall situation. He had no doubt that he did not want all of Spain's Pacific and Caribbean empire, only, as affairs stood at the end of the war, Manila, Cuba, and Puerto Rico.

Governing a Caribbean Empire

Cuba had been a prime target of American expansionists since the days of John Quincy Adams. The "apple," as Adams called it, had now fallen. The ironic fact, however, was that U.S. leaders no longer wanted to hold it. Its racial mixture, advanced independence movement, and attendant constitutional problems in Washington made absorption unappealing. Its ninety-mile proximity to the United States, moreover, seemed to make annexation unnecessary. Control could be exerted more indirectly and cheaply. Certainly McKinley wanted control. As Mahan explained in an 1897 essay, the island's domination of three of the four main communication routes in the Caribbean, its short interior lines between ports, its long coastline and many harbors that made blockade nearly impossible — these strategic reasons and the $50 million of U.S. investments in the rich sugar and mining businesses made control necessary.[25]

The problem was how to find the balance between U.S. control and Cuban self-government. "We are dealing with a race that has been steadily going down for a hundred years and into which we have got to infuse new life," General Leonard Wood, McKinley's new commander in Cuba, wrote the president. The Cuban army seemed unfit to rule: "A Cuban camp could always be detected by the nose before it came into view," a disgusted U.S. officer wrote

25 Alfred Thayer Mahan, *The Interest of America in Sea Power, Present and Future* (Boston, 1897), 286–313.

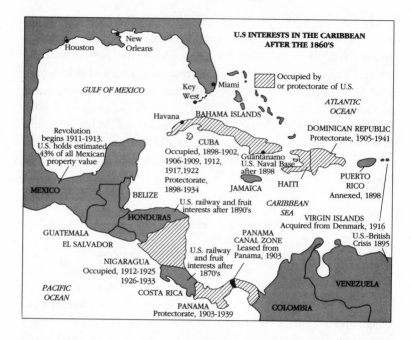

home in mid-1898. Cubans "are very unsatisfactory." Ragtag, steal-
ing from U.S. messes in order to survive, the Cubans were shunted
aside and humiliated. They nevertheless had weapons, an ideology
of independence inherited from Martí, and, after February 1899, the
horrifying example (in U.S. eyes) of the Filipinos rebelling against
their new American masters. The danger was such that the Cubans
were not allowed to participate in the victory parades. Wood ad-
vocated solving the dilemma through outright annexation. Then
a "stable government" could be installed. By stable, he said, he
meant "money at six percent." James Harrison Wilson, who sur-
faced in Cuba as another top U.S. military commander, argued for
a subtler approach: Create indirect political and economic ties
that would, as they had in Hawaii, slowly pull Cuba into the
Union.[26]

26 David Healy, *The United States in Cuba, 1898–1902* (Madison, 1963), 34–6;
   Major-General Joseph T. Dickman to his brother, August 10, 1898, Papers of
   Joseph T. Dickman, Notre Dame University, Notre Dame, Ind.

Elihu Root, whom McKinley had enticed from the top of New York's legal and corporate community to replace the hapless Alger as secretary of war, had to make the choice. No one was better qualified. A gifted administrator, and so well connected that he became the father of the twentieth-century American establishment, Root quickly grasped the reins and cleansed the War Department. He thoroughly reorganized the army by creating the general staff in 1903 and also began the first long-term strategic planning that included an interservice planning group. Root paid special attention, however, to governing the new conquests, a task he and McKinley assumed was a right of the executive with minimal congressional contributions. By late 1899 Root had stalled the Cuban independence forces by buying off individual soldiers and promising their leaders a large amount of self-government. He opted for Wilson's approach: indirect control through economic ties and also through a series of political provisions that included a U.S. naval base at Guantanamo, sanitation policies that would encourage foreign investment, a Cuban debt limit so European creditors could not gain a foothold, and — of special significance — the right of U.S. intervention to guarantee a republican government.[27]

These provisions were written into a U.S.-Cuban treaty by Senator Orville Platt (R.-Conn.). They thus became known, rather misleadingly, as the Platt Amendment, although they were Root's and Wilson's ideas. Root's special touch was to force the Cuban Constitutional Convention to write the Platt Amendment into its governing document in 1900. His task was not easy. He tried to load the convention with pro-U.S. delegates by imposing suffrage requirements of property and literacy. Nationalist elements nevertheless won. When they objected to the Platt Amendment, Wood and Root informed the Cubans the new nation had no choice but to accept it; after all, Root observed, the United States already had the authority to set Cuba aright under the Monroe Doctrine. He now only wanted this authority put into a treaty (and constitution) that would be sanctified by international law. The Cuban Constitutional Conven-

27 H. Wayne Morgan, "William McKinley as a Political Leader," *Review of Politics* 28 (October 1966): 429.

tion capitulated by a vote of 16–11, with four abstentions. A key leader, Estrada Palma, gave in with the hope that outright annexation would soon follow. Others came around after Root promised to give them a reciprocity treaty that would guarantee entry to U.S. markets. At first, Root and the new president, Theodore Roosevelt, could not overcome the opposition of beet-sugar interests to such a treaty. In 1903, however, these interests were literally bought out by the American Sugar Refining interests that had access to Cuban fields. Industrialists and farmers from the United States also supported the treaty, because they received preferences in the island's markets. The United States had apparently padlocked Cubans into its system politically and economically, while giving them the semblance of self-government. As Wood wrote privately to Roosevelt in 1900, "There is, of course, little or no independence left Cuba under the Platt Amendment."[28]

Puerto Rico gave Root an easier time, although early signs were ominous. In 1897–8, the island's people were given a large amount of autonomy by Spain, and even sent delegates to the Cortes in Madrid. The U.S. military governor, General Nelson A. Miles (of Indian-fighting fame), promised "the blessings" of U.S. government, so Puerto Ricans did not oppose the invasion. But they quickly learned that the blessings did not include what they wanted: either self-governing autonomy with access to U.S. markets or full statehood in the Union. The irony became that the United States went into an imperialist war to give Cuba freedom, but ended taking Puerto Rico and stripping its people of many rights they enjoyed under Spanish rule. The annexation was driven by McKinley's quest for strategic naval bases, which indeed he found in Puerto Rico. Washington's rule soon led the people to condemn Miles and his advisers as "czars and sultans."

The key piece of evidence for their case was the Foraker Act of 1900 (named after Ohio Republican Senator "Fire-Alarm" Joe Foraker), which made Puerto Rico an "unincorporated territory" subject only to Congress's whim. The power rested in a governor appointed

28 Richard H. Collin, *Theodore Roosevelt's Caribbean* (Baton Rouge, 1990), 526–7;
     Healy, *U.S. in Cuba*, 132, 143, 153–4, 166–7, 175, 178, 204–5, 214–15.

by the U.S. president. The inhabitants were guaranteed religious freedom (a reason why the Vatican acquiesced in the U.S. acquisition), but no promise of either citizenship or statehood followed. In Washington, Congress passed the measure after a bitter struggle and by only a 172–161 margin. Opponents railed against this new colonialism that allowed McKinley to put the island in a governing limbo. Again, political controls were buttressed by tariff preferences that gave Puerto Rican sugar access to the U.S. market and effectively integrated the island into the mainland's economy. In a series of landmark decisions between 1901 and 1910, known as the Insular Cases, the Supreme Court's majority ruled that the peoples of territories such as Puerto Rico, which had been obtained by conquest, did not have full citizenship rights. They enjoyed only certain "fundamental" rights because they were in an "unincorporated" territory subject to congressional authority. (Puerto Ricans finally received U.S. citizenship in 1917, but nearly a century after the conquest only had commonwealth, not statehood or independent status; the decisions resulting from the Insular Cases meanwhile continued to govern U.S. holdings in the Pacific, such as Guam.) As the Supreme Court made African Americans second-class citizens in *Plessy v. Ferguson* (1896), its Insular Cases made Puerto Ricans inferior by conquest. The 1898 empire marked the first time the United States had annexed a major territory without the intention of granting statehood and citizenship.[29]

Again, the pursuit of opportunity drove U.S. policy. On one level, the quest was for full control over strategic naval bases. On another level, it was, as the Foraker Act indicated, for investment opportunities without local restraints. When the U.S. customs duties on Puerto Rican goods disappeared in 1901, the sugar companies, as British historian Raymond Carr writes, were "allowed to expand their activities in Puerto Rico whatever the social and human costs." A future result, he notes, "was economic catastrophe in the 1930s" for the island. More immediate results of Washington's po-

---

29 Julius W. Pratt, *America's Colonial Experiment* (New York, 1959), 68, 187–8; Louis Henkin, *Foreign Affairs and the Constitution* (Mineola, N.Y., 1975), 268; Raymond Carr, *Puerto Rico: A Colonial Experiment* (New York, 1984), 20–46.

litical and economic policies were chaotic elections ("mob rule" in the 1900 balloting, as Carr describes it) and a full-blown constitutional crisis in 1909 when the nation's leader, Luis Muñoz Rivera, in the best tradition of 1776, challenged U.S. colonial financial control. President William Howard Taft interpreted the challenge as proof that "we have gone somewhat too fast in the extension of political power to them for their own good"; he and Congress took further power away from the Puerto Ricans. Racism again complemented imperialism: "Liberty is a habit," one U.S. observer declared after the unruly 1900 elections, that "tropical peoples" had trouble learning.[30]

The Meaning of Caribbean Empire

The Insular Cases changed U.S. constitutional history for the sake of empire. Meanwhile, McKinley transformed presidential powers by the grace of empire; that is, he and Root especially consolidated power in the executive to an extent unseen since the Civil War. This time, however, the consolidation was to prove more permanent because foreign policy, which the president controlled in the new age of communications and more rapid military movements, was gaining a primary and lasting place on the nation's agenda for the first time in a half century.

Equally interesting is how U.S. officials used this power in making choices. In every major decision they were motivated not primarily by concern for stability and, certainly, not by concern for democracy. Through the Platt Amendment, trade measures, and the Foraker Act, as well as the court cases, they sought control and opportunity. If they had wanted stability first, they would have made Cuba and Puerto Rico parts of the Union. Racial, economic, and constitutional problems, however, prevented such integration and, in any case, U.S. policymakers believed they could have the best of all worlds by more indirect control and the illusion of Cuban self-government. (The racial reasons were sometimes bluntly stated. Major General John T. Dickman related that when Cubans accused

30 Carr, *Puerto Rico,* 37, 44–51.

Americans of wanting to annex them, "you ought to see them squirm when I tell them that your Uncle Samuel has too many niggers already.")[31]

The responsibility for maintaining order could have also been given fully to Cubans and Puerto Ricans. It was not given, however, again because of the economic, strategic, and racial results of the Second Industrial Revolution. As a direct consequence of this policy of opportunity, Cubans vented their frustrations over unbalanced economic development and lack of control over their own political affairs by erupting in civil war and even attempted revolution during the next thirty-five years. The United States responded with military force as early as 1906, and thus only sharpened the imbalances and the Cubans' charges that it was the United States, not themselves, who prevented the working out of the nation's problems. For the sake of control and opportunity, the United States became, in both Cuba and Puerto Rico, not the agent of order but the focal point for protest and disorder. For the next two generations, Washington nevertheless refused to reconsider its policies but only tried to protect its economic and strategic opportunities through the often reluctant but continued use of military force under the command of the new presidency.[32]

31 Dickman to his brother, May 24, 1899, Dickman Papers.
32 Lloyd Gardner, "From Liberation to Containment," in William Appleman Williams, ed., *From Colony to Empire* (New York, 1972), 220.

8. Pacific Empire – and Upheaval

"We are all jingoes now," the *New York Sun* wrote immediately after the 1898 war, "and the head jingo is the Hon. William McKinley." The term "jingo" came from an 1878 British music hall song about "jingo" Englishmen who were aching to fight Russia. The term also came from the Japanese empress, Jingo, who sometime before the fourth century A.D. invaded Korea in an uproar of nationalism, war, and all-out expansionism.[1] By the late 1890s it was a household term. Given the lineage, however, McKinley was no "jingo." He disdained seizing parts of the Spanish empire and approached Cuba, Puerto Rico, and – above all – the Philippines incrementally and with a superb politician's sensitivity to the need for consensus. His objective was not a colonial empire but the minimum territory needed to obtain his conquest of world markets, along with the taking of strategic points necessary to protect that conquest. To achieve such a conquest, however, McKinley was willing to endure disorder and bear upheavals, even full-scale insurrection in the Philippines, or the threat of becoming involved in war on the Asian mainland.

Destroying Order for Opportunity:
Annexing the Philippines

On May 4, 1898, even before he received official word of Admiral George Dewey's conquest of Manila, the president ordered 5,000 troops to embark for the occupation of the Philippines "and such service as may be ordered hereafter." These troops quickly encountered the forces of Emilio Aguinaldo, who had led the Filipino

1 *Des Moines Register,* April 17, 1985, 9A; Paul F. Boller, Jr., *Presidential Anecdotes* (New York, 1981), 191–3.

independence fight in 1896–7 against Spain. After a brief interlude, the struggle reerupted with such fury in March 1898 (six weeks before U.S. forces appeared) that the U.S. consul told Washington that "insurrection is rampant," and that despite Spanish "barbarity," the rebels verged on conquering Manila itself. Just twenty-eight years old in 1898, Aguinaldo had been born to a poor farmer and his wife, who was one-half Chinese. He had shown brilliance, ruthlessness, and leadership, as well as an ardent nationalism. In late May 1898, Admiral Dewey reported that Aguinaldo's forces were able to render valuable military services. Within a month, however, as McKinley's determination to seize Luzon and Manila hardened, U.S. officials in the islands were instructed to have nothing to do with any of Aguinaldo's "political claims." His forces had now grown to 37,000 troops. By midsummer, as the Filipino noted that Americans were not preparing to leave despite the end of the war, tension heightened. McKinley had walked into a trap. He ordered Dewey to make no deals with Aguinaldo, but the rebel seemed to need none. By July his forces practically controlled the most strategic island, Luzon (which is nearly as large as New York State), except for Manila; were spreading their authority over other islands; and had conquered large elements of Spain's army.[2]

McKinley nevertheless decided to try to hold all the Philippines until he could figure out exactly which spoils of war U.S. interests required. The touchstone was Asian trade. Acting Secretary of State William R. Day and Massachusetts Republican Senator Henry Cabot Lodge penned memorandums in June 1898 (after, it might be noted, conversations with each other). Day assumed that the recent industrial surpluses required "an enlargement of foreign markets," especially in China where European colonization threatened American interests. Lodge's memorandum, written to Day on June 6, 1898, seemed to borrow heavily from Lodge's close friend, Brooks Adams, who had developed a historical theory that world power

2 U.S. Senate Document no. 62, *A Treaty of Peace Between the United States and Spain . . .,* 55th Cong., 3d Sess. (Washington, D.C., 1899), 320–1, 329; Long to Dewey, May 26, 1898, Papers of George Cortelyou, Library of Congress, Washington, D.C.; Dewey to Long, July 4, 1898, ibid.; Lewis L. Gould, *The Spanish-American War and President McKinley* (Lawrence, Kan., 1982), 63, 67.

followed the center of money exchanges. Those centers, Adams argued, had moved constantly westward, and now the United States was in a position to seize world economic power from Great Britain if Americans could dominate Asia, the largest and cheapest of all markets. If, Lodge warned, Europeans instead divided China and "we fail to establish ourselves with a large port and with territory in the East," catastrophe loomed: "We must have new markets unless we would be visited by declines in wages and by great industrial disturbances, of which signs have not been lacking. The old theory of competing in foreign markets merely by the price of the product is no longer practicable." Now "a navy, coaling stations and ports in the East . . . have become essential conditions in our time." Lodge urged that, at a minimum, Luzon be U.S.-controlled.[3]

McKinley's thoughts clearly had been running along the same lines, as had those of many others, including John Hay whom the president had ordered to return from London in mid-1898 to become secretary of state. To ensure his freedom of action, and to pull off a political coup that set an important historical precedent, McKinley named a five-man peace commission that not only had a majority of expansionists but included key senators who would later have to vote on their own handiwork. Senators Cushman Davis (R.-Minn.) and William Frye (R.-Maine) were imperialists; Senator George Gray (D.-Del.) was an avowed (but as McKinley understood, a malleable) antiexpansionist. Day, who headed the commission, was not considered an imperialist, but he did want Manila, although little else of the Philippines. Above all, however, Day would do whatever his longtime Ohio friend, the president, asked him to do, as would the fifth member, Whitelaw Reid, owner of the powerful Republican newspaper the *New York Tribune*. On October 28, 1898, McKinley finally ordered them to demand all the Philippines; in return the United States would pay an indemnity of $20 million for recent improvements Spain had made in the islands.

---

3 William C. Widenor, *Henry Cabot Lodge and the Search for an American Foreign Policy* (Berkeley, 1980), 93–8; Thomas McCormick, *China Market* (Chicago, 1967), 114, 164–5; I am indebted to Professor Richard Werking for the Lodge document.

McKinley reached this fateful decision for many reasons. He had already determined that Manila had to be kept as the strategic U.S. port for protecting interests in Asia. After talking with specialists on the islands, and with military advisers providing confirmation, the president decided that Manila's defense against possible attacks from other powers (such as Germany) required all of Luzon, and that Luzon's defense required controlling the rest of the 7,100 Philippine Islands. In addition, Aguinaldo's forces could apparently not be trusted. Dewey cabled on October 13, "The natives appear unable to govern." U.S. consuls' reports through the summer contradicted Dewey's view. On the other hand, the consuls sent numerous letters from wealthy Filipinos begging for annexation to the United States; in early September one such dispatch concluded, "if we [Americans] evacuate, anarchy rules." As early as August, McKinley had ordered "no joint occupation with the insurgents," only unilateral U.S. control. Meanwhile he kept a careful eye on European powers who coveted the islands, and the Japanese who subtly sounded out the State Department about a cooperative role "in the interest of commerce and peace." McKinley wanted no part of a policy that would give advantages to his chief competitors. In the autumn he undertook a political swing through the American heartland. Ostensibly it was to sound out public opinion while stumping for Republican candidates in the 1898 campaign. In reality, he had already decided to take the islands. His speeches were structured not to consult but to arouse that opinion to fulfill "the responsibility that has been put upon us by the results of the war," as he declared in one speech. McKinley returned to Washington to report that the people agreed that the United States had a mission in Asia.[4]

As the president reached this momentous conclusion, one development was of special importance: Based on the evidence he had at hand, McKinley would have had difficulty arguing that Americans had to annex Luzon for the purpose of restoring order. Aguinaldo had apparently already begun to accomplish that objective. The

---

4 Robert C. Hilderbrand, "Power and the People . . . 1869–1921" (Ph.D. diss., University of Iowa, 1977), 138–9; U.S. Senate Document no. 62, *A Treaty of Peace*, 333–5.

U.S. consul general in Hong Kong, who was in close contact with Aguinaldo, told Washington in mid-July 1898:

[Aguinaldo] organized a government of which he was a Dictator, an absolutely necessary step if he hoped to maintain control over the natives, and from that date until the present time he has been uninterruptedly successful in the field and dignified and just as the head of his government.

The diplomat stressed that the Filipino "had taken up the reins of the Spanish government and controlled the island of Luzon outside of Manila; had complete telegraphic communications with the chieftains of the provinces . . . and established a revolutionary government which was apparently acceptable to the Filipinos of the Island." In the crucial province of Batangas, south of Manila, for example, Aguinaldo's decrees governed by June (and would continue to do so – with the help of upper-class Filipinos – until U.S. troops finally invaded to destroy the government in early 1900).[5]

McKinley did not have to annex Luzon to impose order; nor did he have to "uplift and civilize [the Filipinos], and by God's grace do the very best by them," as he explained his decision to a group of Methodist church visitors. The Filipinos had been the subjects of Christian missionaries and governments for three hundred years. His central reason was revealed in another remark made to the Methodists: "We could not turn them over to France or Germany – our commercial rivals in the Orient – that would be bad business and discreditable." Actually, major European powers led by the British and French pushed the president to annex the islands so their imperialist colleagues, especially the Germans, would not be able to yield to temptation. Annexation also made sense in the context of McKinley joining the British to counter other imperial powers who were maneuvering to exploit the crumbling Manchu dynasty. The decision made little sense as a policy to impose order, Christianity, or American-style democracy.[6]

5 Quoted in "Mark Twain on American Imperialism," *Atlantic* 269 (April 1992): 59–60; also U.S. Senate Document no. 62, *A Treaty of Peace*, 337; Glenn Anthony May, *A Past Recovered* (Quezon City, Philippines, 1987), 115–16.

6 Lazar Ziff, *America in the 1890s* (New York, 1966), 221; Horace Porter to McKinley, September 6, 1898, container 57, Cortelyou Papers.

Aguinaldo's forces and U.S. troops exchanged gunfire on February 6 and the island exploded in revolution against McKinley's policy. Who fired the first shot remains difficult to determine, although there is no doubt that on the president's orders U.S. troops were moving into key port cities held by the Filipinos and assuming the powers of government. Until the exchange of gunfire, some close observers doubted whether the Senate would ratify the peace treaty. One of these observers was Andrew Carnegie, who so hated the thought that Americans were following in the footsteps of his despised British imperialists that he wrote highly insulting letters to his friend in the White House ("Your friend personally, but the bitterest enemy you have officially," one read). The steel magnate offered to buy the islands for $20 million so he could restore their independence. Other critics warned that such a colonial policy would undermine the Constitution. Most of these critics, however, wanted to exploit Asian trade and somehow neutralize the Philippines so they could be used (in the phrase of antiimperialist Edward Atkinson) as a "sanctuary of commerce."[7]

Acting as McKinley's floor leader to pass the peace treaty, Lodge noted pointedly that the pact's opponents refused to discuss the fundamental issue – "the enormous material benefits to our trade, our industries, and our labor dependent upon a right settlement of this question." They instead "placed their opposition on such high and altruistic grounds" as constitutionality. Lodge willingly confronted them on their grounds, but he regretted that because the opponents refused to deal with the most fundamental policy, he lacked the opportunity to touch on "the commercial advantages to the country involved in the question of these islands, or the far greater question of the markets of China, of which we must have our share for the benefit of our workingmen." Other supporters of the peace treaty were outspoken. Control of at least parts of the Philippines, said Senator John L. McLaurin, who spoke for South Carolina textile firms, "is our only safeguard for our trade interests in the East." A southern textile owner thought the constitutional debate

---

7 Carnegie to McKinley, November 28, 1898, container 57, Cortelyou Papers; *The Anti-Imperialist* 1 (no date): 45–6.

irrelevant: "We have had colonies in this country ever since we ceased to be colonies ourselves." Lodge and the young Republican senator from Indiana, Albert J. Beveridge, pounded home the historical lesson that Americans had long been treating Indians just as they now planned to treat Filipinos. The policy was hardly new. They delighted in noting that the Democrats' patron saint, Thomas Jefferson, had governed not only Indians but all of Louisiana without the inhabitants' consent after he purchased it from France in 1803.[8]

If the annexationists had the best of the economic and constitutional debates, however, both sides could equally exploit the explosive racial issue. As African Americans (including some who had served in the 1898 war) were lynched, burned, or otherwise oppressed in the United States, McKinley and other officials did nothing. A few antiimperialists, such as the articulate Boston lawyer Moorfield Storey, condemned the policy in the Philippines and began to see that African Americans were treated similarly, if not worse, at home; these opponents of the treaty consequently began to champion African-American rights. Storey was appalled when Elihu Root declared that the failed policy of giving African Americans the vote in the United States proved that the Filipinos could not be trusted with it. Most antiimperialists, however, were much less concerned about the treatment of African Americans than they were with the treatment of Filipinos. The racial question, as they saw it, had so torn up three hundred years of American history that they did not want to compound the tragedy by adding in the Filipinos. One interesting variation of the opponents' view came from the American Federation of Labor which argued that "trade unions are possible only in industrial and in civilized countries." Because the Philippines did not qualify, Americans would have to build a costly army and navy to enforce imperialism. A second, more significant, variation appeared in June 1898, when the Anti-Imperialist League formed in Boston. More than half the audience was made up of women. Throughout most of the nineteenth century, women's orga-

8 *Congressional Record*, 55th Cong., 3d Sess., January 24, 1899, 960; Walter L. Williams, "U.S. Indian Policy and the Debate over Philippine Annexation . . .," *Journal of American History* 66 (March 1980): 818–20; Patrick J. Hearden, *Independence and Empire* (DeKalb, Ill., 1982), 135–7.

nizations had shown little interest in foreign policy, but led by suffrage groups, they changed their focus after the 1870s. Many women openly identified with Filipinos who were also to be governed without their consent. (Women's groups played important roles in the growing foreign policy debates between 1898 and 1905.) Imperialists, however, assumed that if the U.S. government had shown it could keep African Americans and Indians (and women) in their place at home without the vote, it could do the same with Filipinos.[9]

The debate, accelerated by the peace treaty signed with Spain December 10, 1898, and sent to the Senate January 4, 1899, raged on with the opponents believing they were gaining strength – until the night of February 4. McKinley then received news that the insurgents had attacked U.S. forces in Manila. He must not have been surprised. As early as October 1898, he had been warned by his consul general, R. Wildman, that there was no good reason for war with Aguinaldo, but "the way we are going on now [in pushing aside the Filipinos], it seems to me we may drift into a miserable war that would be as unnecessary as it would be disastrous." McKinley nevertheless stayed the course and war had erupted. "How foolish these people [the Filipinos] are," the president instantly observed after receiving the February 4 cable. "This means the ratification of the treaty." On February 6, the pact passed along partisan lines by the bare two-thirds required, 57–27, with 40 Republicans, 10 Democrats, 2 Populists, 4 Silverites, and 1 independent for, and 21 Democrats opposed along with 3 Republicans, 2 Populists, and 1 Silverite. The outbreak of war, McKinley's use of patronage and presidential authority, and the Republican dominance in the Senate decided the issue. Less important was William Jennings Bryan's last-minute conversion to supporting the treaty on the ostensible (and puzzling) grounds that the war had to be ended first before he could wage political war on McKinley about the treaty and the issue of imperialism in the 1900 presidential campaign. Bryan

9 William B. Hixon, Jr., "Moorfield Storey and the Struggle for Equality," *Journal of American History* 55 (December, 1968): 533–54; *American Federationist* 6 (April 1899): 38; Judith Papachristou, "American Women and Foreign Policy, 1898–1905," *Diplomatic History* 14 (Fall 1990): 498–505.

could not decisively turn many Senate votes; Lodge, Mark Hanna, and the powerful Rhode Island Senator Nelson Aldrich could and did. McKinley and the Republican leadership threw a sop to the opposition, and covered their political flanks, by passing the McEnery Resolution that promised in an unspecified "due time" the Philippines would receive independence.[10]

Deeply embittered, Carnegie denied the war had "entrusted to us" the Philippines, as McKinley claimed. "This is the President's own Pandora box," Carnegie charged, and it was entirely his doing. More accurate was the *Philadelphia Press*'s prescient assessment in late June 1898. Its editorial, "The Inevitable Expansion," argued that the "first cause" in obtaining a Philippine foothold had not been the war but the soaring export of manufactures from $150 million to nearly $300 million in just five years. "The time has come for the United States to look out and not in. . . . These things are inevitable. They have not been caused by the Spanish war and its close will not change them. They create new responsibilities, and the United States must meet them."[11] To meet such responsibilities, McKinley sought what he termed "benevolent assimilation." He instead received a three-year war.

Part Two of a War for Empire

To protect its Asian interests, the United States fully involved itself in imperial conquest, and not only in the Philippines. Hawaiian annexation had resulted from the war. So too did a renewed clash in Samoa with Germany. It did not help that Germany had been pro-Spain throughout the crisis, and that Dewey's ships and a small German fleet had nearly come into conflict in Manila Bay.[12]

---

10 Widenor, *Lodge,* 116–17; "Extracts from confidential letter of R. Wildman . . . dated Oct. 15," container 57, Cortelyou Papers; diary, February 4, 1899, container 52, ibid.

11 Joseph F. Wall, *Andrew Carnegie* (New York, 1970), 707; *Philadelphia Press,* June 29, 1898, 6.

12 Alfred Vagts, *Deutschland und die Vereinigten Staaten in der Weltpolitik,* 2 vols. (New York, 1935), 1: 780–97; the German context, especially the "social imperialism" perspective, is succinctly given in Gustav Schmidt, *Der europäische Imperialismus* (Munich, 1989), 73–81.

American power focused, however, on the Philippines and the Asian mainland. When Aguinaldo's troops refused to obey, McKinley did not hesitate to escalate U.S. troops' presence in the islands until they numbered over 30,000 at one time, and totaled 120,000 during the three-year conflict. For all of his messages to Congress and Methodist church leaders about ideals, McKinley, like Woodrow Wilson, the two Roosevelts, and others who followed him to the White House, used the new U.S. military power created by the Second Industrial Revolution, and used it decisively, without visible qualms, and as forcefully as required.[13] Nearly 2,000 Americans died in the war, 1,500 more than the number who died in combat in the 1898 war, but McKinley never seriously considered pulling back, striking a compromise with Aguinaldo, or allowing the Philippine leader to reclaim the control of his people that the U.S. consul believed he had demonstrated through much of 1898. Meanwhile, at least 200,000 Filipinos died in the struggle.

McKinley's objectives, he declared in mid-1899, were fourfold: "Peace first, then a government of law and order honestly administered, full security to life, property, and occupation under the Stars and Stripes." As the fighting escalated, however, brutalities on both sides intensified and casualties mounted. The president found himself fighting a bloody conflict, with no end in sight, just as the 1900 presidential election began to be discussed. He had excellent military forces whose officers had been promoted because of their success in hunting down Indians during the 1865 to 1890 years. Of the thirty generals who served in the war between 1898 and 1902, twenty-six, or 87 percent, had dealt with the Indians. Three of the remaining four were from the West. Moreover, the best people in the Philippines seemed to be on the American side. "Leading Filipinos express confidence in early pacification of the islands," General Elwell Otis cabled home in May 1900. Those "leading Filipinos," most living in upper-class Manila neighborhoods and with a fear of Aguinaldo based on class hatred, had earlier given McKinley

13 D. Cameron Watt, *Succeeding John Bull* (Cambridge, 1984), 188, is important on the U.S. view of using force.

bad advice about "Philippine views" and helped the president miscalculate throughout 1898.[14]

The president tried to regain control first by sending increasing numbers of forces, then personally censoring the news of those forces' activities. His minute attention to newspaper correspondents' access to news, and the stories given out by the administration, was impressive. When reporters in the Philippines finally complained that the censors were changing the meanings of their stories before publication, McKinley devised an artful announcement that managed to place the blame on General Otis. The stakes were considerable. Between 1890 and 1909 the total circulation of U.S. daily newspapers nearly tripled. Americans were literate and took their news seriously, especially from the highly partisan journals with which they happened to agree. McKinley carefully created the first White House press operation to ration news to this vast media. He spent time cultivating reporters, as did Secretary of State Hay, who was the first in his position to hold regular weekly meetings with journalists.[15]

McKinley also tried to create the proper record, and gain public support, by appointing a special commission in January 1899 (just before the Senate vote on the peace treaty) to investigate the Philippine crisis. It was headed by Cornell University President Jacob Gould Schurman, who was publicly known as an antiexpansionist; however, McKinley privately knew (because of a Schurman letter to the president) that he ardently believed that the conquest of China's trade "is undoubtedly our most important foreign question at the present time." The president again carefully screened the Schurman Commission's work, but he need not have worried. To the surprise of many, the commission urged the retention of the Philippines until, as Schurman phrased it, the Filipinos could exercise "the rights and duties of independent sovereignty." After all, as he wrote to a friend in 1900, "the *effect* of our tenure of the Philippine Islands has, in my

14　Note apparently by McKinley, about August 2, 1899, container 58, Cortelyou Papers; Williams, "U.S. Indian Policy," 828; Otis to Adjutant General, May 4, 1900, Papers of William McKinley, Library of Congress, Washington, D.C.

15　Hilderbrand, "Power and the People," 161–6; Otis to Adjutant General, April 19, 1899, container 58, Cortelyou Papers.

judgment, been the improvement of trade opportunities in the Orient" — although the "sole aim" in both the Philippines and Puerto Rico, Schurman immediately added, "must be the welfare of the natives." Secretary of State Hay sympathized with Schurman: "It is heart breaking to see how much punishment those misguided Filipinos insist on, but it must go on until they learn the things that belong to their peace. Then will come the time for you to put forth the bases of an orderly and beneficent government for them."[16]

In March 1901, U.S. officers discovered Aguinaldo's mountain hideout, used native troops to track him down, and when those troops nearly perished from starvation and Aguinaldo sent them food, the U.S. mission shot the Filipino guard and captured their leader. Fighting had died down by 1901, and in that year the United States moved into the great naval base at Subic Bay, where, with the exception of 1942–4, it remained until 1991. The fighting, however, never stopped. American troops continued to war on other islands, especially between 1902 and 1910, and, in the case of the Moros on Mindanao, until 1935. After that confrontation, Washington officials allowed the U.S.-trained Philippine Constabulary to try to eradicate the revolt. The Constabulary failed. As a high-ranking U.S. Army officer wrote home in 1909, long after the revolution had supposedly ended: "We have established civil government, so called, but everybody carries arms on all occasions, even when bathing in the sea. . . . The civil government is a farce to placate sentiment in the states and could not last a minute without military force."[17]

The disorder and bloodshed continued for many reasons. The United States refused to leave; instead, under the 1901 commission headed by William Howard Taft, it established a government con-

---

16 Schurman to McKinley, December 10, 1898, container 58, Cortelyou Papers; Schurman to White, March 12, 1900, Papers of Jacob Gould Schurman, Cornell University, Ithaca, N.Y.; Hay to Schurman, June 19, 1899, ibid.

17 Russell Roth, *Muddy Glory: America's "Indian Wars" in the Philippines, 1899–1935* (West Hanover, Mass., 1981); Major General John T. Dickman to his brother, June 11, 1909, Papers of John T. Dickman, Notre Dame University, Notre Dame, Ind.

trolled by Americans. After 1905, the executive power was in the hands of a governor-general appointed by the president of the United States. The only Filipinos included were from the upper classes. In 1906, the first provincial leaders were allowed to participate. Many formed a party that demanded immediate independence. These leaders, in turn, were opposed by more radical guerrillas who, in fighting U.S. control, carried on the many wars in the thousands of outlying islands. Economically, Washington imposed land and tariff measures that replicated the unequal distribution of property that had been established under Spanish rule. Huge chunks of the best land fell into American hands. The U.S. sugar trust bought 80,000 acres in 1910, and Taft himself had earlier invested in a promising holding. In all, the United States had celebrated a victory in 1901; in 1906, the *Chicago American* even linked the national pastime to the national policies by claiming that baseball's individualism "is one of the reasons why American soldiers are the best in the world [and] capable of going into action without officers."[18] But the war raged on.

Not even baseball-trained or Indian war–hardened U.S. military could impose order on the upheaval. Or, if some U.S. diplomatic dispatches were to be believed, they could not reimpose order. The Filipinos, according to American consul generals, were on their way to creating their own order in 1898. McKinley's interests were elsewhere; he searched for an answer to what Schurman called "our most important foreign question," that is, finding opportunities in Asia. As for Aguinaldo, he managed his plantations until World War II when he cooperated with the Japanese invaders against General Douglas MacArthur, the U.S. commander in the Pacific. MacArthur was the son of Arthur MacArthur, Aguinaldo's conqueror in 1901.

18 John A. Lankin, "Philippine History Reconsidered," *American Historical Review* 87 (June 1982): 621–4; Eufronio M. Alip, *Philippine Government* (Manila, 1939), 79–87; Renato Constantino, *A History of the Philippines* (New York, 1975), 34, 251–99, 319; the best overall treatment is Glenn Anthony May, *Social Engineering in the Philippines* (Westport, Conn., 1980); George Will, *Men at Work* (New York, 1990), 240. I am indebted to Leslie Hilgeman for her work on the Philippines.

Wars to Open Doors

During his early 1898 run-up to the war with Spain, McKinley closely associated the crises in the Caribbean and Asian theaters. As revolution threatened Cuba, so European imperialism endangered China. The U.S. business community tried to keep Asia in the forefront of the nation's debate. Exports of cotton cloth to China more than doubled to $7 million in a single year, the New York *Commercial Advertiser* reported in January 1898. "The Orient is just beginning to be a purchaser in our markets for things which every civilized nation has always bought to its capacity." Thus it was imperative to "retain free entry into the China market. . . . It must be clearly understood that while armed Europe is welcome to steal Chinese territory . . ., we cannot submit to being excluded from trade in that territory." Other observers noted that kerosene exports to China had reached $4.5 million and the market seemed unlimited, as it did for exports of flour, iron, and steel. A metaphor for post–Civil War U.S. industrial development was the Cordova, Alabama, cotton mills, whose 25,000 spindles were built by Boston capital, and whose entire product in 1897 went to China.[19]

As John Hay returned home from London in late summer 1898, he was, as McKinley knew, fully conversant with the threats that endangered America's Open Door to China. He also had learned firsthand that all of Europe seemed about to explode because of imperial rivalries. The British Empire in Africa was being undermined by costly wars in Khartoum, South Africa, and by the crisis between British and French forces who met on the upper Nile at Fashoda in 1898. The growing confrontation in Asia was part of these global rivalries. Besieged abroad by German, French, and Russian militarism, and by American and German marketplace triumphs, Great Britain followed a policy of appeasement not only toward the United States but, to McKinley's and Hay's horror, toward the Russians when the two European nations agreed in April 1898 to stake out zones in China for railroad monopolies. The

19 New York *Commercial Advertiser*, January 26, 1898, 6; *Chattanooga Tradesman*, December 15, 1897, 59.

Russians seemed to be closing off their Manchurian ports. The Open Door was imperiled. The new secretary of state was determined to reopen the door with a joint U.S.-British push.

The gigantic stakes at issue were outlined by Hay's and Roosevelt's close friend, Brooks Adams, in the August 1898 issue of *The Forum*. In "The Spanish War and the Equilibrium of the World," Adams used trade figures and money-flow statistics to demonstrate that the 1898 war marked the point at which the world's money centers since 1815, London and Paris, were shifting either east to Berlin and St. Petersburg, or west to New York. The great question would finally be decided by which side controlled Asian markets; it would be a battle "between the maritime and unmaritime races." Adams demanded an alliance between the British and Americans to push back the "unmaritime" Russians and Germans; otherwise, the inability to get rid of U.S. surplus goods would "run the risk of [American] suffocation." If, on the other hand, the alliance worked,

Probably human society would then be absolutely dominated by a vast combination of peoples whose right wing would rest upon the British Isles, whose left would overhang the middle provinces of China, whose centre would approach the Pacific, and who would encompass the Indian Ocean as though it were a lake, much as the Romans encompassed the Mediterranean.[20]

Hay needed little encouragement to accept such a thesis. A former private secretary of Abraham Lincoln, diplomat, popular poet and novelist, and steel executive, he understood American society, its needs and limits. Hay believed in the workings of the marketplace. He further believed that, by working through it, the natural political and economic aristocracy America had spawned, of which he was a valued member, would control the fulcrum of world affairs – if the marketplace was allowed to work. The problem was that the tsar and the kaiser, especially, wanted to close off parts of Asia's markets, and that now, out of an acute sense of self-preservation, the British, and perhaps Japanese, were joining the race to colonize and cordon off large, strategic parts of a fragmenting

20 Brooks Adams, "The Spanish War and the Equilibrium of the World," *Forum* 25 (August 1898): 641–51.

China. Hay believed in the marketplace, but he was not so naïve as to believe that free markets, or laissez-faire approaches, determined world affairs. The great industrial and financial complexes that now competed for vast economic and strategic prizes required the support, and often the direction, of strong central governments. Germany appeared especially threatening. It had replaced Great Britain as the major danger to U.S. interests in the Caribbean and the southwest Pacific. Authorities ranging from Mahan to the germanophile U.S. ambassador to Berlin in 1897, Andrew Dickson White, warned, in White's words, that by the 1898 war, "German feeling toward us had become generally adverse and, in some parts of the empire, bitterly hostile." A clash impended. Germany could be friendly when Americans were preoccupied with settling a continent, wrote an 1897 *North American Review* essayist, but with "a reinforced Monroe Doctrine, great navy," and U.S. interests clashing with Germany's at pivotal parts of the globe, the relationship had necessarily changed.[21]

Most of all, however, Hay and other U.S. officials watched the course of Russian power. Once informally allied with Americans, the St. Petersburg government now alienated U.S. opinion when, after the 1881 assassination of Tsar Alexander II, it reversed many of Alexander's reforms to crack down on internal dissent. Anti-Semitic policies accelerated; these included the arrest of Jews who had been born in Russia and then returned as agents of U.S. corporations. Singer Sewing Machine and McCormick Harvester, both of which had political influence in Washington, especially suffered from these arrests, and U.S. officials threatened to abrogate the 1832 treaty of commerce and navigation unless Russia changed its policies. At the same time, the historic movement of Slavic peoples across Russia and into Siberia (as many as four million moved between 1880 and 1900), and the building of the Trans-Siberian Railway with its rich contracts for U.S. steel and locomotive builders, offered a chance to repair the frayed relationship. Tsar Nicholas II, however, threatened

21 Andrew Dickson White, *The Autobiography of Andrew Dickson White*, 2 vols. (London, 1905), 2:144–8; Poultney Bigelow, "The German Press and the United States," *North American Review* 164 (January 1897): 12–23; Marilyn B. Young, *Rhetoric of Empire* (Cambridge, Mass., 1968), 15.

to destroy this chance by using the railway as part of a power grab in Manchuria. Such a policy seemed to be made more imperative by an economic depression that struck Russia in mid-1899 and remained for nearly a half-dozen years.

Against this background the tsar called for the first Hague Conference to discuss arms limitation and the peaceful settlement of disputes. The United States attended, but Mahan, as one of the U.S. delegates, led the successful fight against any American agreement to obligatory arbitration. Washington's vital interests were better decided by force, he argued, than by submitting them to the tender mercies of non-American judges. Also against this background, U.S. analysts and officials concluded by 1899–1900 that Russia posed the greatest danger to the proper workings of the Asian marketplace, and that it was the United States, rather than an overextended Great Britain, which would have to blunt that danger. The great struggle, wrote a scholarly essayist in late 1898, was between "Slav and Saxon," with the Americans and British having to unite "against the advance of the Russian Macedon." One of the few prominent voices who disagreed was that of Henry Adams, Brooks's brother and an intimate of Hay. "If Russia breaks down now," Henry wrote the secretary of state in 1900, "I'm not dead certain but that the whole flowery menagerie might break loose."[22]

Hay and McKinley chose Brooks's analysis over Henry's warning. The Chinese marketplace had to be saved by explicit agreement, or the Open Door principle – which Hay defined as "a fair field and no favor" – could be obliterated. The growing trade, especially in manufactured goods (which now accounted for up to 90 percent of U.S. exports to China), gave point to the belief that although the trade accounted for only 1 percent of overall U.S. commerce, its rise from $7 million of exports in 1896 to $12 million in 1897 and $14 million in 1899 portended rich future profits. Only a few, such as Worthington C. Ford, former head of the Treasury Department's Bureau of Statistics, disagreed. China was so poor, Ford argued, that

22 Schmidt, *Der europäische Imperialismus*, 44–50; H. W. Powers, "The War as a Suggestion of Manifest Destiny," *Annals* 12 (September 1898): 186–92; Henry Adams, *The Letters of Henry Adams*, 2 vols., ed. Worthington C. Ford (Boston, 1930–8), 2:289–90.

it could never become a great U.S. market. And God forbid that China industrialized and developed, he implied, because with its cheap labor it could undersell the West everywhere. Hay could not take the chance that Ford might be right. Domestic political and economic demands, the growing doubts about the British being able to maintain the Open Door on their own, were too pressing. In 1899, Hay issued the first set of Open Door notes asking that the powers not violate existing interests inside leased territories they acquired, that they not discriminate against other nations in setting port and railway rates, and that the Chinese tariff duties apply within each new sphere of interest. No one was pleased with Hay's initiative outside of Washington, not even the British, who had hoped that he would instead ally himself directly with them against the other Europeans. London, however, realizing this was the best it could obtain, finally went along, then the Japanese agreed, and, finally and with great reluctance, the Germans, Russians, and French signed up.[23]

Whether Hay's request (that everyone publicly declare themselves against sin) might have actually saved the Open Door principles was not tested. Hardly had Hay settled back to enjoy his apparent triumph than the Boxers United in Righteousness stormed toward the Chinese capital of Peking, leaving dead Christians and destroyed Western property in their wake. The Boxer uprising of 1898 to 1900 was one in a series of upheavals dating from the eighteenth century that were aimed at overthrowing the Qing dynasty. The greatest had been the Taiping and Nian uprisings, which had begun to wash away the intellectual and military foundations of the Qing. Then had come disastrous defeats in wars against the French and, notably, the Japanese. But the triggers for the Boxers were the 1897–8 German grab of Shantung, the Russian movement into Manchuria, the new French claims in the south bordering Indochina, and the British taking of Weihaiwei harbor on the Shantung Peninsula to offset the German conquest. In response, Chinese na-

23 U.S. Department of Commerce, Bureau of the Census, *Historical Statistics of the United States* (Washington, D.C., 1961), 550; David Healy, *U.S. Expansionism* (Madison, 1970), 166.

tionalism accelerated just as the United States became heavily involved in this imperial shoot-out. Recruiting peasants and playing on growing antiforeign feelings, the Boxers targeted Christian missionaries and their relatively few Chinese converts. Women, led by the Red Lanterns Shining group, became key members of the Boxers. By 1900, the rebels were in Peking killing not only converts, but French and Belgian engineers and leading U.S. missionaries. When the Western powers tried to send in more troops to protect their legation compounds, the Boxers were able to stop them. After the German minister was killed in June 1900, the empress dowager rallied to the Boxers' side and declared war herself against the foreigners. As the terror spread, foreigners in Peking were besieged. Some twenty thousand troops from Japan, France, Great Britain, Russia, and the United States finally reached the capital and lifted the siege. McKinley used his new base, Manila, to send five thousand troops into the battle.[24]

The question then became how to get the foreign armies out of a quickly decaying China. "Your open door is already off its hinges, not six months old," Henry Adams teased Hay. "What kind of door can you rig up?" On July 3, Hay tried to rehinge his policy by issuing his second Open Door notes. He asked the powers directly to declare that they supported China's "territorial and administrative integrity." They finally did so declare, but not until a crisis in August–September 1900 forced McKinley to assume that the tsar would keep troops in Peking until the weakened dowager empress would give him all Russia wanted in Manchuria, and perhaps in other parts of China as well. The Russians especially were holding on to the port of New Chwang, which Hay privately called "bold robbery." Faced with a bitter reelection campaign against William Jennings Bryan, who was making much of McKinley's wars for imperialism in the Philippines and China, the president actually considered, for a moment in September 1900, either pulling out of China or joining in the rush for Chinese ports and territory. Either

24 Jonathan Spence, *The Search for Modern China* (New York, 1990), 139–40, 230–5; Michael Hunt, *The Making of a Special Relationship: The United States and China to 1914* (New York, 1983), 185–8.

way, the Open Door principles would disappear into history. Secretary of War Elihu Root argued that the U.S. troop withdrawal would protect Americans against becoming "but a chip floating on the surface of the currents of intrigue and aggression of other Powers," and keep "us out of complications which might discredit our policy among our own people" – a powerful argument for McKinley at that point in the presidential campaign.[25]

Hay, however, supported by Mahan and the leading U.S. diplomatic authority on China, William C. Rockhill, turned McKinley back around. Faced with the defeat of his own, Seward's, and indeed a half century of U.S. diplomacy in China, and writing from a sickbed in New Hampshire, the secretary of state argued that the Open Door required that U.S. troops remain until all the foreign powers backed down from their demands. In one of the most realistic notes ever penned by an American official, Hay wrote:

The dilemma is clear enough. We want to get out at the earliest possible moment. We do not want to have the appearance of being forced out or frightened out, and we must not lose our proper influence in the final arrangement. If we leave Germany and England in Peking, and retire with Russia, who has unquestionably made her bargain already with China, we not only will *seem* to have been beaten, but we run a serious risk of being *really* frozen out. . . . There is, therefore, not a single power we can rely on, for our policy of abstention from plunder and the Open Door. . . . The inherent weakness of our position is this: we do not want to rob China ourselves, and our public opinion will not permit us to interfere, with an army, to prevent others from robbing her. Besides, we have no army. The talk of the papers about "our preeminent moral position giving us the authority to dictate to the world" is mere flap-doodle.

Hay hoped that some kind of alliance with the British might "make our ideas prevail," but he knew this was politically impossible. He was publicly joined in this stay-the-course policy by leading cotton interests. "Cotton is king," the *Atlanta Constitution* announced, "and we must remain in Peking to see him duly crowned."

25 Adee to McKinley, August 25, 1900, container 59, Cortelyou Papers; Root to McKinley, September 11, 1900, McKinley Papers; Adams, *The Letters of Henry Adams*, 2:290.

In 1901, the powers finally retreated from the capital, as they pledged allegiance to Open Door principles. But they simultaneously extracted the huge indemnity of $333 million from China for the Boxers' massacres and destruction of property. Rockhill led the drive to reduce the indemnity; he knew it could further weaken China and serve as leverage for more foreign demands. Unsuccessful in this attempt, in 1907 President Theodore Roosevelt pledged to return part of Washington's share to the Chinese for use in sending their students to U.S. schools. (TR's decision was not philanthropic. He sought to achieve specific goals: Calm violent anti-American feelings being fanned by Chinese nationalism over U.S. exclusion acts; try to loosen Japan's stranglehold on educating young Chinese who studied abroad; and teach the younger generation about American virtues and economics. "A Chinese who acquires his education in this country," a State Department official announced, "goes back predisposed toward America and American goods.")[26]

The widely read humorist Finley Peter Dunne had his "Mr. Dooley" declare that "what China needs is a Chinese exclusion act." It might have worked better than the Open Door. For the Open Door principles, duly sworn to by all the powers, legitimized the growing foreign competition over the potential riches of the China market, led to military intervention and colonial positioning so participants could better compete, and even convinced McKinley and Hay themselves to ask China for rights at Samsah Bay — a request the Chinese rejected by quoting back Open Door principles. Such intervention, not least the presence of growing numbers of Christian, especially Protestant missionaries, helped breed such anti-Qing groups as the Boxers. Faced with this growing upheaval and imperialist competition, McKinley explicitly rejected Root's suggestion of retreat and accepted Hay's argument that the United States had to pay the price

26 Hay to Adee, September 14, 1900, McKinley Papers; *Public Opinion*, September 6, 1900, 292; McCormick, *China Market*, 161–75; Delbert McKee, "The Boxer Indemnity Remission," *Society for Historians of American Foreign Relations Newsletter* 23 (March 1992): 1–19.

for maintaining opportunities in China, regardless of possible strains that might result in U.S. policy or in China itself.

To maintain access to those Open Door opportunities, moreover, McKinley took a historic step in creating a new, twentieth-century presidential power. He dispatched the five thousand troops without consulting Congress, let alone obtaining a declaration of war, to fight the Boxers who were supported by the Chinese government. That government even declared war against the United States, although the president and Congress did not bother to notice the declaration. Presidents had previously used such force against non-governmental groups that threatened U.S. interests and citizens. It was now used, however, against recognized governments, and without obeying the Constitution's provisions about who was to declare war. After the 1898 war, England's *Spectator* (as duly noted by McKinley's private secretary, George Cortelyou) believed that the Civil War and the 1898 war had shown that the presidency had become "neither more nor less than elective monarchy, limited as to duration, and regulated as to finance, but otherwise nearly unfettered. . . . The formless people when excited always hunger for a leader, and they get one." In the China crisis, the elective monarchy's power further expanded.[27]

A political postulate was taking shape: the more the United States expanded, the more disorderly and revolutionary those parts of the world seemed to become for U.S. interests and, consequently, the more a strong commander in chief was required. Expansion and disorder abroad equaled centralization at home. A precedent had been set for Theodore Roosevelt, Woodrow Wilson, and later presidents.

But then, McKinley obviously thought the game was worth such a risk. He was playing for the entire market of China, not for just isolated colonial enclaves. He also had placed his political life on the line to continue a half-century-old quest for vast opportunities that were reachable, Americans thought, through open doors.

27 *Spectator*, July 30, 1898, in container 56, Cortelyou Papers; Arthur Schlesinger, Jr., *The Imperial Presidency* (Boston, 1973), 80–90.

The Ratification of 1900

Reflecting with friends on a September Sunday night in 1899, McKinley observed:

One of the best things we ever did was to insist upon taking the Philippines and not a coaling station or an island, for if we had done the latter we would have been the laughing stock of the world. And so it has come to pass that in a few short months we have become a world power, . . . and it is vastly different from the conditions I found when I was inaugurated.[28]

The election fourteen months later, observers generally agreed, was to determine whether Americans wanted to carry the burdens of such power. By May 1900 the president believed imperialism was to be "the paramount and dominating issue in the campaign," as Schurman paraphrased McKinley. His major opposition was to come from Democratic nominee William Jennings Bryan, who was backed not only by Bryan's traditional prosilver allies but also by the money and political power of the antiimperialist groups of Boston, Chicago, Indianapolis, and other major cities, most of them east of the Mississippi. Andrew Carnegie's millions funded the antiimperialist attacks on McKinley. It was, however, a strange romance. Carnegie detested Bryan's class appeal and devotion to free silver. The nominee flatly refused the steelmaker's plea to make foreign policy the single issue of the campaign. Carnegie even tried to buy a third party into existence, but failed. Bryan gave him hope with an acceptance speech in 1900 that indeed did single out imperialism as the issue, and the Democratic party platform blasted as well British imperialism (especially in South Africa), but when the campaign began, Bryan continued to discuss the silver and trust issues. Former House Speaker Thomas B. Reed (R.-Maine) laughed that "Bryan had rather be wrong than President." The silver issue had been settled by the inflow of the yellow metal since 1896 and the Gold Standard Act. The trust issue was an ineffective attempt to exploit class differences by pointing to the growing number of corporate trusts the Republicans allowed to form after 1897. Even on the imperialist issue, however, Democrats, led by Bryan, blurred the

28 Diary, September 17, 1899, container 52, Cortelyou Papers.

choices by pledging to give the Filipinos better government, not promising immediate independence, and swearing to uphold vital U.S. interests in the Far East. Bryan, moreover, had finally supported the peace treaty in 1899.[29]

The Democrat's attempt to court the labor and lower-middle-class vote sent confused signals. On the one hand, U.S. laborers did not go along with the working-class imperialism that so marked British and Western European politics. American laborers were too much divided by ethnic and religious affiliations to unite in back of any major political issue, other than demands for better wages and conditions. Labor also opposed the taking of Cuba and Hawaii because of the cheap labor that would be able to have access to the mainland. On the other hand, urban laborers in particular were paid in currency based on gold, and they did not want their weekly wages diluted with Bryan's cheaper silver.[30]

McKinley exploited these contradictions in Bryan's appeal, changed the terms of the debate by defining imperialism as an honorable American tradition, and carried out a foreign policy in late 1900 that first forced Bryan to drop the imperialism issue, and then swamped the Nebraskan in the balloting. The president's most dramatic move was to name the loudest of all imperialists, Governor Theodore Roosevelt of New York, as his vice-presidential nominee. Roosevelt went on such a rousing cross-country tour that he finally lost his voice. He even went to Bryan's home state of Nebraska and delivered forty speeches in four days. The message was always much the same: Bryan's political patron, Jefferson, had been one of the first great imperialists; the United States was governing the Philippines in the American tradition and in the natives' best interests, which may not be what "the inhabitants at the moment prefer"; force was necessary because only to power will "the barbarians . . .

29 Schurman to McKinley, June 1, 1900, Schurman Papers; Bryan to Carnegie, December 30, 1898, Papers of William Jennings Bryan, Library of Congress, Washington, D.C.; Robert L. Beisner, *Twelve Against Empire* (1968; reprint, New York, 1985), 121–2, 204.

30 Philip Taft, *The AFL in the Time of Gompers* (New York, 1957), 291–2. The comparative view is Bernard Semmel, *Imperialism and Social Reform: English Social-Imperial Thought 1895–1914* (Cambridge, Mass., 1960).

yield"; and if whites were "morally bound to abandon the Philippines, we were also morally bound to abandon Arizona to the Apaches" – a reference that again tied together the expansion of the 1830s to 1880s with that of the 1890s. As for the vaunted constitutional principles, "Bryan cannot be acquitted of hypocrisy when he prattles about the 'consent of the governed,' in the Philippines," Roosevelt wrote, "and profits by the denial of this same so-called right in [the Democratic party–controlled states of] North Carolina and Alabama."[31]

McKinley meanwhile bravely used force to protect Americans from the Boxers and the Russian imperialists, although voters never realized how torn he actually was over this crisis. He and his campaign manager, Mark Hanna, explicitly tied imperialism repeatedly to "traditional and distinctively American grounds" until their policies in the Far East seemed more like a continuation of four hundred years of American history than any un-American departure. McKinley turned the class argument against Bryan: "I rejoice" that those favoring "public law, sound currency and industrial prosperity" are "arrayed against those who are inciting class hatred . . . among the people of our happy country." The American empire thus was built on consensus, morality, and tradition, unlike European empires, according to McKinley. The U.S. domination of foreign peoples, in any event, was incidental to realizing America's commercial and cultural destinies. While the British seized 4.7 million square miles of territory between 1870 and 1900, and Germany 1 million, the United States needed only 125,000. As McKinley blurred the issues and protected Americans in Peking, Carnegie surrendered and came out against Bryan and the Democrat's demands for silver and an income tax. Other Republicans, who disliked McKinley's policies, despised Bryan more and showed, as one newspaper said of former President Benjamin Harrison, "brilliant flashes of silence." Winning the largest plurality of votes until that

31 Theodore Roosevelt, *The Letters of Theodore Roosevelt*, 8 vols., ed. Elting E. Morison et al. (Cambridge, Mass., 1951–4), 2:1385, 1404–5; Williams, "U.S. Indian Policy," 825–6.

time in a presidential election, McKinley also garnered twenty-one more electoral votes (292 to 155) than he had obtained in 1896. He and Roosevelt even won Nebraska.[32]

The 1900 election was no mandate on imperialism because by October Bryan had concluded it was a losing issue for him; he consequently downplayed it and began emphasizing the trust question. Hanna and McKinley were delighted; they knew that in the middle of the new prosperity few Americans were concerned about trusts. Bryan had so muddled his campaign that, except for the woebegone silver issue, many did not understand what he did espouse. "Mr. Dooley" suggested that the Democrats run an advertisement: "Wanted: a good, active, inergetic dimmycrat . . . must be in favor iv sound money, but not too sound, an' anti-impeerylist but f'r holdin' onto what we've got, an inimy iv thrusts but a frind iv organized capital."[33]

McKinley was not ambiguous. In the draft for his speech at Berkeley, California, in May 1901, he demanded more educated people "with technical and scientific knowledge" to run America's Second Industrial Revolution, because "industry has become a science." And because Americans had "passed beyond the period of exclusion and isolation the mastery of languages is an essential qualification to the pioneer of new markets. . . . The superficial student is less in demand than he ever was." Four months later, he told those attending the Pan American Exposition in Buffalo that the nation's "almost appalling wealth" dictated that "isolation is no longer possible or desirable." He passionately pleaded for a broader reciprocity trade policy before American surpluses suffocated the system. He ended the speech with a demand for a modern merchant marine, a Pacific cable, and an isthmian canal.[34]

32 McKinley to William L. Strong, November 1, 1900, container 59, Cortelyou Papers; David Green, *The Shaping of Political Consciousness* (Ithaca, 1987), chap. 2; Beisner, *Twelve Against Empire*, pp. 186–7.

33 Finley Peter Dunne, *Mr. Dooley's Opinions* (New York, 1901), 96.

34 Draft of May 1901 speech, container 60, Cortelyou Papers; R. Hal Williams, *Years of Decision* (New York, 1978), 157; Tom E. Terrill, *The Tariff, Politics, and American Foreign Policy, 1874–1901* (Westport, Conn., 1973), 206.

The next day he was killed by an assassin. Hanna and the party bosses had kicked Theodore Roosevelt upstairs from the New York governorship into the virtually powerless vice-presidency in order to stop his crusading in the state. The Rough Rider, the most vociferous defender of American imperialism, had become president.

9. Theodore Roosevelt:
Conservative as Revolutionary

Distinguished scholarly work on Theodore Roosevelt has concluded that his conservatism, moralism, and keen sense of balance-of-power international politics are the keys to understanding this highly popular and influential president. On the centennial of his birth, he was celebrated with a *Time* magazine cover story in March 1958, at the nadir of the Cold War. *Time* applauded his use of "a new kind of power — deterrence" to "promote the U.S. self-interest in . . . world order." One biographer notes "that a deep-seated conservatism formed his basic political outlook." Another concludes that "he believed in change, but gradual change; change within established institutions." A third argues that it was not TR's blustering and quick use of force that marked his diplomacy as much as careful balance-of-power calculations. A fourth, taking a cultural approach, believes that "TR's willingness to use civilization as a political guideline marked him as a major figure in the rise of American internationalism," and his view of "civilization," which belonged to a simpler past, made him "the last traditional American statesman." One of the first analysts of his statecraft, Alfred L. P. Denis, who remains one of the best, observed that "his apparent impulsiveness . . . obscured in some ways the essentially conservative quality of his statesmanship."[1]

If these arguments are correct, two questions arise: Why did TR's conservative diplomacy time and again result in upheaval, imbalance, and even revolution, and why did he interpret his presidential

1 John Milton Cooper, Jr., *The Warrior and the Priest* (Cambridge, Mass., 1983), 33; John Morton Blum, *The Republican Roosevelt* (Cambridge, Mass., 1954), 5–6; Howard K. Beale, *Theodore Roosevelt and the Rise of America to World Power* (Baltimore, 1956); Frank Nincovich, "Theodore Roosevelt: Civilization as Ideology," *Diplomatic History* 10 (Summer 1986): 223, 245; Alfred L. P. Denis, *Adventures in American Diplomacy, 1896–1906* (New York, 1928), 6.

powers in foreign affairs so radically that he would probably have upset his great conservative hero, Alexander Hamilton? If the argument, as some advance it, is that the context of his time drove this conservative to extremes, then that context has to be carefully and fully developed. For a central irony of modern American diplomatic history is that between the 1890s and World War I, the United States became a great world power – that is, one of the three or four most powerful nations, and thus a supposed supporter of the status quo and the maintenance of a favorable balance of power – at the same time important parts of the world exploded into revolution. Roosevelt and the United States certainly did not cause this revolutionary outbreak, but in certain cases – for example, Panama, the Dominican Republic, Mexico in 1911–13 – the American role was notable and in several instances determinative. In nearly every case, however, Roosevelt's policies worsened, rather than made more orderly, the conditions that triggered the upheaval.

Progressives, such as those with whom Roosevelt identified, might have sought order and their parochial definition of "civilization" as a priority at home but it was not their first priority abroad. In every instance, Progressive diplomacy first aimed at the creation of opportunity (as in Panama and the Russo-Japanese War), or the maintenance and expansion of opportunity (as in the Dominican Republic, Cuba, and Mexico). They were driven not in the first instance by the quest for a more democratic stability, as were some Progressives at home, but by a search for markets, the perceived need for strategic outposts, and a racism that emerged naturally from their history while blending with, and complementing, their overseas imperialism. When this search resulted in upheaval, Roosevelt, resembling William McKinley before him and William Howard Taft and Woodrow Wilson later, used military force to try to repair the damage, or to ensure – if U.S. interests were already paramount (as in Cuba) – that they remained paramount and the status quo was preserved. As commander in chief of this force, the president was in a position to make immense claims for his authority, claims that (as Wilson himself noted in a series of lectures in 1908) created a new presidency that had little relation to that of the nineteenth-century chief executive, and even less to the office visu-

alized in the eighteenth-century Constitution. Without meaning to
do so, but because of his reading of American history and his myopic
nationalism, the conservative Roosevelt played a role in creating a
revolutionary, war-wracked world, instead of creating a balance-of-
power complex that maintained a healthy, gradually evolving international system.

New York Versus Washington

Henry Adams, a close friend and even closer observer of Roosevelt,
realized these ironies that were at the heart of TR's statecraft and,
indeed, that form a historical climax in Adams's autobiographical
account of America's rise to world power after 1865. Adams set the
context for Roosevelt's presidency:

Washington was always amusing, but in 1900, as in 1800, its chief interest
lay in its distance from New York. The movement of New York had
become planetary – beyond control – while the task of Washington, in
1900 as in 1800, was to control it. The success of Washington in the past
century promised ill for its success in the next.[2]

Between 1897 and 1904, New York moved further out of control.
In the ten years before 1904, an average of 301 firms annually
disappeared into mergers. Between 1898 and 1902, however,
mergers reached numbers never topped in American history: 1,028
companies disappeared in 1899 alone. In 1897 the worth of firms
merging into great companies amounted to $1 billion; in 1903 it
was $7 billion. During this era of mergers the corporation assumed a
new form. U.S. Steel, formed by J. P. Morgan on the base of
Andrew Carnegie's plant, absorbed 138 other companies. International Harvester (formerly McCormick) controlled 85 percent of the
harvesting-machine market; American Can Corporation sold nine of
every ten cans used in the country; and American Sugar Refining
(one of the greatest of all trusts) controlled the nation's entire sugar
market. Tens of dozens of railways in the 1880s had been combined
into six giant transportation networks by Morgan, John D. Rockefeller, E. H. Harriman, and a few others. These men were not

2 Henry Adams, *Education of Henry Adams* (Boston, 1930), 436.

railway (or steel) entrepreneurs. They were capitalists who used their power as investment bankers to reorganize the nation's corporate system, make it more efficient and monopolistic, and gain great personal profit. By 1904, 78 corporations controlled more than 50 percent of the production in their particular industry. Twenty-eight firms controlled more than 80 percent of their industry's production. New companies continued to appear, many others went bankrupt, and even some of the richest investors wilted under the strain, but Americans had never remotely seen such consolidation of production and capital in their history.[3]

A number of causes could be identified. The survivors of the post-1873 depression years (led by Carnegie and Rockefeller) had found the business methods necessary to "run full," as Carnegie phrased it, and nevertheless sell the resulting glut of goods at a profit. Many came together to try to avoid further traumas and to monopolize markets to the greatest possible extent. Most of all, however, the merger movement was driven by new technology (the changes from steam to electricity, iron to steel alloys, telegraphs to telephones, simple machines to dynamos and internal combustion engines) that required much capital to develop, as well as large markets in which to sell profitably. The markets, as the most successful entrepreneurs had long since demonstrated, had to be international. This realization led to other kinds of cooperative ventures, such as U.S. Steel's attempts to divide the world steel-rail market with its European and American competitors. The monopoly capital that reorganized the economic bases of American society also used its profits to invest abroad after 1897, although about half of those investments remained in the Caribbean–South American arena.[4]

Roosevelt was president at the peak of the merger movement. His policies, as opposed often to his rhetoric, demonstrated little recognition that this mutation of the Second Industrial Revolution had far-reaching significance for domestic politics. As many scholars

3 Ron Chernow, *The House of Morgan* (New York, 1990), 81–6; Stuart Bruchey, *Enterprise* (New York, 1990), 341; George E. Mowry, *The Era of Theodore Roosevelt, 1900–1912* (New York, 1962), 7–8.
4 Eric Hobsbawm, "The Crisis of Capitalism in Historical Perspective," *Socialist Revolution* 6 (October–December 1976): 84–5.

have shown, his fame as a trustbuster far outran his actual accomplishments, especially when compared with Taft's presidency, which in four years initiated about twice as many antitrust suits as were started during Roosevelt's seven White House years. Profoundly careful in this regard during the first six of those years, TR either built on McKinley's already established policies in regard to the Caribbean, the Asian balance of power, and the expansion of presidential authority, or he refused to deal with central issues that McKinley had tackled head-on – most notably, the need for new tariff policies. "Thank God I am not a free-trader," TR wrote his close friend Henry Cabot Lodge in 1895. "Pernicious indulgence in the doctrine of free trade seems inevitably to produce fatty degeneration of the moral fibre."[5]

As New York governor in 1899, Roosevelt believed that because "we have . . . tremendous problems in the way of the relations of labor and capital to solve," it was necessary "to pay far more attention to this than to any question of expansion for the next fifty years." He added he believed "this although I am an expansionist."[6] Like the American Tory he was, Roosevelt sought to use government means, not least the tariff and his White House "bully pulpit," to carry out enough gradual reform to ensure political peace, bridge the growing gap between classes, and link those objectives to his foreign policies. Hannah Arendt's famous dictum that "the alliance between capital and mob is to be found at the genesis of every consistently imperialist policy" is too overstated to fit Roosevelt's policies well. Nevertheless, as a self-described member of the nation's governing class, he understood that foreign policy could provide both the bread and the circuses needed to maintain political calm.

His good friend Brooks Adams (whom he invited at times to stay in the White House) explained the dynamic interrelation of domestic and foreign policy directly to Roosevelt. In 1901, Adams argued that the high tariff could be kept only if Americans built a great military force that could defend U.S. interests in the inevitable

5 Chernow, *House of Morgan*, 130–1; Theodore Roosevelt, *The Letters of Theodore Roosevelt*, 8 vols., ed. Elting E. Morison et al. (Cambridge, Mass., 1951–4), 1:504.
6 Roosevelt, *Letters*, 2:1053.

commercial battles over Asian and Latin American markets. "In a word," Adams wrote the president on July 17, 1903, "to live this country must keep open the highways leading west, at equitable rates, and must command the terminus in Asia – and if we fail in this we shall break down." (At another point, Adams cried: "We must have a new deal . . ., and have a centralized administration, or we shall wobble over.") Roosevelt was quite taken with the letter; he replied the next day: "It is necessary for us to keep the road of trade to the East open. In order to insure our having terminals we must do our best to prevent the shutting to us of the Asian markets. In order to keep the roads to these terminals open we must see that they are managed primarily in the interest of the country, that is of the commerce of the country."

Roosevelt's definition of "interest" was interesting. He refused, however, to open the veins of the Republican party by fighting to lower the tariff. He was thus left with Brooks's advice to push legislation to centralize and make more efficient the regulation of railroads, which he succeeded in making law, and to prepare for a series of military encounters. "There is a homely adage which runs, 'Speak softly and carry a big stick, you will go far,'" he told a Minnesota audience at nearly the same moment McKinley was assassinated. "If the American nation will speak softly and yet build and keep at a pitch of the highest training a thoroughly efficient navy, the Monroe Doctrine will go far." Or, as he phrased it earlier, "Diplomacy is utterly useless where there is no force behind it; the diplomat is the servant, not the master, of the soldier." He preferred, however, to wage war on the less industrialized nations. Wars between the more "civilized" countries would grow "rarer and rarer." But "in the long run civilized man finds he can keep the peace only by subduing his barbarian neighbor." This American toryism had thus concluded that domestic peace and overseas commercial expansion were interlinked, as was that expansion connected to the need to wage wars against the less industrialized regions (especially Asia and Latin America) that increasingly became the commercial and strategic targets.[7]

7 B. Adams to Roosevelt, July 17, 1903, Roosevelt to Adams, July 18, 1903, both

En route to fighting Spaniards in Cuba, Roosevelt read Edmond Demolin's *Supériorité des Anglo-Saxons*. The Rough Rider believed in Darwinian theory in science, but he had little faith in social Darwinism in the political and economic world. Such skepticism probably increased when he noted the number of social Darwinists who were antiimperialists in 1899–1900. He seemed to draw his racial views from two sources. The first was Lamarckism, which stressed the slow environmental reform that could improve the race, rather than a social Darwinism that often emphasized laissez-faireism and sudden change. A tory such as TR demanded slow change, and he also believed in a strong role for individual will (he had, after all, built himself from a sickly, pampered boy to a husky Rough Rider), and training in morality. The second source was his reading of American history, especially that of the West, which he chronicled in a multivolume work. Those histories, as one writer has noted, were "palpably white supremacist." He placed himself among the "men of sane and wholesome thought" who believed the continent had a greater manifest destiny than to be a mere hunting ground for savages: "I don't go so far as to think that the only good Indians are dead Indians, but I believe nine out of every ten are, and I shouldn't like to inquire too closely into the case of the tenth." His imperialism, then, came more out of traditional values than any Darwinian categories – out of American history, not science. He read the white settlement of the continent as had Turner, whose work on the so-called frontier inspired TR, and with whom he struck up a correspondence.[8]

Roosevelt consequently saw Great Britain as a natural ally. Common racial destinies seemed to have swept aside, finally, the two

in Papers of Theodore Roosevelt, Houghton Library, Harvard University, Cambridge, Mass.; Lloyd Gardner, "From Liberation to Containment," in William Appleman Williams, ed., *From Colony to Empire* (New York, 1972), 223; J. Bartlett, *Familiar Quotations* (Boston, 1980), 687; Theodore Roosevelt, "Washington's Forgotten Maxim," *Proceedings of the U.S. Naval Institute*, 23, no. 3, (1897): 458; David Healy, *U.S. Expansionism* (Madison, 1970), 151–3.

8 Thomas G. Dyer, *Theodore Roosevelt and the Idea of Race* (Baton Rouge, 1980), is crucial; David Burton, *Theodore Roosevelt* (Philadelphia, 1969); Roosevelt, *Letters*, 1:363.

nations' differences in the New World and aligned them, along the Open Door principles, against Russia and Germany in Asia. He and his secretary of state, John Hay, were dismayed when the British suffered losses in their war against the South African Boers. The debacle only proved to TR that "England is on the downgrade" and that Americans were becoming dominant in the Anglo-Saxon partnership. He and Hay hoped that their heartfelt support for Britain's travails would lead London to espouse the Open Door for U.S. goods in South Africa, but after peace was restored, the door effectively shut. The British were more cooperative, however, on the issue of a disputed slice of territory between Alaska and Canada that became more valuable when gold was discovered in the region after 1896. When TR sent troops to enforce his claims, an arbitration panel of three U.S. and three British "jurists" was created. The president named not jurists but politicians who shared his view. The chief British judge voted with them, more for the sake of Anglo-American harmony than for equity. Much to the Canadians' fury and disgust, their territorial claim was sacrificed to London's new appeasement policy.

With the British so cooperative, Roosevelt most feared the Russians, whose system was corrupt and whose policies sought to control the Eurasian landmass. He also targeted the Germans, whom he wanted to "wish well where they do not conflict with the English-speaking peoples." Such conflict seemed to be growing – in Asia; on the oceans, where the kaiser's battleship-building program challenged both large English-speaking nations; and in the Caribbean, where U.S. war plans posited possible war against Germany. Berlin, for its part, was actually pushing the Western Hemisphere farther down its list of strategic priorities. Henry Adams, as usual in foreign affairs, was close to the mark:

Nothing is more curious to me than to see the sudden change of our national susceptibilities [Adams wrote his intimate friend Elizabeth Cameron in March 1903]. Down to 1898 our *bête noir* was England. Now we pay little or no attention to England; we seem to regard her as our property; but we are ridiculous about Germany. The idea of a wretched little power like Germany, with no coast, no colonies, and no coal, attacking us, seems to me too absurd for a thought, but Cabot [Senator Lodge] and Theodore

[Roosevelt] and the Senate . . . seem to have it on the brain and we are spending a great many millions of dollars in providing against it.[9]

Roosevelt, as usual, listened more closely to Brooks's advice and ignored Henry's. To save the race, Brooks believed, the "terminals" of the East had to be kept open, Russia and Germany rolled back, and those he considered uncivilized become civilized, while – above all – maintaining class peace and economic expansion within the United States. Such a tall order required tutoring the public and Congress about their new responsibilities, a task TR considered formidable because, in his view, both constituencies were parochial and ignorant. He further termed Congress institutionally ill-equipped to undertake foreign policy responsibilities. A central theme of Progressivism was educating, managing, and actually controlling the public so it would understand the virtue, as Progressive leaders saw it, of governmental leadership in cleansing and raising up society. To this end, Roosevelt used and courted the press in a manner previously unmatched, even by McKinley. Roosevelt sought control of the news, and he understood how to go far in achieving it, even in peacetime. His was the first major career in American politics to be developed by the use of modern journalism. When the White House (the term itself came into common use during his presidency) was refurbished in 1902, he ensured the building of a room for the press. He tried to manipulate journalists until some refused to talk with him unless a friend came along to witness. His outspoken views and colorful language were hidden from the public to some extent. Edith Wharton concluded that such secrecy by the press proved how "he was loved and respected." (Even this sophisticated novelist was taken aback, however, when she heard him say at a large luncheon party, "If only we could revive the good old Roman customs. I know a bath in Senator _____'s blood would set me right in no time.") The press's self-censorship perhaps also came from fear. Roosevelt unsuccessfully once tried to quiet a critical

9 Beale, *Roosevelt*, 450; Thomas J. Noer, *Briton, Boer, and Yankee* (Kent, Ohio, 1978), 5–20, 135; Alfred Vagts, *Deutschland und die Vereinigten Staaten in der Weltpolitik*, 2 vols. (New York, 1935), 1:618–21; Henry Adams, *Letters of Henry Adams (1892–1918)*, ed. Worthington C. Ford (Boston, 1938), 401–2.

publisher by twisting a law so it could serve to jail the man under federal criminal libel statutes. It seemed the tighter control at home was necessary for control abroad.[10]

The Revolutionary in Panama

Certainly Roosevelt intended to control the Caribbean–Central American passageways, especially the future canal at the isthmus. After the British endured their series of military catastrophes in South Africa during late 1899, the secretary of state pushed them to sign the Hay-Pauncefote Treaty of February 1900. The pact finally abrogated the 1850 Clayton-Bulwer Treaty and gave the United States the sole right to build and control – but not fortify – a canal linking the Atlantic and Pacific. To Hay's amazement, the Senate refused to ratify on the grounds that the United States had to have the right to fortify a canal. Roosevelt, then governor of New York, helped lead the criticism of this Republican handiwork, and Henry Cabot Lodge headed the Senate attack on the treaty because of his own intense nationalism and sense that Great Britain was vulnerable. Above all, however, Lodge and other Republicans involved in the 1900 election campaign were not going to be accused of being soft on the British. The wounded secretary of state offered to resign, but McKinley would not hear of it. He instead ordered Hay to obtain the rights to fortify. The second Hay-Pauncefote Treaty included such rights, and it sailed through the Senate in November 1901.[11]

As Roosevelt assumed power, he was fully conversant with the need for a canal, not least because his good friend Alfred Thayer Mahan had been drubbing into him the passageway's commercial and strategic importance. The question became whether the canal's location would be in Nicaragua, as recommended by commissions since the 1870s because of its cheapness and relative lack of engineering problems, or in Panama, where some rights were held by a

10 Cooper, *Warrior and Priest*, 27–9; George Juergens, *News from the White House* (Chicago, 1981); Edith Wharton, *A Backward Glance* (New York, 1934), 314.

11 William C. Widenor, *Henry Cabot Lodge and the Search for an American Foreign Policy* (Berkeley, 1980), 148; *Washington Post*, June 10, 1990, F6.

French company that had become the descendant of de Lesseps's failed attempt to build a canal in the 1880s. The company was under the control of two powerful, if devious, figures, Philippe Bunau-Varilla and Wall Street lawyer William Cromwell. In 1902, these two men helped reverse long-standing U.S. policy and lobbied through the Senate the Spooner Amendment (named after Senator John Spooner, R.-Wis.), which gave the president the power to pay $40 million to the French company and purchase canal rights from Colombia, which claimed Panama as its province. Hay then negotiated the Hay-Herrán Treaty, which gave Colombia $10 million plus $250,000 annually for a six-mile-wide zone.

The pact arrived in Bogotá amid civil war and while the government was under the control of a regime that was skeptical of modernization, Yankees bearing supposed gifts, and the value of linking the two great oceans. Colombia finally rejected the money offer as insufficient. Roosevelt became nearly apoplectic. He could not return to obtain more money from the Senate because of the power of John T. Morgan (D.-Ala.), who long had held strong personal interest in building a Nicaraguan passageway. Bunau-Varilla and Cromwell, closely in touch with State and War Department officials, then timed a Panamanian uprising against Colombia in November 1903 when they knew a U.S. warship would be in the area. The Panamanians needed little encouragement. Separated from Colombia by impenetrable jungle, they had been rebelling against Colombia's control since the mid-nineteenth century. Because of the 1846 U.S.-Colombia treaty in which Washington guaranteed passage across the isthmus, U.S. warships had often mediated the flare-ups. When the U.S. Navy intervened to stop an uprising in 1901, just before rebel, anti-Colombian forces were about to invade Panama City itself, it was clear that the United States, not Colombia, was the decisive power on the isthmus. One historian has calculated that between 1850 and 1903, U.S. forces occupied Panama for a total of two hundred days. In late 1903, Roosevelt used U.S. ships and sailors to prevent Colombia from putting down the revolt. He clearly violated the 1846 pact that assumed Colombian sovereignty in the region. No matter; Hay quickly negotiated with Bunau-Varilla (not with Panamanians) an amazing treaty that gave the United States "titular sovereignty" (as Hay later called it) in a ten-mile-wide strip that cut the new nation in half. Panama received $10 million plus $250,000 annually for the rights. Roosevelt justified the coup by saying that Colombia had "misgoverned and misruled" Panama, and so when the Colombians rejected a fair treaty, "the people of Panama rose literally as one man."[12]

Roosevelt had sought control. He had instead stirred up revolution in Panama and passions in both Central America and Washington. The Panamanians, furious at Bunau-Varilla's sellout of their rights so he could protect his company's investment, finally quieted temporarily when the United States simply bought out their ragtag army with gold pieces. Directly and indirectly, U.S. officials ran Panama from the Canal Zone until the 1930s and 1940s when nationalism again arose to demand a new, fairer relationship. Roosevelt encountered more problems at home. He had carefully used newspaper friends to prepare Americans for the taking of a canal area. Such prophylactic propaganda, however, did not prevent an outpouring of criticism, led by the *New York Times* and Hearst newspapers, that called TR's seizure "nefarious," and "a rough-riding assault upon another republic over the shattered wreckage of international law." A *New York World* story revealed Bunau-Varilla's role and the millions of dollars that were at stake. Senate Democrats tried to block the treaty just as the 1904 presidential election campaign appeared on the horizon. Terming the opponents a "small body of shrill eunuchs" who represented only effete northeast mugwumps, Roosevelt blasted back and pushed the treaty through the Senate in early 1904 after a hard fight. Hay, long in failing health, was further depressed by the experience and died in early 1905. The episode reinforced TR's sorry view of the Senate: "It is evident that the Senate is a very poor body to have as part of the treaty-making power," he wrote in mid-1905.[13]

---

12 Roosevelt, *Letters,* 3:675; Michael L. Conniff, *Panama and the United States* (Athens, Ga., 1992), 33–4, 60–1; Richard H. Collin, *Theodore Roosevelt's Caribbean* (Baton Rouge, 1990), chaps. 7–8; for a well-argued view, see especially Richard Lael, *Arrogant Diplomacy; U.S. Policy Toward Colombia, 1903–1922* (Wilmington, Del., 1987).

13 *Public Opinion,* November 19, 1903, 645; Miles P. DuVal, *Cadiz to Cathay*

Engineers meanwhile began the greatest job of earth moving and lock building in history. Scientists and medical workers achieved a comparable miracle by eradicating the causes of yellow fever and malaria, the two destroyers of de Lesseps's earlier venture. The Frenchman had also failed, however, because he tried to do the world's greatest engineering job with private capital; Roosevelt understood the limits of the private marketplace and knew that in this case the advancement of private opportunities in trade required twentieth-century mercantilist government involvement. In 1906, he became the first president who left the country while in office when he visited the project and sat at the levers of the giant machines. In 1914 the canal's opening reduced the New York to San Francisco shipping distance from 13,600 to 5,300 miles.

The Dominican Intervention

The United States repeatedly dispatched warships and landed military forces in the Caribbean–Central American region in the nineteenth century, but after 1898 the pace quickened. Between 1898 and 1920 U.S. Marines entered Caribbean countries no fewer than twenty times. The new canal's security was only one of many reasons for the interventions. Some two years before the Canal Zone was obtained, Roosevelt declared in his 1901 annual message that such interventionism among "barbarous and semi-barbarous peoples" was "a most regrettable but necessary international police duty which must be performed for the sake of the welfare of mankind." Privately, however, he hoped both North Americans and Europeans would restrain themselves. Nevertheless, "if any South American State misbehaves toward any European country, let the European country spank it." He further apparently limited U.S. power by telling the German ambassador, and close friend, Speck von Sternburg in late 1901, "I regard the Monroe Doctrine as being the equivalent to an open door in South America." By mid-1903, however, TR wrote a friend that the Monroe Doctrine's proper sphere

(Stanford, 1947), 411–12; Cooper, *Warrior and Priest,* 71; Roosevelt, *Letters,* 4:1286.

was the Gulf of Mexico, Caribbean, and both entrances to the canal.[14]

This distinction between applying the Monroe Doctrine to the Caribbean–Central American region and the Open Door principles to the remainder of Latin America helps explain TR's furious activity in the former, and his somewhat more relaxed attitude toward the latter. As U.S. overseas investments soared from less than a billion dollars in 1897 to $3.5 billion in 1914, nearly half went into Latin America, especially into Mexico and the rest of Roosevelt's Monroe Doctrine–protected region. The U.S. military officers charged with protecting their nation's citizens and property were appalled at the region's misgovernment. They and American journalists urged the State Department to intervene more frequently, to teach the native peoples how to behave and progress according to Anglo-Saxon standards. The State Department responded sufficiently so that these peoples began to call the Marines "State Department troops." Cuba received special attention: U.S. officials earnestly wanted the island to run its own affairs, but order and the Platt Amendment had to be upheld when, invariably, the Cubans' attempt to govern their island without having either real political or, especially, economic control resulted in upheavals. Valuing self-government and Cuban-determined order some, but the privileges under the Platt Amendment more, Roosevelt and his secretary of war, William Howard Taft, used troops in 1906 to maintain, as well as to exercise, those privileges – while publicly stressing that the Marines were used at Cuba's request. Indeed, they had been landed with the approval of both the government and the rebels trying to overturn it. In the many-mirrored illusion of Cuban self-government, the United States appeared as both a protector of the government and an advocate for the rebels. It was not an illusion that would reinforce order.[15]

Along with the Panama incursion, however, Roosevelt's most important and instructive intervention occurred in Santo Domingo

14 Roosevelt, *Letters,* 3:116, 527; Cooper, *Warrior and Priest,* 71–2.
15 Richard D. Challener, *Admirals, Generals, and American Foreign Policy, 1898–1914* (Princeton, 1973), 167; Allan R. Millett and Peter Maslowski, *For the Common Defense* (New York, 1984), 319; Robert C. Hilderbrand, "Power and the People . . ." (Ph.D. diss., University of Iowa, 1977), 195–7.

in 1904–5. Analyses of this episode usually begin with the rivalry between U.S. and European trading companies, the resulting instability, and TR's dispatching troops to restore order as an "international policeman." The causes and implications, however, are deeper.

In 1900, the Dominican Republic's society was being thrown into turmoil by the emergence of two agrarian systems: a northern commercial class dependent on exports of tobacco and then cocoa, and a southern class dependent on sugarcane plantations. Both were being destabilized, the first by the replacement of tobacco culture by cocoa, the second by a large influx of U.S. and Cuban capital, which developed sugar plantations but drove peasants off the land and caused food shortages. The sugar elite became a driving force for the use of U.S. troops to maintain order – that is, for preservation of its new economic power. The carrying of its sugar, and the importation of its goods, became a profitable business. Thus the San Domingo Improvement Company of New York moved into the country during the 1890s to control the busy customshouses, and the U.S.-owned Clyde Steamship Line became the main carrier. The new North American investments, not European threats, initially created the conditions for U.S. intervention. The $20 million of U.S. investments, about one-third in sugar, finally prompted European investors, led by German and French interests, to try to stop the North American penetration. The problem revolved around economic development and its attendant dislocations, not a threat to U.S. regional strategic concerns. That strategic threat was largely conjured up by U.S. Minister William F. Powell who, along with other North Americans, had been demanding for years that Washington annex the country.[16]

By early 1904, Roosevelt was acutely sensitive to the Dominican concerns because of crises elsewhere in the region. In 1902–3, the British, Germans, and French used force to collect debts from a corrupt Venezuelan regime. Roosevelt had been consulted by the Europeans, but followed his policy of letting Europeans "spank"

16 Michael Baud, "The Origins of Capitalist Agriculture in the Dominican Republic," *Latin America Research Review* 22, no. 2 (1987): esp. 148–9.

Latin Americans and gave his blessing for the spanking. To his surprise, American public opinion became infuriated at the European incursion. The International Court of Justice, moreover, approved the use of force, a precedent that threatened to trigger similar interventions. As Roosevelt grew uneasy, Speck von Sternburg suggested that the president exercise police powers so Europeans would not have to intervene. The idea, Roosevelt replied in March 1903, "is new to me. I will try it out. . . . A second attempt of foreign powers, to collect their debts by force, would simply not be tolerated here." When, therefore, the State Department warned him in early 1904 that the American-European competition in the already unstable Dominican Republic threatened revolutions that could harm U.S. interests, Roosevelt was prepared to act. "I want to do nothing but what a policeman has to do in Santo Domingo. As for annexing the island, I have about the same desire to annex it as a gorged boa constrictor might have to swallow a porcupine wrong-end-to." He intended to move because "the attitude of the Santo Domingans has been one of half chaotic war towards us."[17]

An arbitration commission in mid-1904 gave Roosevelt what he wanted: recognition of the San Domingo Improvement Company's rights. When, however, the Dominican government defaulted in its payments to the company, and the company took over a key customshouse to collect for itself, the Europeans again complained. The company, U.S. diplomats, and a compliant Dominican regime (which received a $1.2 million subsidy for its cooperation) asked the United States to take over the customshouses. Roosevelt dispatched ships to protect the country's government, which had just struck the deal with Washington, against its own irate citizens. The president then arranged a January 1905 treaty that guaranteed the nation's territorial integrity in return for the United States receiving the right to collect all customs. Fifty-five percent of the receipts were to pay the foreign creditors, while 45 percent were to be used for the Dominicans. To TR's chagrin, the U.S. Senate rejected the pact. Opponents disliked the territorial guarantee. Moreover, they began

17 Dexter Perkins, *The Monroe Doctrine, 1867–1907* (Baltimore, 1937), 394, 408–9; Roosevelt, *Letters*, 4:734.

to suspect that foreign bondholders, not U.S. or Dominican national interests, were to be the real beneficiaries. Defying the Senate and the Constitution, Roosevelt put the pact into effect through an executive agreement between himself and the Dominican regime. The takeover was not sufficient to ensure order. The president had to instruct the U.S. Navy to stop any revolutionary outbreak. Because U.S. agents ran the customshouses, in 1907 two New York banking powers, J. P. Morgan and Kuhn, Loeb and Company, funded the entire Dominican debt and so brought it under total U.S. control. With the course fixed, foreigners effectively excluded, and the now unneeded territorial guarantee provision removed, the Senate finally ratified TR's work in 1907.[18]

The president justified his actions by announcing a Roosevelt Corollary to the Monroe Doctrine in his 1905 annual message. Denying any intention of U.S. "aggrandizement," he declared that the United States only wanted "the other republics on this continent" to be "happy and prosperous," which, in turn, required that "they maintain order within their boundaries and behave with a just regard for their obligations toward outsiders." The United States would intervene in "the interest of peace as well as in the interest of justice." (In an unintended irony, TR added that the new policy "will give the people of Santo Domingo the same chance to move onward and upward which we have already given to the people of Cuba.") Privately he wrote that the Monroe Doctrine could no longer be "used as a warrant for letting any of these republics remain as small bandit nests of a wicked and inefficient type."[19]

In reality, Roosevelt had not supported, but had inverted, the Monroe Doctrine: In 1823 it had been created to protect Latin American revolutionaries against foreign intervention; in 1905, he redefined it to protect U.S. interventionism against Latin American revolutionaries. The one common theme was, as Elihu Root (Hay's successor as secretary of state) phrased it, that since the Doctrine rested on the U.S. right of self-protection, the United States could

18 Perkins, *Monroe Doctrine*, 413–14, 427, 435–6; Burton, *Roosevelt*, 115–17.
19 James D. Richardson, *Messages and Papers of the Presidents*, 20 Vols. (New York, 1897–1922), 16:7375–8; Roosevelt, *Letters*, 4:1286.

define it unilaterally. Washington made the same point when it conditioned its signature to the Hague Conference conventions of 1899 and 1907 for the Permanent Court of Arbitration. Roosevelt, moreover, redefined the doctrine through a use of executive power that greatly enlarged presidential authority and diminished Congress's already shrinking role in foreign policy. Executive agreements dated back to 1817, but they had been used infrequently before Roosevelt's 1905 policy was implemented. He opened the door to their increased use until, by the end of the century, such agreements were employed many more times than treaties to define U.S. relations with other nations. Roosevelt justified this extension of power not only with his belief that the Senate was ill-equipped to handle foreign policy but also with the rationale that the president "is the steward of the people." The chief executive could carry out his will even if a specific constitutional authorization to do so was lacking, as long as "such action" was not "forbidden by the Constitution or by the laws."[20]

Protecting U.S. opportunities in such areas as the Caribbean thus led to foreign challenges and internal upheavals that, in turn, helped create the imperial presidency of the twentieth century. Root perhaps best explained the original causes. With North Americans for the first time accumulating "a surplus of capital beyond the requirements of internal development," the secretary of state declared in 1906, and with "that surplus increasing with extraordinary rapidity," there have opened "great opportunities for peaceful commercial and industrial expansion to the south." The Americans, he continued, have come to complement each other; they consequently should follow "the pathway marked out by the far-sighted statesmanship of Blaine for the growth of America, North and South, in the peaceful prosperity of a mighty commerce." Root had earlier called Roosevelt "the greatest conservative force for the protection of property and our institutions in the city of Washington."[21]

20 Albert K. Weinberg, *Manifest Destiny* (Baltimore, 1935), 429; Charles Evans Hughes, *Pathway of Peace* (New York, 1925), 122–39.
21 *Foreign Relations of the United States, 1906*, 2 parts (Washington, D.C., 1909), 2:1457–61; Roosevelt, *Letters,* 4:730.

Certainly not only TR's "conservative force" but the force of his successors was needed to realize Blaine's policy in Santo Domingo. For the Roosevelt Corollary brought not order, but more upheaval to the Dominicans. With Washington's help, foreigners dominated the key agricultural export industry of sugar and the more general export-import businesses. Except for these foreigners and the small Dominican elite that depended on the foreigners, the overwhelming majority of the country's population remained dirt poor as many of the nation's resources remained undeveloped – not least the production of staple foods for the people. The transportation system was colonial, that is, it was built not to link Dominican cities and markets, but to expedite export crops to the harbors for overseas sales. Increasingly exploited by class, race, foreign domination, and neocolonial institutions, the Dominicans came to believe that only revolution could give them a chance. The Roosevelt Corollary of 1905 thus led to vast opportunities for North Americans but also to the disorder that Woodrow Wilson's intervention of 1916 and eight years of U.S. military occupation would seek to cure.[22]

Asia: The Shutting of Open Doors

If, in the Caribbean, his attempt to impose military order was not to be confused with success, Roosevelt's attempt to play a delicate game of balance-of-power politics in Asia was not to be confused with a quest for order. In neither case did he demonstrate an awareness of the root causes of the disorder he despised, but at least in Asia TR finally came to realize the inability of U.S. power to unravel the complexities of Chinese politics and Japanese motivations. Unfortunately, he came to this realization only after trying to protect U.S. Open Door opportunities in Asia with policies that were based on miscalculations that had historic implications.

The aftermath of the Boxer uprising and the Foreign Intervention (as later Chinese historians termed it) left Russia in a dominant bargaining position with China. Japan and the United States were left searching for an opportunity to block the tsar's expansionism.

22 Bruce J. Calder, *The Impact of Intervention* (Austin, Tex., 1984), esp. xxiv–xxxii.

American interest in Russia leaped; between five and ten books on Russia had been published in the United States between 1890 and 1894, but more than forty books appeared between 1900 and 1904. Widely read journals such as the *North American Review* and *Atlantic Monthly* contained firsthand accounts and essays on the topic. Ties of friendship remained, especially as Count Witte and his Trans-Siberian Railway agents purchased tons of cheap U.S. steel for rails. Witte also removed tariffs on some farm machinery, and U.S. firms, such as International Harvester, increased their market share from 21 percent to 28 percent from 1901 to 1903. The reasons for the growing animosity between the two giant nations lay elsewhere, especially in the tsar's refusal to pull back, as he had promised, from Manchuria in early 1903. China, with the other powers' encouragement, protested unsuccessfully. American cotton exporters again warned Washington about the loss of key Northeast Asian markets to Russian cotton interests. American officials saw that Witte could not carry through his policy of avoiding clashes in Asia, at least avoiding them until the railroad was finished and an era of calm gave Russia time to develop industrially. "Our strength in Russia is . . . not with the military or diplomatic sections of the Government," Hay wrote the U.S. minister in Peking in mid-1903, "but with Mr. Witte and the whole financial world of Russia." The growing mistrust accelerated in 1903 when the terrible pogrom at Kishinev was revealed; public meetings in New York City and elsewhere condemned the tsar and quickly raised $368,000 to help Russian Jews.[23]

The Japanese had meanwhile concluded that a clash with the tsar's ambitions in Manchuria and Korea was probable. Pro-Russian officials in Tokyo were bypassed, war preparations began, and in January 1902, a treaty of alliance was signed with Great Britain. Fearful of Germany's rise in Europe and Russia's in Asia, the British had found common cause with Japan's determination to block the kaiser's and the tsar's expansionism, as well as to avenge the humiliations those two leaders had heaped on Japan in 1895–7. Roosevelt

---

23 George Queen, "The United States and the Material Advance in Russia, 1881–1906" (Ph.D. diss., University of Illinois, 1942), 158–66, 179.

thought of himself as an informal partner in the Anglo-Japanese alliance. He shared the fear of Russia and, he thought, the Anglo-Japanese commitment to Open Door principles. As Japanese-Russian tensions rose in 1903, the United States consistently sided with Tokyo. When Japan suddenly struck in 1904 and destroyed much of the tsar's Pacific fleet, Roosevelt was pleased. "The Japs will win out," he told Hay in July 1904. "The Japs have played our game because they have played the game of civilized mankind. . . . We may be of genuine service if Japan wins out, in preventing interference to rob her of the fruits of her victory" – a reference, of course, to the Europeans' treatment of Japan after the 1894–5 war. Some U.S. bankers, led by Jacob Schiff of Kuhn, Loeb, agreed. Bitter over the tsar's pogroms, they joined with their British counterparts to finance the Japanese military. U.S. publicists, led by George Kennan, also whipped up public opinion to favor Japan. He had once been pro-Russian, but his ten-month trip through *The Siberian Exile System,* as his book was called, turned him into perhaps the leading and best-known North American critic of the tsar's policies. He and TR were close. "If everyone regarded this [war] as Mr. Kennan and I do," Roosevelt announced at a White House luncheon, "I know where our warships would be."[24]

A few Americans dissented. James Harrison Wilson continued to warn that the key to a stable, developed Asia was U.S.-Russian friendship. He became "more and more persuaded," Wilson told U.S. diplomat (and China specialist) William Rockhill in mid-1904, "that any national attitude of undue sympathy with the Japanese or of policy which estranges Russia from us is a great mistake." He argued for a deal with Russia that would ensure an "open door to Manchuria," and one with Japan that would allow Tokyo to control the Philippines in return for commercial preferences for U.S. traders. Then, he believed, "we shall have called a New Empire into existence to readjust the balance of the world! We now hold the

24 Roosevelt, *Letters,* 4:865; W. G. Beasley, *The Rise of Modern Japan* (New York, 1990), 150; Frederick F. Travis, *George Kennan and the American-Russian Relationship, 1865–1924* (Athens, Ohio, 1990); Taylor Stults, "Imperial Russia Through American Eyes, 1894–1904" (Ph.D. diss., University of Missouri, 1942), 222–3.

powers which control the game." Strong currents, however, ran against Wilson and those who agreed with him. One of the strongest was exemplified in a paper presented at London's Royal Geographical Society in January 1904 by Halford Mackinder. Entitled "The Geographical Pivot of History," it argued that with the world fully discovered, expansionism would be replaced by power emanating from development and central geographic location. Hence, Mackinder suggested, the British (and, by implication, the American) Navy was becoming of less importance than central Russia, which occupied the world's "pivot area" and was being developed so it had the potential to control the great Eurasian landmass. If Mackinder was correct, Mahan's warning about the Russian menace might be accurate, but the American strategist's solution – a huge battleship fleet – could be irrelevant. Russia had to be contained, its power broken up, on the Eurasian mainland itself.[25]

By early 1905, the tsar was indeed using the completed sections of the Trans-Siberian Railway to move several times more men and equipment to the war front than he had at the start of the conflict. The Japanese clearly lacked the resources to win decisively in a much longer war. The outbreak of a revolution against the tsar in St. Petersburg on "Bloody Sunday," January 9, 1905, however, and a second Japanese naval victory, demonstrated that both sides needed peace. Roosevelt offered mediation, and at Portsmouth, New Hampshire, peace terms were hammered out, with great difficulty, in mid-1905. Despite its weakness at the end of the fighting, Japan attained most of its goals: exclusive rights in Korea; the takeover of the vital South Manchuria Railway, which blocked Russian movement to the south; and the southern half of strategic Sakhalin Island. Because Japan did not also obtain an indemnity, riots erupted in Tokyo. Both nations agreed to restore Chinese authority in Manchuria, although given the Russian railway concession in the north and Japan's in the south, this gesture to the Open Door was empty.

Roosevelt won the Nobel Peace Prize for his mediation, but he

25 J. H. Wilson to Rockhill, June 30, 1904, Papers of William W. Rockhill, Houghton Library, Harvard University, Cambridge, Mass.; H. J. Mackinder, "The Geographical Pivot of History," *Geographical Journal* 23 (April 1904): esp. 421–3, 433–6, 442.

failed to gain either a Japanese commitment to the Open Door principles or a balance of power that could protect U.S. interests in Asia. He had to recognize that not only had Japan emerged as the most powerful nation in northeastern Asia, but it was refusing any longer to protect American markets, most notably in Korea, where Roosevelt ignored the 1882 U.S.-Korean treaty pledge to help protect Korea's independence (at least by offering "good offices"). He instead did nothing in 1905 when Tokyo made the country into a protectorate. The most TR extracted was the Taft-Katsura deal (another executive agreement), in which the United States recognized Japan's power in Korea in return for Tokyo recognizing U.S. control of the Philippines. But for Roosevelt worse lay just ahead. The 1905 revolution in Russia, triggered by the Japanese-inflicted defeats, became one in a series of revolutions that were to mark the opening of the twentieth century: Vietnam, Persia in 1906, Turkey in 1908, China and Mexico in 1911, and finally Russia in 1917.[26]

George Kennan was delighted by the St. Petersburg uprising in 1905, especially after he had worked to indoctrinate Russian prisoners of war in 1904–5 with antitsarist doctrines. The Bolshevik Revolution of 1917, however, turned out to be more than he had wanted or expected. Like Roosevelt, Kennan came to be surprised by the path on which his antitsarist beliefs had taken him.

The Aftermath

Roosevelt's Asian policies received two other decisive jolts in 1905. The first originated in U.S. discrimination against Chinese immigrants in the post-1880 era. These acts climaxed at the 1904 St. Louis Exposition, where official Chinese delegates were abused. Peking retaliated by refusing to renew its immigration treaty with the United States. Merchants in major Chinese ports joined by totally boycotting U.S. goods. The boycott was not discouraged by European and Japanese competitors of American products. Roosevelt was amazed. His low opinion of these people was marked by his

26 Geoffrey Barraclough, *Introduction to Contemporary History* (New York, 1964), 101–4, 150.

tendency to call a particularly inefficient and unsuccessful person a "Chinese." He demanded that the Qing officials force the merchants to drop the boycott. The Qing dynasty responded positively, then revealed its true feelings by posting upside down, in many cities, the proclamation to end the boycott. The boycott finally ended, but Roosevelt had confronted a new type of Chinese antiforeign movement. The second blow landed in 1904 when he begged J. P. Morgan and other U.S. bankers to save American control of the important Hankow-Canton railway concession. Unknown to TR, Morgan had actually secretly helped the original concessionaires, the American China Development Company, sell out at immense profit to King Leopold of Belgium. The deal broke the U.S. promise to China that the railway would be controlled only by Americans. As the Chinese and Roosevelt protested the sellout, Morgan reluctantly agreed to repurchase the concession. China, now believing the Americans were as untrustworthy as other foreigners, demanded the return of the concession. Roosevelt asked Morgan to stand firm. The banker, seeing an opportunity to sell the concession once more at a profit, and not showing explicit confidence in TR's grasp of Asian diplomacy, sold out to Peking.[27]

Roosevelt's vaunted balance-of-power diplomacy in Asia, undermined by racism, Japanese military victories, U.S. bankers' lack of concern, and the antiforeign zeal of the gathering Chinese revolution, lay in ruins. He had better luck mediating a crisis between France and Germany in Morocco in 1906. Determined to help maintain French-British alliance ties and contain Germany, TR achieved both objectives. But there was little in this mediation for broader U.S. interests. He had tried without much success to have the parties accept an Open Door pledge for the benefit of U.S. producers interested in North Africa. The failure in Asia, however, threatened to bring about historic consequences, given the rhetoric and expressed needs of U.S. exporters and officials since the days of Sew-

27 Sherman Cochran, "Commercial Penetration and Economic Imperialism in China," in John K. Fairbank and Ernest R. May, eds., *America's China Trade in Historical Perspective* (Cambridge, Mass., 1985), 190–4; Jonathan D. Spence, *The Search for Modern China* (New York, 1990), 237–8; Michael H. Hunt, *The Making of a Special Relationship* (New York, 1983), 277–8.

ard. In 1907, Japan tightened its grip on Korea by excluding many U.S. goods. The pro-Japanese Rockhill claimed Tokyo was simply trying to get rid of war surpluses, but the tightening was actually a step toward full annexation of Korea in 1910. Also in 1907, Japan and Russia effectively divided Manchuria between themselves. Roosevelt was also bedeviled by anti-Japanese riots that erupted in California because of the rising number of Japanese living in the state. He finally worked out a gentleman's agreement in which Tokyo promised to control emigration and Washington tried to protect Japanese already in America. Especially surprising, however, was TR's candid admission that the furor in California "is a race question. . . . I did not see this at the outset."[28]

In 1906, U.S. officials evaluated their position in the "Orange," or Asiatic, war plan. They concluded that in case of war with Japan, the Philippines could not be held and U.S. forces would have to be pulled back to Hawaii. Congressional refusal to build up the distant Pacific bases at Guam and the Philippines, as well as bitter interservice rivalries that made the development of a common strategy difficult, combined with the growing Japanese power to shape the plan. Roosevelt tried to display his military reach by sending the U.S. Navy (now containing twenty-two modern battleships) on an around-the-world voyage in 1907–8 that notably scheduled special stops in Japan. The Japanese were most friendly, and the ships proved seaworthy, but the trip did nothing to change the balance of power. In 1899, Roosevelt had condemned opponents of Philippine annexation as "men of a bygone age." Now, in 1907, he was forced to admit that the islands had to be given independence earlier than he preferred: They "form our heel of Achilles. They are all that make the present situation with Japan dangerous." The last sentence indicated that he had given up trying to maintain the Open Door in the great markets of Manchuria. All doubts were removed in 1908 when he helped shape the Root-Takahira deal (another executive agreement), in which the United States recognized Japan's interests in

28 Akira Iriye, *From Nationalism to Internationalism* (London, 1977), 144; Hugh Seton Watson, *The Russian Empire, 1801–1907* (Oxford, 1967), 682; Cooper, *Warrior and Priest,* 111–12.

Manchuria. The Root-Takahira agreement ended the attempt of an imaginative Chinese official, Yüan Shih-k'ai, to entice U.S. and other foreign interests into Manchuria to block Japan.[29]

Some Americans, headed by wealthy internationalists such as Hamilton Holt, founded the Japanese Society amid the 1907 crises in an effort to build networks of understanding between the two peoples. Roosevelt's views evolved in the next five years. He warned friends that Western powers must not try to stop Japan's "natural expansion" into the Asian mainland, because otherwise Japanese would move in large numbers to Canada and the United States. Simultaneously, he became more radical politically by coming out in favor of inheritance and income taxes, stronger regulation of interstate businesses, fixing railroad rates, and building up the labor movement. He condemned "malefactors of great wealth" in 1907 (even as he worked with J. P. Morgan to end an economic panic), condemned as well "predatory wealth," demanded federal regulation of stock exchange practices, and gave his Nobel Peace Prize money to a foundation for industrial peace.[30]

Coming to terms with his failures in Asia seemed to coincide with Roosevelt's domestic reform program, the "new deal" that his friend Brooks Adams had earlier demanded. Brooks, however, had asked for it in conjunction with, rather than as a substitute for, U.S. exploitation of Asia. The coincidence of Roosevelt's political turn may have been unrelated to his new views of Asia. Less questionable is that between 1898 and 1905 his foreign policies that aimed at gaining U.S. commercial and strategic opportunities in Asia were undermined by his myopic nationalism, a racism that caricatured Chinese (and prevented him from understanding the racism against Japanese in California), a misunderstanding of Japan, an underestimation of Russia's fragility, an overestimation of U.S. military power, and an inability to maneuver the balance of power in Asia to

29 John M. Dobson, *America's Ascent* (DeKalb, Ill., 1978), 130; Akira Iriye, *Across the Pacific* (New York, 1967), 120; Paolo E. Coletta, *The Presidency of William Howard Taft* (Lawrence, Kan., 1973), 209–10; Cooper, *Warrior and Priest,* 112.
30 Warren F. Kuehl, *Seeking World Order* (Nashville, 1969), 106; Walter Scholes and Marie Scholes, *The Foreign Policies of the Taft Administration* (Columbia, Mo., 1970), 121–2; Mowry, *Era of Roosevelt,* 220–22; Roosevelt, *Letters,* 6:1539.

his country's advantage.[31] Attempting to forward American opportunities, his policies – from encouraging Japanese exploitation of Korea and Manchuria to his actions in the Chinese boycott, the Hankow-Canton concession issue, and the Root-Takahira agreement – helped feed Chinese nationalism, disorder, and revolution.

31 Beale, *Roosevelt*, pp. 456–9.

10. William Howard Taft and the Age of Revolution

President William Howard Taft and Secretary of State Philander C. Knox were responsible for conducting U.S. foreign policy when, between 1909 and 1913, two generations of American diplomatic history climaxed in Canada, Central America, Mexico, and Asia. Viewed by many scholars, not incorrectly, as sometimes lethargic and often unimaginative, Taft and Knox shared a love for the law, and the respect for property, precedent, compromise, peaceful settlements, and the power of money that are common to many lawyers. Taft was happiest not as president but later when he served as chief justice of the Supreme Court. "The truth is," he said then, "that in my present life I don't remember that I ever was President."[1]

Taft had a superb legal mind. Knox, like his predecessor, Elihu Root, ranked at the top of the best corporate lawyers in a nation dominated by corporations. Taft, moreover, sported a résumé that included being governor-general of the Philippines, secretary of war, Theodore Roosevelt's diplomatic troubleshooter, and the successor handpicked by TR himself. The Rough Rider quickly regretted his selection, although he probably would have been disappointed regardless of whom he had chosen to succeed him. Roosevelt, moreover, along with his several predecessors in the White House, had bequeathed to Taft and Knox foreign policies that finally triggered a series of disorders, indeed revolutions in several instances, that neither Taft nor anyone else could understand and resolve. The uprisings over the tariff and in Central America, Mexico, and China were fitting conclusions to the previous half century. Taft and Knox had the misfortune to be in the White House and the State Department when many of those deeply rooted policies bore bitter fruit for the United States.

1 James Barber, *Presidential Character* (Englewood Cliffs, N.J., 1972), 175.

Croly, Taft, and the Promise of American Life

As Taft entered office in 1909, Herbert Croly, a hitherto little-known editor of an architectural journal, published *The Promise of American Life*. Roosevelt called the book "the most profound and illuminating study of our national conditions which has appeared in many years." Political observers soon began to see Croly's influence on Roosevelt's thinking as the restless former president shaped a new program to recapture the White House in 1912. The book became a landmark in progressivism because it used an interpretation of the past to present striking insights into the future. Croly believed three themes from that history had become central by 1909: a nationalism whose post–Civil War surge made the state more than the sum of its political and economic factions; a democracy that had to be rethought in a frontierless, newly industrialized society; and an efficiency that determined who survived in cutthroat international competition. Although each was sometimes viewed as contradictory to the other two, Croly argued that in the twentieth century only a strong, Hamiltonian, nationalist state could secure both a Jeffersonian democracy and capitalist efficiency. Breaking with those Progressives who preached more democracy through the use of the referendum and recall, Croly argued that modern democracy required the protection of a centralized national state. Within that state the pivotal unit, the corporation, would not be controlled by antitrust measures (for they produced inefficiency), but by federal regulation and the countervailing powers of legal, strong labor unions. Croly thus tried to reconcile the tensions that lay at the heart of American political debate during the Second Industrial Revolution: The American "people collectively have become more of a democracy in proportion as they have become more of a nation. Their democracy is to be realized by means of an intensification of their national life."[2]

Croly's belief that centralization at home produced more democra-

---

2 Herbert Croly, *The Promise of American Life* (New York, 1909), 270–1; Eric Goldman, *Rendezvous with Destiny* (New York, 1952), 147; David W. Levy, *Herbert Croly of the New Republic* (Princeton, 1985), 94–141.

cy (supposedly through the grace of an efficient, disinterested federal bureaucracy) was nothing more than an act of faith. Roosevelt, however, wanted to believe it, and many Progressives were relieved that perhaps their politics had fewer contradictions in an industrialized America than they had feared. In foreign policy, however, Croly's program seemed even more consistent and attractive. That realm of affairs was run by nation-states, the most efficient of which could dominate world affairs and spread the blessings of democracy globally (if one assumed the United States was, as it indeed appeared, the most efficient). Croly offered nothing less than a new, twentieth-century mission for Americans. Unlike John Winthrop's "City on a Hill" of 1630, however, Croly's was a nation in the arena of imperialism. He argued for an end to higher tariffs and for the efficiency forced by lowering tariffs; for a commitment to exercising military power (oceans do not provide security but have "multiplied the possible sources of contact"); and, in all, for internationalism. The willingness to wage war for the sake of nationalism and democracy had to be assumed: "The Christian warrior must accompany the evangelist." If, Croly warned, Progressives were not prepared to use the new nationalisms and modern warfare for decent democratic purposes, evil-minded conservatives lurking in the shadows would use nationalism and weapons for nondemocratic ends.[3]

A specific foreign policy agenda naturally followed. International commitments were inevitable because "a decent guarantee of international peace [was] precisely the political condition which would . . . release the springs of democracy." In Europe, he wrote in interesting prophecy, Americans must be ready to renounce "neutrality" and intervene "to tip the scales in favor of a comparatively pacific settlement of international complications." As regards Latin America, which received the most detailed attention, he assumed that the Monroe Doctrine was outdated and the Roosevelt Corollary of the doctrine most applicable; that is, U.S. and European interests in Latin America ran parallel, and Washington officials should therefore act as police to maintain order and collect debts. Much could be accomplished by working "with the best element in South American

3 Croly, *Promise of American Life.* 255–7, 289, 305, 210.

opinion," but some states lacked such enlightened elites and had to be handled more forcefully. He especially worried about "revolutionary upheavals" in the pivotal nation of Mexico. Canada had to be separated from Great Britain so it could find its natural home in a North American system, perhaps through a trade treaty. Croly thus envisioned a political and economic empire stretching from the northern borders of Canada into Latin America, with the United States as its cockpit. In Asia, he recognized the Philippines as a weakness in the U.S. diplomatic armor, but he believed the islands had to be defended with a great Pacific fleet so the Open Door principles could be upheld. China could then be protected by "a great deal of diplomacy and more or less [*sic*] fighting." Americans would also become better educated about their high stakes in "the future development of China and Japan." Colonialism, as in the Philippines, was good because it served "not as a cause of war, but as a safety-valve against war. It affords an arena in which the restless and adventurous . . . can have their fling."[4]

As one of his biographers has noted, Croly combined "an internationalized imperialism with democratic nationalism."[5] It was this combination that so many Progressives, as well as some conservatives, found irresistible. The formulation justified what they were doing at home and hoped to do abroad. Taft and Knox bought much of this argument, but they were selective. Taft's view of nationalism was more skeptical than Croly's, as was his confidence in democracy, either at home or, especially, abroad. The 320-pound president was not one for undertaking too many missions. He admitted both an "indisposition to labor as hard as I might" and an inability to keep up with his work (which, as his chief aide noted, meant Taft might "be about three years behind when the fourth of March, 1913, rolls around"). He was also full of self-doubt, especially in having to follow Roosevelt. On inauguration day morning, a cold storm hit Washington. Roosevelt said it was a fitting way to end his presidency. Taft replied, "You're wrong. It is my storm. I always

4 Charles Forcey, *The Crossroads of Liberalism* (New York, 1960), 30–1; Croly, *Promise of American Life*, 261, 293–312.
5 Forcey, *Crossroads of Liberalism*, 170.

knew it would be a cold day when I became President of the United States."[6]

The new president, nevertheless, roused himself to diverge from Croly's recommendation and far surpass Roosevelt in enforcing antitrust acts. He broke up Standard Oil, U.S. Steel, International Harvester, and the tobacco trust, among others. He did establish a Department of Labor and a Federal Children's Bureau, but he was considerably more doubtful about the virtues of big government's controlling big business than was Croly or the later Roosevelt. He preferred as a good lawyer to enforce antitrust legislation, and, as a good administrator, to make the State Department more efficient in helping the corporations. Based in part on the British Foreign Office's organization chart, the reorganized State Department now had specialists heading some geographic bureaus (such as that for the Far East), and a more streamlined decision-making system that, in Taft's view, would "make it a thoroughly efficient instrument in the furtherance of foreign trade and of American interest abroad."[7]

Taft followed Croly's analysis in regard to tariff revision and Canadian reciprocity, and paid dearly. The Payne tariff bill passed the House in 1909 with a free list and lower rates that pleased exporters and importers. In the Senate, however, protectionist interests retaliated; the resulting Payne-Aldrich bill hardly met Croly's standards for a moderate tariff. Taft made it worse, however, by failing to restore the free list, then praising the results. His remarks alienated industrial exporters, raw material importers, and Progressive tariff revisionists. Roosevelt had not helped. He refused to fight these battles earlier and now did little to help Taft. But worse lay ahead.

Taft believed that foreign trade was increasingly vital to U.S. prosperity, and that trade, as well as investment, was rapidly moving north. In 1909, Americans sent $207 million worth of goods to Canada, or twice the amount sent to the second best customer, Great Britain. Since 1900, U.S. investment in Canada (especially in mines

---

6 Robert C. Hilderbrand, "Power and the People . . ." (Ph.D. diss., University of Iowa, 1977), 221; Paolo E. Coletta, *The Presidency of William Howard Taft* (Lawrence, Kan., 1973), 47.

7 Stuart Bruchey, *Enterprise: The Dynamic Economy of a Free People* (Cambridge, Mass., 1990), 388.

and forests) had nearly quadrupled to $750 million. Washington officials, moreover, searched for a weapon to destroy Canadian-British economic links, especially after 1907, when Canada's new tariff favored the great British markets and discriminated against the giant southern neighbor. Neither Taft nor Prime Minister Wilfred Laurier wanted to face a possible trade war, but the Americans had another agenda driving their policy. As Charles Pepper of the Bureau of Trade Relations informed Knox in a memorandum entitled "The Open Door to Canada," removing Canada from the British trade orbit could undermine the entire British imperial preferential tariff system and change the course of trade "from west to east and from east to west" to "north to south and south to north." Taft fully endorsed such a rerouting. He privately told Roosevelt that if a Canadian reciprocity pact could be negotiated, it "would make Canada only an adjunct of the United States." Taft pushed through his bill to begin to realize a North American continental market, but in Ottawa, Conservatives, strongly supported by British interests and helped by ill-timed remarks by Washington politicians about the probability of future annexation of Canada, defeated the legislation. Croly's nationalism had been too blatant, too impolitic, to realize one of its greatest foreign policy objectives.[8]

Taft's way with words, or, more accurately, his apparent lack of concern about them, repeatedly hurt him. Unlike McKinley and Roosevelt, he cared little about managing news releases, saw few reporters, withheld information, and took the position that the public had little right to be informed. Critics thus attacked the administration with ever smaller fears of retaliation. A prime example was the coining of the term "dollar diplomacy" by a hostile reporter to describe Taft's foreign policies. The term had the connotations of exploitation and Wall Street domination. Taft was sensitive to the charges, not least to the allegations of being controlled by Wall Street, which he once declared was, as an aggregation, "the

---

8 This account draws heavily from Robert E. Hannigan, "Reciprocity, 1911: Continentalism and American Weltpolitik," *Diplomatic History* 4 (Winter 1980): 1–18; an important interpretation is Paul Wolman, *Most Favored Nation: The Republican Revisionists and U.S. Tariff Policy, 1897–1912* (Chapel Hill, 1992), esp. 136–67.

biggest ass that I have ever run across." But as he did nothing to counter the term's use, officials, including the powerful assistant secretary of state Francis Huntington Wilson, began to use it to describe Taft's search for peaceful solutions – "the substitution of dollars for bullets." Taft finally used the term himself in his last annual message to Congress. The phrase was indeed accurate except that it overstated the president's reluctance to use force. During the 1894 Pullman strike, federal judge Taft had been willing to give orders to "shoot to kill" the strike's leaders. As Roosevelt's man in Cuba and the Philippines, and as president ordering troops into Nicaragua, he also did not blanch at the use of force. One of his key agents in Asia, Willard Straight, rightly defined dollar diplomacy as "the financial expression of John Hay's 'open door' policy." From Seward to Hay, U.S. officials had not hesitated to use bullets when dollars proved inadequate.[9]

Indeed, dollar diplomacy, as Taft realized, was a misleading term for two reasons. It not only did not preclude the use of force, but the effect of dollars in Central America, the Caribbean, Mexico, and Asia was so destabilizing that it required the use of force to restore conditions for opportunity. Using dollars, moreover, did not connote turning foreign affairs over to bankers. United States officials were sufficiently attuned to the new mercantilism, during the age of the Second Industrial Revolution and imperialism, to understand that government played at least as fundamental a role in building railroads in China or Central America as the government had played in the United States during the 1860s and 1870s. Imperialism was, at bottom, a clash of governments, that is, of Croly's nationalisms. For example, the long American attempts to turn imperialism into a kind of free-market, open-door competition in Asia had collapsed amid the Chinese nationalism on the bullet-riddled streets of Peking during 1900, if not long before. Free-market competition paradoxically required ever greater state participation. To call U.S. policy "dollar diplomacy," Taft himself observed, "is to ignore entirely a most useful office to be performed by a government in its dealings with foreign governments." Hence the president created the Bureau of Foreign and Domestic Commerce in the Commerce Department

9 Hilderbrand, "Power and the People," 214–15, 244–6, 261–2.

to help individual firms compete overseas. [10] Dollar diplomacy, in all, was a partnership among the government, bankers, military, and the wealthy native *comprador* elite that had integrated itself into the American system. Dollar diplomacy was Croly's powerful national state wedded to the Second Industrial Revolution, and it was therefore an incestuous, and thus highly dangerous, relationship.

Taft and Knox tried to remove one large obstacle from the foreign affairs process in 1910 when the president shocked a New York audience by urging that "matters of national honor" should be referred to an arbitration court, just as were questions of property. After internationalist and peace organizations quickly supported this initiative, Knox signed two trial treaties with Great Britain and France, which declared that all justiciable disputes were to be arbitrated, while all other issues could be referred to a joint high commission, which would decide whether arbitration or some other means of settlement would be exercised. A major, indeed historic, breakthrough in the long quest for imposing order and fair process without resort to arms seemed ready to bless the globe. Taft, however, had not reckoned with Roosevelt or the Senate. Roosevelt blasted the treaties for "sloppy thinking," and was joined by Alfred Thayer Mahan in claiming that vital U.S. interests (such as the Monroe Doctrine) could not be entrusted to joint commissions until international law was further developed. Taft neglected consulting the Senate. Lodge consequently pushed the treaties through the Senate 76–3, but only after Progressives joined him in stripping the pact of any teeth or the power to rule on important issues. Order through due process of law was a good objective in theory, but it had little relationship to U.S. foreign policy's search for opportunity abroad. [11]

10 Martin J. Sklar, *The United States as a Developing Country* (New York, 1992), 88, a book that has influenced this chapter's interpretation; Henry F. Pringle, *The Life and Times of William Howard Taft,* 2 vols. (New York, 1939), 2: 678–83; Emily Rosenberg, *Spreading the American Dream* (New York, 1982), 57, 59.

11 Warren F. Kuehl, *Seeking World Order* (Nashville, 1969), 137–41; William E. Leuchtenberg, "Progressivism and Imperialism: The Progressive Movement and American Foreign Policy, 1898–1916," *Mississippi Valley Historical Review* 39, no. 3 (1952): 491.

From Opportunities to Revolution
to Marines in Central America

That search reached one climax in Central America between 1906 and 1912. Since the second Hay-Pauncefote Treaty and the Roosevelt Corollary, Central America had become Washington's reserve, in large part. French, British, and especially German economic inroads did not change the extent of U.S. domination of the region's affairs but only made it more important to Washington officials to enlarge their power in the area. The soon-to-be-opened Panama Canal had the same effect. Yet throughout 1906–12, North American policies toward the region revolved not around a quest for stability and the status quo but around the encouragement of a series of revolutions. Thus the United States set out to create disorder in Central America, especially in El Salvador, Honduras, and, above all, Nicaragua.

Since 1893 José Santos Zelaya had sought to use dictatorial rule to develop Nicaragua. He dreamed of spreading his power over a united Central America, a dream that had not been realized since the first, heady days of independence in the 1830s. Washington's decision to build the canal in Panama smashed Zelaya's hope of using U.S. dollars to enrich his nation and make it a pivot of global trade. He approached Europeans and Japanese about financing a Nicaraguan canal, gave concessions increasingly to non-U.S. groups, and waged a series of wars to recoup his fortunes by bringing other nations, especially El Salvador, under his control. After 1906, U.S. officials covertly helped a revolutionary group in El Salvador, which duly promised to be friendly to Washington. The North Americans also urged Costa Rica to attack Nicaragua.[12] Zelaya's major competitor, however, was Guatemala's leader, Estrada Cabrera, who tried to organize coalitions against Nicaragua. During a war between Honduras (supported by Guatemala) and Nicaragua in 1907, Theodore Roosevelt and Mexican dictator Porfirio Díaz intervened just as Zelaya was gaining the upper hand. The mediation led to the creation of a Central American Court (based in a handsome Costa Rican

---

12 Thomas Schoonover, *The United States in Central America, 1860–1911* (Durham, N.C., 1991), 171.

structure built by Andrew Carnegie's millions), which was to stop future wars through processes of law. The court lasted until 1916 when its decisions ruled against U.S. claims in the Nicaraguan region, and the United States then effectively destroyed it.

Meanwhile, Washington also destroyed Zelaya. In late 1909, a revolt erupted in eastern Nicaragua that was sponsored by North American interests. When Zelaya tried to regain control, Knox (who personally had considerable investments in Central American fruit plantations) sent in four hundred U.S. Marines – in effect, to protect the revolt. Zelaya made the fatal error of executing two U.S. mercenaries he caught trying to blow up some of his troops. An enraged secretary of state instituted a "hard-Knox" policy: He dispatched warships to show his and Taft's resolve, demanded Zelaya's immediate exit, and the dictator sailed off to Spain. The U.S. involvement, however, had only begun. Washington's chosen government for Nicaragua did not meet the approval of many Nicaraguans, especially after the puppet regime turned over majority interest in the nation's railroads and the national bank to New York financiers in return for large loans. The surprised U.S. minister, Elliott Northcott, expecting on his arrival in 1911 to be greeted as a savior, wired home that not only Guatemala and El Salvador opposed the new Managua regime, but "the natural sentiment of an overwhelming majority of Nicaraguans is antagonistic to the United States" – an antagonism expressed when citizens tried to blow up the government's palace and arsenal the day of Northcott's arrival. In 1912, when a revolt led by a respected general erupted against Washington's handpicked president, Adolfo Díaz, Taft landed 2,600 troops to put down the uprising and keep Díaz in power. Marines remained in Nicaragua until 1925 when their withdrawal set off another revolt. As their overthrow of Zelaya and activities elsewhere in the region indicated, U.S. officials had nothing against the principle of revolution. In certain circumstances, Taft and Knox, resembling Roosevelt, even preferred revolution over order. They only sought to discriminate among those who were, and were not, to be favored by Washington-sponsored upheavals. [13]

13 José Madriz to Taft, June 13, 1910, *Foreign Relations of the United States, 1911* (Washington, D.C., 1915), 655–6; Coletta, *Taft,* 188.

A historic turn in Honduras also demonstrated how North Americans favored opportunity over order. A poor country, Honduras nevertheless had enough land, fairly distributed, to support most *campesinos* until the late 1880s. A banana plantation boom then occurred in reaction to the new markets opening for the fruit in the Americas and Europe. By 1910, 80 percent of the banana plantations were controlled by U.S. companies. These firms not only held the nation's best lands and transportation networks but instigated wars in order to control the government. When Huntington Wilson complained that "Honduras has politically, financially, and economically about as bad a record for stability as can be found on the face of the earth," it was as much a judgment on North Americans as on Hondurans. Headed by Sam "the Banana Man" Zemurray, U.S. investors and adventurers headed out of New Orleans in early 1911 to seize power. When President Miguel Dávila asked for help, Knox offered it in return for the U.S. right to intervene and control Honduran customshouses. The Honduran Congress, surrounded by angry mobs who threatened the representatives with death if they accepted the Knox-Dávila deal, unsurprisingly rejected it. Zemurray then effectively took power, combined with the United Fruit Company of Boston (or "the Octopus," as Latin Americans soon termed it), and turned Honduras into the prototype of a banana republic.[14] When revolts produced power for U.S. citizens and interests, such uprisings were much to be preferred over stability – especially stability imposed by native governments that Washington believed were weak, as well as suspect in their appreciation for the Monroe Doctrine and its recent corollary.

The Mexican Revolution

Since the 1870s, Mexico's dictator, Porfirio Díaz, had ensured that his nation would not be a banana republic, but his welcoming of U.S. investment nevertheless made Mexico into a dependent of the

14 William H. Durham, *Scarcity and Survival in Central America* (Stanford, 1979), 115–18; C. D. Kepner, Jr., *Social Aspects of the Banana Industry* (New York, 1936), 53–4; C. D. Kepner, Jr., and J. H. Soothill, *The Banana Empire* (New York, 1935), 107–12.

northern republic. The dollar flow increased as the ruler's colleagues grew older, more satisfied, and less flexible. A 1902 report revealed that North Americans had invested a half-billion dollars, with over one-half entering in just the previous six years. The money went into oil concessions, silver and other mining operations, and huge plantations, including those developed for rubber growing and export agriculture. But this was only a prelude. Between 1903 and 1910 investments skyrocketed to three times those of 1876 to 1900. By 1910, the nearly $2 billion of U.S. investment owned 43 percent of Mexico's property; 15 million Mexicans owned 33 percent, and other foreign investors 24 percent. In some sectors, the Americans' presence was overwhelming. For example, they controlled two-thirds of the rubber business, which, with the automobile, was beginning to undergo a global boom in demand. In other fields, such as oil, Americans were in heated competition with other foreign, especially British, investors. American citizens nevertheless seemed to dominate the industry by 1905. A key U.S. banker, James Speyer, told the German ambassador in 1904 that "in the United States there is a pervasive feeling that Mexico is no longer anything but a dependency of the American economy, in the same way that the entire area from the Mexican border to the Panama Canal [all of Central America] is seen as part of North America." After a visit to Mexico, Andrew Carnegie said with delight, "in every corner of the Republic reigned prosperity and an enviable peace."[15]

Carnegie had not looked deeply enough. The massive foreign investments transformed Mexico. As haciendas evolved to export sugar and hemp, landless peasants proliferated and the production of staple food dropped. Mexico grew more corn and beans for domestic consumption in 1867 than in 1910. Prices rose because of imported staples from the more expensive United States and the ability of wealthy urban and rural elites to purchase these items. As agri-

15 Friedrich Katz, *The Secret War in Mexico: Europe, the United States, and the Mexican Revolution* (Chicago, 1981), 15–17, 22; William Schell, Jr., "American Investment in Tropical Mexico . . . , 1897–1913," *Business History Review* 64 (Summer 1990): 217–54; Ramón Eduardo Ruiz, *Triumphs and Tragedy: A History of the Mexican People* (New York, 1992), 292.

cultural exports increased in the early 1900s, U.S. and Mexican capitalists intensified their drive to seize peasant lands. American-built railroads carried the goods to ports, but also penetrated and threatened communal life, especially in northern Mexico. Discontented peasants had long been known in the country, but by 1910 there were many more than had existed twenty years before, and they were joined by rural laborers who were more rootless and more radical. In the cities, the influx of capital created a new, literate, and politically aware middle class. The group was not radical, but by 1910 it had developed several demands: more Mexican control over Mexican affairs, and more young blood (like its own) to replace the gerontocracy that surrounded Díaz, who had now ruled nearly four decades.[16]

The U.S. panic of 1907 demonstrated the price of dependence on the giant northern neighbor. As New York capital dried up, Mexican exports dropped, investment disappeared, thousands of Mexican immigrants to the United States suddenly began to return home, and unrest spread. Having begun to understand the dangers of dependence after the stunning U.S. victory in the 1898 war and the quick imperialism that had struck Cuba, Puerto Rico, and Panama, Díaz had already moved to loosen the U.S. economic grip. He grew especially concerned that the U.S. firms moving in were no longer medium-sized and manageable but the outsized products of the post-1897 merger movement, such as Standard Oil and the railroads, which could not be easily managed. He nationalized many of the U.S.-controlled railroad lines (but not the British), imposed duties that raised the price of raw materials headed for the northern border, during 1907–8 worked to attract European capital to fill the vacuum left by the New York panic, and launched a special attack on Standard Oil by excluding it from rich oil fields while cutting its share of Mexico's illuminating and machine oil market from 99 percent to 44 percent between 1904 and 1910. Díaz meanwhile gave increased preference to British oil, especially to Lord Cowdray,

16 Friedrich Katz, "Rural Rebellions After 1810," in Friedrich Katz, ed., *Riot, Rebellion and Revolution: Rural Social Conflict in Mexico* (Princeton, 1988), 543–50; John Mason Hart, *Revolutionary Mexico* (Berkeley, 1987), 247–8.

whose powerful interests checked Standard Oil and by 1910 controlled 58 percent of Mexico's petroleum production. [17]

Roosevelt and Taft did not complain to Díaz. Investors from the United States, however, not only complained; following the lead of James Stillman, president of National City Bank of New York, they began to note the attractiveness of Francisco Madero who, in his mid-thirties, had challenged Díaz. Madero was no revolutionary. Born to great wealth, he wanted to join Díaz, not depose him, but when the old dictator rejected the proposal and then said he might not run again for the presidency, the younger man launched his own campaign. Díaz reversed himself, won in a fixed election, and suddenly confronted a political tornado. Vowing to overthrow Díaz, Madero issued his own moderate platform to appeal to, and empower, the new middle class. He was joined by two quite different, more radical, figures, Emiliano Zapata and Pascual Orozco, who mobilized peasants and rural laborers in the south and north respectively, and particularly in areas where foreign investment pressures were greatest. Conditions were ripe. By 1900, perhaps 82 percent of the *campesinos* had no land, while 1 percent of the population owned 97 percent of the fertile land. The growing revolutionary movement was marked less by antiforeign violence (few attacks on foreigners — except Chinese — occurred even during the bloodiest outbreaks) than by the Mexicans' hatred of Díaz for dealing so much of their wealth to North Americans and the British. As Díaz's power slipped, Taft and Knox signaled that the old president had fallen from favor; one clear signal was their allowing Madero's supporters to obtain arms in the United States. Díaz realized that he had to depart before the moderate opposition turned into an unpredictable uprising. "Madero has unleashed a tiger!" the old man observed. "Now let us see if he can control it." [18]

He could not. Obtaining power in June 1911, Madero unsurprisingly retained many of Díaz's advisers. He did nothing about major

17 Friedrich Katz et al., *La servidumbre agraria en México en la época porfiriana* (Mexico City, 1976), 15–17, 60–61; Hart, *Revolutionary Mexico,* 247–9; Katz, "Rural Rebellions After 1810," 544.

18 Hart, *Revolutionary Mexico,* 238–49; Ruiz, *Triumphs and Tragedy,* 292–316; Katz, "Rural Rebellions After 1810," 551; Katz, *Secret War in Mexico,* 39–40.

land reform or foreign capital, which was also not surprising, given his closeness to Stillman, U.S. railroad entrepreneurs, and powerful Texas bankers who had protected him during his struggle against Díaz (the Madero family's males and many of these American businessmen's sons had even been educated in the same classrooms at Culver Military Academy in Indiana). Standard Oil, scholars much later discovered, had probably offered Madero between $500,000 and $1 million to help overthrow Díaz. Furious at the absence of land reform that would return haciendas to the *campesinos,* Zapata and his officers issued the Plan of Ayala in November 1911. Joined by Orozco in the north, the Zapatistas pushed events to a new, more radical stage. As the revolt of rural and urban working classes spread, accompanied by growing violence, Madero found he had also lost the support of army officers who had remained loyal to Díaz. Strikes, fighting, land seizures erupted. Madero could do little, however, until he placed General Victoriano Huerta in charge of his army. Huerta stopped the Zapatistas, but came to realize that Madero was too weak to rule. The general also learned that Madero's failures had angered U.S. Ambassador Henry Lane Wilson, an experienced, deeply conservative diplomat whom Taft had brought in from the American post in Chile to deal with the spreading problems in Mexico. Wilson quickly disliked and mistrusted Madero for not being able to maintain peace and uphold property rights. American policy, diplomatic observers in Mexico City noted, turned against Madero for many reasons: his unwillingness to make a favorable reciprocity trade treaty with Washington; his willingness to move closer to Europeans and even encourage European immigration; his whipping up of Mexican nationalism, which, for sound historical reasons, was anti-Yankee; his legitimation of trade unions and strikes against U.S. firms; and his reluctance to give Standard Oil and U.S. railway representatives the concessions they thought they had paid for when they helped Madero gain power.[19]

On September 15, 1912, Wilson sent Madero a note that in tough language outlined Washington's grievances. It demanded the

19 Hart, *Revolutionary Mexico,* esp. 245–8; Bruchey, *Enterprise,* 389; Katz, *Secret War in Mexico,* 46–8.

capture and punishment of all those involved in murdering U.S. citizens (forty-seven of whom had been killed between 1910 and 1912), ordered that discriminations against U.S. property be stopped, and warned that the "lawlessness and chaos" must be halted immediately. The Mexican foreign minister denied the charges and demands. Given Wilson's intimacy with the Guggenheim mining interests, the Madero regime probably doubted the ambassador's detachment. In 1911, as the fighting had spread, Taft had placed twenty thousand troops on the border to protect property and lives inside the United States. Trying to defuse the crisis, the president dissembled by announcing that the troops were only on spring maneuvers. Given his record for using force in the Philippines, Cuba, and Nicaragua, this explanation could have been doubted, and the president found himself whiplashed between those who wanted the United States to keep its hands off Mexico and those who wanted dollars supplemented with bullets. He further tried to contain the revolt by imposing an arms embargo, but now offered to lift the embargo if Madero responded favorably to Wilson's September 15 demands.[20]

Madero had lost control of his "tiger" and the support of his giant neighbor. Taft was apparently moving toward Wilson's violent anti-Madero feelings. Knox disagreed; he mistrusted Wilson and did not want any U.S. military intervention, especially after the Taft administration was defeated in the 1912 presidential race and was a political lame duck. In February 1913 General Huerta made a deal with the ultraconservative nephew of Díaz, Felix Díaz, and turned against Madero. Felix Díaz and Wilson were so close that the German ambassador in Mexico City wired Berlin in February: "American ambassador working openly for Díaz, told Madero in my presence he was doing so because Díaz is pro-American." Huerta captured Madero, then asked Wilson what to do with the captive. Wilson was deeply involved; in his offices Huerta and Díaz had made the "Pact of the Embassy" to seal their new partnership. The ambassador told Huerta he must "do whatever you think best for the country." When

20 Taft to Williams, March 28, 1911, William Howard Taft Papers, Library of Congress, Washington, D.C., microfilm reel 365.95A.

Madero's wife pleaded for her husband's safety, Wilson replied he could not interfere in a "sovereign nation's" problems. On February 21, 1913, Huerta's men killed Madero and an associate. Immediately a pro-Madero revolt erupted in the north, led by Venustiano Carranza. Taft told Wilson that given the fluid situation, Huerta's inability to settle U.S. property claims quickly, the British refusal to recognize Madero's murderer, and his own lame-duck status, no recognition of the new president was to be granted. President-elect Woodrow Wilson would have to make that decision. Huerta lasted little more than a year; Woodrow Wilson's pressure, climaxing with the landing of U.S. forces at Vera Cruz in 1914, helped drive him from power. Ironically, Carranza then moved to take over the country and directly challenged U.S. oil holdings.[21]

As historian John Mason Hart has observed, the "basic antagonism" in 1911–12 "was between village communalists and agricultural workers on the one side and hacendados and foreign landowners in defense of their commercial holdings on the other." With their billion dollars of investments, U.S. citizens constituted most of those foreign landowners. They had first worked with Porfirio Díaz to transform Mexico from a largely self-sustaining nation based on a liberal 1857 constitution into a country with deepening class divisions that was dependent on exports and New York capital. (By 1912, the U.S. chargé d'affaires could bitterly complain of the "unintelligent demands of the proletariat.") When Díaz finally tried to offset the American commercial invasion, U.S. investors, led by some of the most powerful progenitors of the new Industrial Revolution, supported Madero's overthrow of the old dictator. But Díaz was doubly damned; his earlier long cooperation with Americans had aroused deep nationalist feelings that, especially after the 1907 panic, Madero could exploit. The 1910 outbreak, one close observer noted, "had a decidedly Boxer character . . . directed primarily against the . . . interests of the United States."[22] When Madero

---

21 Coletta, *Taft*, pp. 178–81; Alan Knight, *U.S.-Mexican Relations, 1910–1940* (San Diego, 1987), 57–78, is an important alternative view; Katz, *Secret War in Mexico*, 94–6, 103.

22 Quoted in Ruiz, *Triumphs and Tragedy*, pp. 301–2.

could neither control the rising tide of armed peasant and urban-labor protest, or bring powerful *Porfirioistas* to heel, Henry Lane Wilson worked with Huerta to overthrow the new president. Taft, to his credit, had withstood immense pressures and kept U.S. troops out of Mexico. But the post-1865 American quest for opportunity had helped establish the conditions in Mexico for a major twentieth-century social revolution, and then, to protect those opportunities, had accelerated the revolution. The well-informed German ambassador to Washington Count von Bernstorff placed the episode in historical context: Taft and Henry Lane Wilson pursued "the usual American policy of replacing hostile regimes with pliable ones through revolutions without taking official responsibility for it."[23]

China: The Door Closes, the Revolution Begins

Much the same process that produced revolution in Mexico produced upheavals in China, although in this more complex case the United States was but one of a half-dozen powers that had tried to exploit China economically and culturally. Again, U.S. officials found that the central government could not both meet foreign demands and protect national interests; that foreign economic encroachments and threats mobilized strong indigenous opposition; and that, finally, the opposition triggered a revolution, much more antiforeign in China than in Mexico, that turned into one of the historic shifts of the twentieth century.

American interests were minute when compared with, for example, those of Japan and Russia. The United States did have 3,100 Protestant missionaries in China (and only 3,770 in all, worldwide), but exports that had risen to $53 million in 1905 were dropping toward $24 million in 1912, and they amounted to only 1 percent of total U.S. export trade. Investments were in the $40 million to $50 million range, but again accounted for less than 2 percent of all U.S. overseas investments. Americans even suffered an unfavorable trade balance with China because they imported $30 million of goods in 1912. With Japan, on the other hand, Americans shipped

23 Quoted in Katz, *Secret War in Mexico,* 113.

$53 million in exports and took in $81 million in imports in 1912.
Obviously the Japan market was less mythical, but more profitable,
than the fabled China market. American officials, however, were
good cosmopolitans who were planning for the long term, not
shorter-sighted business types who cared about the ledger-book figures only at the end of each day, and for the long term they were
determined to find outlets that would prevent another era of horrors
comparable to the 1873–97 era. Knox and Taft also devoutly believed they were upholding a near-sacred principle in China. "This
administration," Knox announced, "inherited from its predecessors
the policy of the open door and maintenance of Chinese territorial
integrity." The key to upholding that principle, he believed, was to
ensure "the participation of American capital" in the "great Chinese
railway and other enterprises." Washington would then have the
necessary "voice" that "will go far toward guaranteeing the preservation of the administrative entity of China." But there was even more
at stake than the whole of the China market: "So long as the U.S.
holds the Philippines," Knox believed, "the domination of China by
other nations to our exclusion would be fraught with danger, and it
is unthinkable that this country should be squeezed out of any
combination [of powers] exercising an influence at Peking."[24]

American trade had thus not fulfilled its potential in China because, the secretary of state argued, the U.S. government had done
too little to shield it against the onslaughts of foreign powers who
carefully coordinated their private enterprise and governmental pressures. Such a view was, of course, a direct criticism of Roosevelt's
decision in 1907–8 not to confront the new Japanese-Russian division of the Manchurian railway system and Tokyo's takeover of Korea. It also signaled strong support for Willard Straight's faith that
with enough Kiplingesque courage and Sino-American cooperation,
the United States could help China check and drive back the imperialists and open the whole of Chinese markets to the more natural

---

24 Warren Cohen, *America's Response to China*, 2d ed. (New York, 1980), pp. 81–2;
    Akira Iriye, *Pacific Estrangement: Japanese and American Expansion, 1897–1911*
    (Cambridge, Mass., 1972), 123; the quotations are in A. Whitney Griswold,
    The Far Eastern Policy of the United States (New York, 1938), 144–5.

working of American efficiency. Since his firsthand observation of Japan's conquest of Korea in 1905, and the Japanese defeat of his Chinese plans of 1908 to check Tokyo's control of the South Manchurian Railroad, Straight had, as he said as early as 1904, found "myself hating the Japanese more than anything in the world." Racism again played a major role: "The Russians are white and that means much." Straight thus believed that, with rail magnate E. H. Harriman's riches and contacts in Russia, a deal could be developed to buy the Chinese Eastern Railroad in Manchuria that St. Petersburg controlled, use that as leverage to force Japan to sell the South Manchurian, and hence at once restore Chinese control and U.S. opportunity. Putting the plans together as the first chief of the new Division of Far Eastern Affairs in the State Department during 1908–9, Straight worked with Knox and New York bankers to prepare the offensive. Nor did he change course after Harriman suddenly died in 1909.[25]

Knox and Straight decided to play for it all, and they thought they had strong Chinese support. In reality, Straight's most important supporters, Yuan Shih-k'ai and T'ang Shao-yi, had lost power in 1909, although Chinese officials continued to hope they could use the Americans to counterbalance the Europeans and Japanese. Straight, believing he also had the support of British capital, returned to Asia in 1909 to plan how a U.S. banking group could build a trans-Manchurian railroad (the Chinchow-Aigun). China agreed with his proposal. In Washington, however, Knox decided to try to expand this foothold into a play for all Manchuria. His plan called for the neutralization or internationalization of all Manchurian railroads. The stunning proposal hinged on British cooperation, Russian willingness to sell the Chinese Eastern, Japan's consent to give up the South Manchurian, and the Chinese government's ability to hold its nation together against rising nationalism and intensified foreign pressures. All four of these assumptions promptly collapsed. The major British interest was India, not northern China, and London was willing to allow Japan to do much as it pleased in the latter area as long as Tokyo cooperated with British policies in

25 Michael Hunt, *Frontier Defense and the Open Door* (New Haven, 1972), 144–5.

the former region. The Russians, for their part, had no intention of selling the essential eastern end of the Trans-Siberian Railway system, especially if they could – as they did in 1910 – combine with Japan to confirm their joint division of Manchuria and shut out the irritating Americans. Knox's dream of checking Japan, in historian Warren Cohen's words, "like so many dreams . . . failed to survive the rising sun." On the same day (November 13, 1909), Knox proposed his plan, Japan approached Russia with the possibility of more formally dividing Manchuria. Their agreement was signed, ironically, on July 4, 1910. Determined "to forestall any arrangement between Russia and Japan," Knox instead had driven these former enemies closer together.[26]

But the collapse of Knox's and Straight's final assumption proved most important. Blocked from Manchuria, Taft pressured a European Consortium, formed to build railways in China, to admit U.S. capital. The Europeans objected because admitting the Americans would inevitably lead to Japan and Russia demanding entrance. Taft prevailed. So did the Russians and Japanese. The president now found himself as one of six allied foreign imperialists embarked upon building the Wuhan-Canton and Wuhan-Chengdu railways. Since the 1890s, and especially since the Boxers had shown the military importance of railways, a "rights-recovery" movement had grown to demand that only Chinese capital and engineers build the vital lines. The consortium's move, and the Qing's cooperation, triggered antiforeign protests in mid-1911 that quickly spread (especially in the Wuhan area), and received the support of highly nationalist officers of the reformed Chinese Army. Missionaries were again targeted; a mob murdered eight members of a British Baptist group in Hankow. The Qing court asked Yuan Shih-k'ai to leave his forced retirement and restore order. Taft and Straight were pleased. The president hoped the Manchus could survive, but Straight knew they were doomed. Both men greatly preferred the soldierly Yuan to the

26 Cohen, *America's Response to China*, 78–81; Paul A. Varg, *The Making of a Myth: The United States and China, 1897–1912* (East Lansing, Mich., 1968), 104; Straight's bitterness against Japan appears in Straight to J. P. Morgan & Co., February 11, 1912, Willard Straight Papers, Cornell University, Ithaca, N.Y.

rebels, for, as Straight told Wall Street friends, "if a Republic is established, there will be chaos, constant disturbance, and but little satisfactory business for the honest bankers unless the foreign powers actively intervene." Yuan at first replaced the Manchus by agreeing with the rebels to establish a republic. He then turned on the rebels and established his own personal rule.[27]

In 1912, the key leader of the reform movement, Sun Yat-sen, formed the Kuomintang (KMT). Knowing the United States well, and claiming that the KMT drew inspiration in part from American institutions, Sun directly asked for Washington's support. Taft and Knox were not interested. They mistrusted the KMT, liked the strong hand that Yuan wielded, and believed he could best protect U.S. and other foreign claims in China. The two U.S. officials, in the spirit of William Seward, also wanted to present a solid front with the other powers to protect foreign claims, as well as to prevent the Chinese from playing their traditional policy of countering foreigner with foreigner. The powers sided with the authoritarian Yuan. President Woodrow Wilson remained with Yuan. After the dictator's death in 1916, U.S. officials watched as the KMT took China into its post-1919 revolution. To Taft, Knox, and Wilson, Yuan seemed a good choice to serve some of the same functions as the new U.S. presidency served in the Caribbean, Mexico, and Central America: After Western and Japanese capital acted as a catalyst for Chinese nationalism and antiforeign outbreaks, Yuan was to restore order and preserve such foreign claims as the Open Door.[28]

The alternative to the Taft-Knox policy was noted by Roosevelt in a letter to Taft in late 1910. Roosevelt, resembling most westerners, had little sense of how the foreign pressures were accelerating the disintegration of the already undermined Qing, and how the powers' constant intervention provided a focal point for the antiforeign protests of the rights-recovery movement and other nationalists. He had, however, learned the hard way about Japan, and he told Taft

---

27 Jonathan Spence, *The Search for Modern China* (New York, 1990), 251–66; Daniel M. Crane and Thomas A. Breslin, *An Ordinary Relationship: American Opposition to Republican Revolution in China* (Miami, Fla., 1986), 38–51, esp. 49.

28 Crane and Breslin, *An Ordinary Relationship*, 160–2.

that Manchuria and Korea were vital interests of the Japanese. "We cannot interfere in those areas unless we have an army as good as Germany's or a navy as good as Britain's. The Open Door policy in China was [*sic*] an excellent thing," but it "completely disappears as soon as a powerful nation determines to disregard it." Roosevelt was willing to allow the Japanese to have the run of Manchuria in return for controlling their troublesome emigration to California and Canada. Taft and Knox rejected this alternative view. They were concerned about Chinese territorial integrity, but – as their neutralization plan and demands on the consortium vividly demonstrated – they also demanded expanded American opportunities in the vast China market. In China, Straight candidly admitted to his employers at J. P. Morgan that "the Apple Cart received a blow in the solar plexus" when the rebels brought down the Manchus, and he had not seen it coming. He nevertheless assured Morgan that Yuan's victory was welcome because his group favored "the development of China by foreign capital." Old dreams died hard. As U.S. officials had been discovering for a generation, Taft, Knox, and Straight could not have both opportunity and order in China. Along with the other five imperial powers, they helped create the disorder and xenophobia of early revolutionary China.[29]

Roosevelt was perhaps more pleased with one footnote to Taft's policies. Although the pogroms had largely stopped by 1906, Russia continued to refuse to recognize the U.S. passports of Jews, Roman Catholic priests, and Protestant ministers. Led by Jacob Schiff of Kuhn, Loeb, demands grew that Taft retaliate by abrogating the 1832 treaty regulating U.S.-Russian trade. The president, as usual, moved slowly, but the House of Representatives, with only one dissenting vote, resolved to end the pact. Taft then informed St. Petersburg that the treaty had to be terminated, although he hoped a new agreement would replace it. The two governments never wrote such an agreement, and American-Russian relations continued their long, post-1867 decline.

---

29 Walter V. Scholes and Marie Scholes, *The Foreign Policies of the Taft Administration* (Columbia, Mo., 1970), 121–2; Straight to Harry P. Davison, October 28, 1911, Straight Papers.

The Taft-Knox experiences in China aptly climaxed the major thematic developments of U.S. policy during the 1865–1913 era. Uninterested in more territory, and believing they had the best interests of foreign peoples at heart, Americans tried to separate themselves from the European and Japanese imperial objectives. But with their determination to protect present opportunities and to create new ones, they used U.S. power extensively. At times, as in China and Canada, Taft exercised exclusively economic and political power. In other instances, as in Nicaragua and Mexico, U.S. officials found that dollars and bullets went together.

The Taft administration's foreign policies are of major significance in U.S. diplomatic history – although they have not received a treatment full scale in both detail and context that they deserve – because they so perfectly illustrate the quest for overseas markets that were needed to deal with the requirements of the Second Industrial Revolution (or post–Darwinian missionary enterprises), and how that quest led to disorder and even revolution. Known in the pages of American history as a near-classic U.S. conservative, especially for his non-Rooseveltian conception of presidential powers and his near-religious veneration of the law, Taft nevertheless followed out the logic of American post–Civil War expansion to find that he had become involved in a dollar diplomacy that developed not orderly societies but nationalist revolutions. Croly demanded a modern Hamiltonian system at home to spread Jeffersonian democracy and American economic successes abroad. Taft instead had to work with a new industrial society whose policies helped produce the dangerous nationalisms and "revolutionary upheavals" that Croly most feared.

Conclusion: The 1865–1913 Era Restated

The historiography of 1865–1913 has been heavily influenced by the belief that Americans sought order and stability, acted as an antirevolutionary force, and – notably for some who were undergoing supposed "psychic crises" – searched for a return to supposedly more settled, precorporate times. The influential work of Richard Hofstadter, Robert Wiebe, and biographers of Theodore Roosevelt (especially John Morton Blum and Howard K. Beale) have made the argument for writing the history with some, if not all, of these characteristics.[1]

Such themes may have characterized important parts of the domestic society and policy in the Gilded Age and early Progressive Era. They had little to do with foreign affairs. Nor do they characterize the officials who made overseas policy. The central theme of post-1865 U.S. history is that the nation developed into a great world power, one of the four greatest militarily and the greatest of all economically. These years ushered in the American Century. At the same time, however, major revolts occurred across much of the globe – in Russia, China, Mexico, Cuba, Nicaragua, the Philippines, Panama, El Salvador, and Hawaii, among other places. The rise of the United States to the status of great world power was not dissociated from the causes of these revolutions. American policy played some role in all of these outbreaks, and in most it was a determinative force.

---

1 Richard Hofstadter, "Cuba, the Philippines, and Manifest Destiny," in *The Paranoid Style in American Politics and Other Essays* (New York, 1965); Richard Hofstadter, *The Age of Reform* (New York, 1955); Robert Wiebe, *The Search for Order, 1877–1920* (New York, 1967); John M. Blum, *The Republican Roosevelt* (Cambridge, Mass., 1954); Howard K. Beale, *Theodore Roosevelt and the Rise of America to World Power* (Baltimore, 1956). Richard H. Collin, *Theodore Roosevelt's Caribbean* (Baton Rouge, 1990), is a more recent, but similar, interpretation.

The links that join the emergence of American global power and these upheavals are the Second Industrial Revolution, which accelerated after the Civil War, and a racism that was deeply rooted historically. The racism was so pervasive and many-sided that both imperialists and antiimperialists could reflect it. Driven by these two complementary forces, Americans set out on a quest for opportunities that destroyed order in many of the areas they targeted. The pattern can be outlined: The pursuit of opportunity by modern business groups and missionaries changed indigenous economic systems and cultures; as these economic and cultural changes evolved, so did political changes until the indigenous people split into pro-U.S. (or *comprador*) groups or dissenters. Those who rebelled against the status quo could come from both groups: In Hawaii and El Salvador, for example, they were pro–United States; in the Philippines, China, and Cuba they violently dissented from Washington's policy. A third set of revolutions was also generated. This set, exemplified by the Nicaraguan, Panamanian, and even, at the beginning, the Cuban upheaval, was caused either by the United States directly starting the revolt or warmly encouraging it.

To argue, as some scholars have, that U.S. officials had special sympathy for indigenous nationalists, especially those who opposed European imperialism, is not the essential point. In Cuba, for example, William McKinley was ruthless in destroying the indigenous nationalist movement, as he was again in the Philippines. In China, U.S. officials worked with Chinese leaders only as long as it appeared that the Chinese could help maintain an Open Door against European and Japanese attempts to shut that door through colonization and the establishment of protectorates; when in 1910–12 this Open Door tactic was failing, the United States did not hesitate to force its way into the European Consortium.

Several common threads ran through these episodes. One was the American determination to expand marketplace control and, in some instances (such as China and Hawaii), missionary influence. A second was the appearance of a strong presidency – equipped with the power and communications of the new industrial revolution and self-blessed by its manipulation of the Constitution's commander-in-chief provision – that was needed in nearly every revolutionary outbreak. A new presidency was required either to avoid the trap of involvement (as Fish and Cleveland avoided direct intervention in Cuba during the 1870s and 1890s, respectively) or – considerably more important – to confront the danger or reality of revolution directly and preserve American opportunity through the use of military force if necessary. Woodrow Wilson observed in lectures he gave in 1908, while president of Princeton, that "The war with Spain . . . changed the balance of parts" in the nation's governmental institutions. "Foreign questions became leading questions again, as they had been in the first days of the government, and in them the President was of necessity leader."[2] A stronger executive, however, had been developing in foreign policy since presidential powers reached their nadir during the days of Andrew Johnson. After 1869 the growth of those powers at the expense of Congress (and, at times, of the Constitution) was certainly not linear, but neither was it characterized, nor can it be explained, by cyclical theories of American history. Fish, Evarts, Frelinghuysen, Cleveland, Blaine, Tracy, Harrison, and Gresham set precedents, made treaties, and rammed through Congress legislation that by the mid-1890s had extended the American reach to East Asia, Brazil, Samoa, and West Africa, as well as to Hawaii and the Caribbean–Central American region. Such leading imperialists as Alfred Thayer Mahan understood that for their purposes even more executive authority was needed. In 1897, Mahan complained that "any project of extending the sphere of the United States, by annexation or otherwise, is met by the constitutional lion in the path."[3] To Mahan's satisfaction, McKinley, Roosevelt, and Taft went far in removing the "lion," but the animal had been considerably weakened well before 1897.

These last three presidents of the era had little choice about how to deal with the "lion" given the pressures and logic of American expansion. This expansion grew in large part out of the industrial successes and resulting social and political chaos of the post-1873 series of depressions that lasted until 1897. In this weak, highly

2 Woodrow Wilson, *Constitutional Government* (New York, 1908), 58–9, 78–80.
3 Alfred Thayer Mahan, *The Interest of America in Sea Power, Present and Future* (Boston, 1897), 256–7.

pluralistic state, order was largely restored by executives who used federal forces and state militias, presidents and producers who found solutions in foreign markets, and a new political party alignment after 1894 that helped pacify the system and insulate the corporate and political leadership. The expansion abroad, however, then produced more disorder, and presidents used all the powers they could muster either to exploit the disorder (as in Cuba, Panama, and Nicaragua) or to try to crush it (as in the Philippines, China during 1900, or Santo Domingo). Only in rare instances, such as the Congo in 1884 or the Chinese rights-recovery movement's climax in 1911–12, did the United States tend to back away, and in the instance of China, the retreat was actually a switch to new tactics. The roots of twentieth-century presidential power thus grew between the 1880s and 1913 precisely because so much disorder was produced by U.S. economic and foreign policy, because order was not assumed to be necessarily normal or natural, and because exploiting or – if desired – stopping the disorder required the military force that Mahan, Tracy, McKinley, Roosevelt, and Taft, among many others, espoused. As commander in chief, the president controlled the use of that force.

The presidency was a unique institution among world powers. Nothing in European or Japanese governments resembled it. Nor did U.S. expansion closely resemble European and Japanese expansionism during these years. The United States did not want to become part of a European system or to copy, say, British or German or Japanese imperialism. Ever since 1776, Americans had dedicated themselves to establishing their own system that was adapted to their own evolving needs. That they competed with Europeans for world power was true. That they ultimately proved to be as vulnerable to the demands, even corruptions, of world power as the Europeans and Japanese also was true. That they appeared, with good reason, to Filipinos, Cubans, Chinese, and Central Americans as little different than other imperialists was true as well. Unlike the other major powers, however, the United States had a continent to populate and exploit; it did not desire colonies for surplus population or vast protectorates for raw materials, or (as in the case of Russia) extensive areas that served as passageways to vital new ports for the building of crucial transportation networks. Such characteristics of U.S. expansionism were buttressed by the concern, shared by imperialists and antiimperialists alike, that the Constitution's provisions could not stretch long distances across water, or over non–Anglo-Saxon peoples, without collapsing. Expansionists such as Roosevelt and Lodge indeed believed that the United States could control Puerto Rico or the Philippines not by extending constitutional protection but by giving Congress the power to pick and choose among the document's provisions (as in the case of Puerto Rico) or to treat the newly conquered people as the U.S. government had treated native Americans – by killing or effectively isolating them.

The United States did not want to join the European and Japanese quest for landed, colonial empire. American officials wanted only scattered, relatively small areas of land to serve as bases for their necessary commercial expansionism. Nor did the United States copy the Europeans, or use European or Japanese criteria, in building and measuring their industrial successes. Andrew Carnegie and John D. Rockefeller, among many others, as historian Alfred Chandler has shown, exemplified the leaders of an American complex who were well ahead of their overseas competitors in innovation and systematizing. They also differed significantly from those competitors in terms of their relations with their own government and, especially in the case of Carnegie, in the kind of foreign policy they demanded from national officials.[4]

The 1865–1913 era thus served in substance, as well as in chronology, to establish the conditions for Woodrow Wilson's so-called new diplomacy that has shaped much of international relations, and especially U.S. foreign policy, in the twentieth century. American policy to 1913 shared with Wilson's the dynamic of the successful Second Industrial Revolution; an enormous, complementary home base that included the Caribbean and Central America and that

4 Alfred D. Chandler, Jr., with the assistance of Takashi Hikino, *Scale and Scope: The Dynamics of Industrial Capitalism* (Cambridge, Mass., 1990); some of these problems are dealt with in the 1865–1913 context in Tony Smith, *The Pattern of Imperialism* (Cambridge, 1981), esp. 1–5, 141–6, and in Michael W. Doyle, *Empires* (Ithaca, 1986), esp. 19–47.

could easily be secured by unilateral military force whenever necessary; assurances of cultural, especially racial superiority; a preference for going it alone (otherwise known as isolationism), with only informal political and personal links to those, such as the Japanese or British, who seemed at times to share major American values; a belief in a necessary, but beneficent, presidency to steer foreign policies; the understanding that the presidency sat atop a new set of government institutions that formed a "promotional state" to push and protect all-important economic policies;[5] and – as a logical climax – the fervent belief that, because the United States had shown its undoubted ability to compete, and had done so without old-style European colonial ties or alliances, the new world order was to be economically open (except, of course, in certain Caribbean areas and the Philippines).

The United States, it has been said, was the first twentieth-century nation. The century has been shaped by scientific innovation, rationalized and globalized industrial processes, multinational corporations, centralized political authorities built on modern communications, military interventionism, fervent nationalism, deadly racism, and – of considerable significance – revolution. During the 1865–1913 years, all of these could be found in U.S. foreign policy. And all were closely related in that policy.

5 Emily Rosenberg, *Spreading the American Dream: American Economic and Cultural Expansion, 1890–1945* (New York, 1982), 57–9.

Bibliographic Essay

Richard Dean Burns, *Guide to American Foreign Relations Since 1700* (Santa Barbara, Calif., 1983), supersedes all other bibliography on pre-1981 materials. See also Gerald K. Haines and J. Samuel Walker, eds., *American Foreign Relations: A Historiographical Review* (Westport, Conn., 1981); Robert L. Beisner, *From the Old Diplomacy to the New, 1865–1900*, 2d ed. (Arlington Heights, Ill., 1986), with a superb bibliography; and the footnotes of this book.

Important overviews of the 1865–1900 years include Nell Irvin Painter, *Standing at Armageddon: The United States 1877–1919* (New York, 1987); Eric Hobsbawm, *The Age of Empire* (New York, 1987), surprisingly weak on the United States; Akira Iriye, *From Nationalism to Internationalism: U.S. Foreign Policy to 1914* (London, 1977), an important synthesis; Charles S. Campbell, *The Transformation of American Foreign Relations, 1865–1900* (New York, 1976), the most detailed account, with a detailed bibliography as well; Beisner, *From the Old Diplomacy to the New*, noted already; Dexter Perkins, *The Monroe Doctrine, 1867–1907* (Baltimore, 1937), still a classic; Tennant S. McWilliams, *The New South Faces the World* (Baton Rouge, 1988), especially on the 1880s–1890s; Hans Ulrich Wehler, *Der Aufstiegdes amerikanischen Imperialismus . . . 1865–1900* (Göttingen, 1974), important on the classes that produced imperial policies; Jean Cazemajou, *American Expansionism and Foreign Policy, 1885–1908* (Paris, 1988), a key French scholar's interpretation, especially good on the social implications; Howard B. Schonberger, *Transportation to the Seaboard; The Communication Revolution and American Foreign Policy, 1860–1900* (Westport, Conn., 1971), linking the transport revolution and expansionism; Emily S. Rosenberg, *Spreading the American Dream: American Economic and Cultural Expansion, 1890–1945* (New York, 1982), a pioneering examination of the governmental-cultural interaction; Milton Plesur, *America's Outward*

Thrust . . . 1865–1890 (DeKalb, Ill., 1971), good on cultural as well as political expansion; David Healy, *U.S. Expansionism* (Madison, 1970), lively reading by an important scholar of the era; John M. Dobson, *America's Ascent . . . 1880–1914* (DeKalb, Ill., 1978), good on the spreading-of-democracy ideal; William H. Becker and Samuel F. Wells, Jr., *Economics and World Power* (New York, 1984), essays by respected scholars, with David M. Pletcher's analysis of the late nineteenth century especially important; Philip Darby, *Three Faces of Imperialism: British and American Approaches to Asia and Africa, 1870–1970* (New Haven, 1987), a useful comparative study; two quite different and important books by Ernest R. May, *Imperial Democracy* (1961; reprint, New York, 1991), and *American Imperialism: A Speculative Essay* (New York, 1968); William Appleman Williams, *The Roots of the Modern American Empire* (New York, 1969), a magisterial account that builds on the agricultural sector; Walter LaFeber, *The New Empire* (New York, 1963), which stresses the 1873–97 depression and U.S.-Latin American relations; Edward P. Crapol, *America for Americans* (Westport, Conn., 1973), an innovative look at anglophobia and U.S. economic expansion; Michael H. Hunt, *Ideology and U.S. Foreign Policy* (New Haven, 1987), especially its view of race in the 1880–1910 era; W. Stull Holt, *Treaties Defeated by the Senate* (Baltimore, 1933), still standard on the subject.

For broader studies of imperialism, start with two works by Wolfgang J. Mommsen, *Theories of Imperialism,* trans. P. S. Falla (New York, 1980); and Mommsen and Jurgen Osterhammel, eds., *Imperialism and After* (Boston, 1986); Carl Parrini, "Theories of Imperialism," in Lloyd Gardner, ed., *Redefining the Past: Essays in Diplomatic History in Honor of William Appleman Williams* (Corvallis, Oreg., 1986), especially for the 1890–1905 theorists; Tony Smith, *The Pattern of Imperialism* (New York, 1982), a comparative study, as is Michael W. Doyle, *Empires* (Ithaca, 1986); Richard Koebner, *Empire* (New York, 1961), a classic study; Robert B. Zevin, "An Interpretation of American Imperialism," *Journal of Economic History* 32 (1972): 316–60.

For post–Civil War diplomacy and the takeoff of the U.S. economic system into the early twentieth century, important accounts include Ernest N. Paolino, *The Foundations of American Empire: William Henry Seward and U.S. Foreign Policy* (Ithaca, 1973); John M. Taylor, *William Henry Seward* (New York, 1992); Eric Foner, *Reconstruction: America's Unfinished Revolution, 1863–1877* (New York, 1988); Adrian Cook, *The Alabama Claims* (Ithaca, 1975); Paul Holbo, *Tarnished Expansion: The Alaska Scandal, the Press, and Congress, 1867–1871* (Knoxville, 1983); Alfred D. Chandler, *Scale and Scope* (Cambridge, Mass., 1990), pivotal; Stuart Bruchey, *Enterprise* (Cambridge, Mass., 1989), excellent on economics, questionable on the foreign policy; Mira Wilkins, *The Emergence of the Multinational Enterprise* (Cambridge, Mass., 1970), especially for the 1880s; Robert B. Davies, *Peacefully Working to Conquer the World: Singer Sewing Machines . . . 1854–1920* (New York, 1976), good case study; Mira Wilkins, *The History of Foreign Investment in the United States to 1914* (Cambridge, 1989); Joseph F. Wall, *Andrew Carnegie* (New York, 1970), a model biography; Ron Chernow, *The House of Morgan* (New York, 1990), prize-winning; Martin J. Sklar, *The Corporate Reconstruction of American Capitalism, 1890–1916* (New York, 1988), a superb analysis of the law and capitalist development; William H. Becker, *The Dynamics of Business-Government Relations* (Chicago, 1982), on smaller firms; Patrick J. Hearden, *Independence and Empire* (DeKalb, Ill., 1982), crucial on textile industry and overseas expansion; Tom E. Terrill, *The Tariff, Politics, and American Foreign Policy, 1874–1901* (Westport, Conn., 1973), an important overview; T. Jackson Lears, *No Place of Grace: Antimodernism and the Transformation of American Culture, 1880–1920* (New York, 1981), excellent on the cultural ramifications of the economic turn; Robert W. Rydell, *All the World's a Fair: Visions of Empire at American International Expositions, 1876–1916* (New York, 1985), pioneering; as is James Gilbert, *Perfect Cities* (Chicago, 1991).

On issues of race and social Darwinism, begin with George Fredrickson, *The Black Image in the White Mind, 1817–1914* (New York, 1971); Paul Gordon Lauren, *Power and Prejudice* (Boulder, Colo., 1988); Walter L. Williams, "U.S. Indian Policy and the Debate over Philippine Annexation," *Journal of American History* 66 (1980): 810–31, of signal importance; Robert Wooster, *The Military and U.S. Indian Policy, 1865–1903* (New York, 1988), on the split between military and federal authorities; Robert M. Utley, *Cavalier in Buckskin* (Norman, Okla., 1988), on Custer by a leading historian of the West; Donald C. Bellomy, "Social Darwinism Revisited," *Perspectives in American History*, n.s., 1 (1984): 1–129; and Cynthia Russett, *Darwin in America: The Intellectual Response, 1865–1912* (San Francisco, 1976), now a standard on the Darwinian impact.

Important recent studies on major figures, 1869–96, include William S. McFeeley, *Grant* (New York, 1981); Clifford W. Haury, "Hamilton Fish . . .," in Norman Graebner, ed., *Studies in American Diplomacy, 1865–1945* (Lanham, Md., 1985); David M. Pletcher, *The Awkward Years* (Columbia, Mo., 1962), the place to begin on the 1880s; Justus D. Doenecke, *The Presidencies of James A. Garfield and Chester A. Arthur* (Lawrence, Kan., 1981); Richard E. Welch, Jr., *The Presidencies of Grover Cleveland* (Lawrence, Kan., 1988); Michael J. Devine, *John W. Foster: Politics and Diplomacy in the Imperial Era, 1873–1917* (Athens, Ohio, 1981); H. E. Socolofsky and Allan B. Spetter, *The Presidency of Benjamin Harrison* (Lawrence, Kan., 1987); Alice F. Tyler, *The Foreign Policy of James G. Blaine* (Minneapolis, 1927), still a standard account, although R. Hal Williams is writing a new biography; Charles W. Calhoun, *Gilded Age Cato*, on Walter Quintin Gresham (Lexington, Ky., 1988); Frederick C. Drake, *The Empire of the Seas* (Honolulu, 1984), an important biography of Admiral Robert W. Shufeldt and his attempts to "open" Africa and Korea; Joseph Fry, *Henry S. Sanford* (Reno, 1982), who was at the intersect of business and foreign policy; Henry E. Mattox, *The Twilight of Amateur Diplomacy* (Kent, Ohio, 1989), on the turn in the U.S. Foreign Service in the 1890s.

For Pacific expansion before 1898, starting points are Ralph S. Kuykendall, *The Hawaiian Kingdom*, 3 vols. (Honolulu, 1938–67); Gary Y. Okihiro, *Cane Fires: The Anti-Japanese Movement in Hawaii, 1865–1945* (Philadelphia, 1991); Thomas J. Osborne, *Empire Can Wait: American Opposition to Hawaiian Annexation, 1893–1898* (Kent, Ohio, 1981); Paul M. Kennedy, *The Samoan Tangle: A Study in Anglo-German-American Relations, 1878–1900* (New York, 1974); George H. Ryden, *The Foreign Policy of the United States in Relation to Samoa* (New Haven, 1933); Thomas McCormick, *China Market* (Chicago, 1967); Arthur Power Dudden, *The American Pacific: From the Old China Trade to the Present* (New York, 1992), highly readable.

For Latin America before 1898, important accounts include Perkins, *The Monroe Doctrine, 1867–1907*, noted previously; Lester D. Langley, *Struggle for the American Mediterranean: U.S.-European Rivalry in the Gulf-Caribbean, 1776–1904* (Athens, Ga., 1976); Thomas Schoonover, "Metropole Rivalry in Central America, 1820s to 1929: An Overview," in Ralph L. Woodward, ed., *Central America* (Westport, Conn., 1988); Thomas Schoonover, *The United States in Central America, 1860–1911* (Durham, N.C., 1991), a major contribution; Richard H. Bradford, *The Virginius Affair* (Boulder, Colo., 1980); Joyce S. Goldberg, *The Baltimore Affair* (Lincoln, Neb., 1986), now standard; William F. Sater, *Chile and the United States* (Athens, Ga., 1990), on the historical context; Craig L. Dozier, *Nicaragua's Mosquito Shore* (Tuscaloosa, Ala., 1985), an exemplary case study of Anglo-American competition; J. Valerie Fifer, *U.S. Perceptions of Latin America* (Manchester, 1991), on the "New West" theme; Joseph Smith, *Unequal Giants, Diplomatic Relations Between the U.S. and Brazil, 1889–1930* (Pittsburgh, 1991), important on the pivotal U.S.-Latin American relationship; Achille Viallate, "Les États Unis et le Pan Américanisme," *Revue des Deux Mondes* 51 (1909): 419–45, for a contemporary view noting Blaine's importance.

On U.S.-Canada relations, Lawrence Martin, *The Presidents and the Prime Ministers . . . 1867–1982* (Toronto, 1982), is delightful; Robert Craig Brown, *Canada's National Policy, 1883–1900* (Princeton, 1964); Donald F. Warner, *The Idea of Continental Union . . . 1849–1893* (Lexington, Ky., 1960); James T. Gay, *American Fur Seal Diplomacy* (New York, 1987); and R. A. Shields, "Imperial Policy and Canadian-American Commercial Relations, 1880–1911," *Bulletin of the Institute of Historical Research* 59 (1986): 108–21.

For U.S.-Africa, start with Peter Duignan and L. H. Gann, *The United States and Africa: A History* (Cambridge, 1984); Clarence Clendenen, Robert Collins, and Peter Duignan, *Americans in Africa, 1865–1890* (Palo Alto, Calif., 1966); Stig Förster, Wolfgang J. Mommsen, and Ronald Robinson, eds., *Bismarck, Europe, and Africa: The Berlin Conference 1884–1885 . . .* (London, 1988); Thomas J. Noer, *Briton, Boer and Yankee: The U.S. and South Africa, 1870–1914* (Kent, Ohio, 1978); John Hope Franklin, *George Washington Williams* (Chicago, 1985), an important biography that has the

Congo episode as a turning point; Sylvia M. Jacobs, *The African Nexus: Black American Perspectives on the European Partitioning of Africa, 1880–1920* (Westport, Conn., 1981).

For the U.S. military buildup, places to start include Russell F. Weigley, *History of the U.S. Army,* enlarged ed. (Bloomington, Ind., 1984); Carol Ann Reardon, *Soldiers and Scholars: The U.S. Army and the Uses of Military History, 1865–1920* (Lawrence, Kan., 1990), a different, useful perspective; Kenneth J. Hagan, *This People's Navy: The Making of American Sea Power* (New York, 1991); and Hagan's important *American Gunboat Diplomacy and the Old Navy, 1877–1889* (Westport, Conn., 1973); David F. Long, *Gold Braid and Foreign Relations: Diplomatic Activities of U.S. Naval Officers, 1798–1883* (Annapolis, 1988); B. Franklin Cooling, *Gray Steel and Blue Water Navy: The Formative Years of America's Military-Industrial Complex, 1881–1917* (Hamden, Conn., 1979), a striking study; for Mahan, the basic source is Alfred T. Mahan, *Letters and Papers of Alfred Thayer Mahan,* 3 vols., ed. Robert Seager II and Doris D. Maguire (Annapolis, 1975).

For the British policy context in the late nineteenth century, crucial works include Paul Kennedy, *The Realities Behind Diplomacy: Background Influences on British External Policy, 1865–1980* (London, 1981); Aaron L. Friedberg, *The Weary Titan: Britain and the Experience of Relative Decline, 1895–1905* (Princeton, 1988); John A. S. Grenville, *Lord Salisbury and Foreign Policy: The Close of the Nineteenth-Century* (London, 1964); James L. Garvin, *The Life of Joseph Chamberlain,* 3 vols. (London, 1932–4), a pivotal figure on British tariff and United States policies.

U.S.-Cuban relations, especially in the 1895–1906 years, can be found in two books by Jules R. Benjamin: *The United States and Cuba: Hegemony and Dependent Development, 1880–1934* (Pittsburgh, 1977), and *The United States and the Origins of the Cuban Revolution* (Princeton, 1990); Louis A. Pérez, Jr., *Cuba Between Empires, 1878–1902* (Pittsburgh, 1983), especially good on Cuba's internal changes; Louis A. Pérez, Jr., *Cuba Under the Platt Amendment, 1902–1934* (Pittsburgh, 1986); Philip S. Foner, *The Spanish-Cuban-American War and the Birth of American Imperialism, 1895–1902,* 2 vols. (New York, 1972); Francisco Lopez Segrera, *Cuba: capitalismo*

dependiente y subdesarrollo (1510–1959) (Havana, 1972), a contemporary Cuban view; David Healy, *The U.S. in Cuba, 1898–1902* (Madison, 1963), the standard for U.S. policy; Gerald E. Poyo, *With All
and for the Good of All . . .* (Durham, N.C., 1989), on Cuban nationalism developing in the United States; Roland I. Perusse, *The
United States and Puerto Rico* (Melbourne, Fla., 1990).

For the 1898 war and ensuing debate, begin with Anne Cipriano
Venzon, *The Spanish-American War: An Annotated Bibliography* (New
York, 1990); David F. Trask, *The War with Spain in 1898* (New
York, 1981), the best one-volume history; H. Wayne Morgan, *Amer-
ica's Road to Empire* (New York, 1965), by an authority on the 1890s;
John Dobson, *Reticent Expansionism* (Pittsburgh, 1988), a good syn-
thesis on McKinley; Gerald F. Linderman, *The Mirror of War: Ameri-
can Society and the Spanish-American War* (Ann Arbor, 1974); Anne
Hummell Sherrill and Howard I. Kushner, *John Milton Hay* (New
York, 1977), a good, brief biography with documents; Göran
Rysted, *Ambiguous Imperialism* (Lund, Sweden, 1975), especially
good on domestic politics; Robert L. Beisner, *Twelve Against Empire:
The Anti-Imperialists, 1898–1900* (1968; reprint, New York, 1985,
with new preface), the best monographic treatment of the debate;
Fred Harvey Harrington, "The Anti-Imperialist Movement in the
United States, 1898–1900," *Mississippi Valley Historical Review*
22 (1935): 211–30, the pioneering essay; Philip S. Foner and
Richard C. Winchester, eds., *Anti-imperialist Reader: A Documentary
History of Anti-imperialism in the United States, Volume I: From the
Mexican War to the Election of 1900* (New York, 1984), key primary
sources; James E. Kerr, *The Insular Cases* (Port Washington, N.Y.,
1982), on the critical court decisions; Raymond Carr, *Spain, 1808–
1975* (Oxford, 1982), important for Spain's diplomacy, as is John L.
Offner, *An Unwanted War* (Chapel Hill, 1992).

For the Philippines, Glenn Anthony May's work is pivotal, for ex-
ample, *A Past Recovered* (Quezon City, Philippines, 1987); Kenton J.
Clymer, *Protestant Missionaries in the Philippines* (New York, 1986);
Daniel Schirmer and Stephen Shalom, eds., *The Philippines Reader*
(Boston, 1987); Russell Roth, *Muddy Glory: America's "Indian Wars"
in the Philippines, 1899–1935* (West Hanover, Mass., 1981); Stuart
Creighton Miller, *"Benevolent Assimilation": The American Conquest of*

the Philippines, 1899–1903 (New York, 1982), which especially stresses racism; Brian M. Linn, *The U.S. Army and Counterinsurgency in the Philippine War, 1899–1902* (Chapel Hill, 1989); David H. Bain, *Sitting in Darkness: Americans in the Philippines* (Boston, 1984), especially important for its historical perspective.

For general works on the late 1890s to 1913 era, important accounts include Bradford Perkins, *The Great Rapprochement: England and the United States, 1895–1914* (New York, 1968), the standard on the crucial U.S.-British relationship; Joseph A. Fry, "In Search of an Orderly World: U.S. Imperialism, 1898–1912," in John M. Carroll and George C. Herring, eds., *Modern American Diplomacy* (Wilmington, Del., 1986); Stuart Anderson, *Race and Rapprochement: Anglo-Saxonism and Anglo-American Relations, 1895–1904* (Rutherford, N.J., 1981); Manfred Jonas, *The United States and Germany* (Ithaca, 1984), a good overview. Fritz Blaich, *Amerikanische Firmen in Deutschland, 1890–1914* (Wiesbaden, 1984); Otto Zu Stolberg-Wernigerode, *Germany and the United States During the Era of Bismarck* (Reading, Pa., 1937); and Alfred Vagts, *Deutschland und die Vereinigten Staaten in der Weltpolitik,* 2 vols. (New York, 1935), are three important German accounts, with Stolberg-Wernigerode examining the earlier years. Henry Blumenthal, *Illusion and Reality in Franco-American Diplomacy, 1914–1945* (Baton Rouge, 1986), standard; Charles W. Brooks, *America in France's Hopes and Fears* (New York, 1987), a two-volume pioneering work; Robert C. Hilderbrand, *Power and the People: Executive Management of Public Opinion in Foreign Affairs, 1897–1921* (Chapel Hill, 1981), an innovative and important approach; Calvin Davis, *The United States and the Second Hague Peace Conference . . . 1899–1914* (Durham, N.C., 1976); Warren F. Kuehl, *Seeking World Order: U.S. and International Organizations to 1920* (Nashville, 1969), the important overview; Charles DeBenedetti, *The Peace Reform in American History* (Bloomington, Ind., 1985); Charles DeBenedetti, ed., *Peace Heroes in Twentieth-Century America* (Bloomington, Ind., 1986); Sondra R. Herman, *Eleven Against War: Studies in American Internationalist Thought, 1908–1921* (Stanford, 1969); Sybil Oldfield, *Women Against the Iron Fist: Alternatives to Militarism, 1900–1989* (Oxford, 1989); Judith Papachristou, "American Women and Foreign Policy, 1898–

1905: Exploring Gender in Diplomatic History," *Diplomatic History* 14 (1990): 493–509, important as a prototypical study for later research; Joel Silbey, ed., *To Advise and Consent: U.S. Congress and Foreign Policy in the Twentieth Century*, 2 vols. (New York, 1991), with twenty-eight key articles.

For major figures, 1901–13, the following are important: Raymond A. Esthus, *Theodore Roosevelt and International Rivalries* (Waltham, Mass., 1970); Richard H. Collin, *Theodore Roosevelt's Caribbean* (Baton Rouge, 1990), a highly detailed emphasis on the "context" of TR's diplomacy; Richard H. Collin, *Theodore Roosevelt, Culture, Diplomacy, and Expansion* (Baton Rouge, 1985); Serge Ricard, *Theodore Roosevelt et la justification de l'impérialisme* (Aix-en-Provence, 1986), more critical than Collin; Frederick Marks III, *Velvet on Iron* (Lincoln, Neb., 1979), an interesting interpretation of the diplomacy; David H. Burton, *Theodore Roosevelt: Confident Imperialist* (Philadelphia, 1968); Frank Nincovich, "Theodore Roosevelt: Civilization as Ideology," *Diplomatic History* 10 (1986): 221–45; Howard K. Beale, *Theodore Roosevelt and the Rise of America to World Power* (Baltimore, 1956), still a standard account; Thomas G. Dyer, *Theodore Roosevelt and the Idea of Race* (Baton Rouge, 1980), very important; Lewis L. Gould, *The Presidency of Theodore Roosevelt* (Lawrence, Kan., 1990); Charles E. Neu, *An Uncertain Friendship: Theodore Roosevelt and Japan 1906–1909* (Cambridge, Mass., 1966), key on the immigration issue; Walter Scholes and Marie Scholes, *The Foreign Policies of the Taft Administration* (Columbia, Mo., 1970), the best comprehensive account; Paolo E. Coletta, *The Presidency of William Howard Taft* (Lawrence, Kan., 1973), a good overview; Richard W. Leopold, *Elihu Root and the Conservative Tradition* (Boston, 1954); Kenton J. Clymer, *John Hay: The Gentleman as Diplomat* (Ann Arbor, 1975), a good biography that can be used with John Hay, *The Life and Letters of John Hay*, 2 vols., ed. Roscoe R. Thayer (Boston, 1915); William C. Widenor, *Henry Cabot Lodge and the Search for an American Foreign Policy* (Berkeley, 1980); Kendrick A. Clements, *William Jennings Bryan: Missionary Isolationist* (Columbia, S.C., 1982); Richard W. Turk, *The Ambiguous Relationship: Theodore Roosevelt and Alfred Thayer Mahan* (New York, 1987).

On the U.S.-Asian (especially Chinese) relationship, the most helpful accounts include: Warren Cohen, *America's Response to China*, 3d ed. (New York, 1990); Warren Cohen, ed., *New Frontiers in American–East Asian Relations* (New York, 1983), especially the Hunt, Iriye, Heinrichs, and May essays; Michael Schaller, *The U.S. and China in the 20th Century* (New York, 1990); Michael H. Hunt, *The Making of a Special Relationship: The U.S. and China to 1914* (New York, 1983); David L. Anderson, *Imperialism and Idealism: American Diplomats in China, 1861–1898* (Bloomington, Ind., 1986), for the background; Key Ray Chong, *Americans and Chinese Reform and Revolution, 1898–1922* (Lanham, Md., 1984), crucial for private citizens, such as Homer Lea, and on Sun Yat-sen; James Reed, *The Missionary Mind and American East Asia Policy* (Cambridge, Mass., 1985); Paul Varg, *Missionaries, Chinese and Diplomats . . . 1890–1952* (Princeton, 1958); Patricia R. Hill, *The World Their Household* (Ann Arbor, 1985), on Women's Foreign Mission movement; Jane Hunter, *The Gospel of Gentility: American Women Missionaries in Turn-of-the-Century China* (New Haven, 1984), on "cultural imperialism"; R. Arkush and Leo O. Lee, *Land Without Ghosts: Chinese Impressions of America from the Mid-Nineteenth Century to the Present* (Berkeley, 1989); Daniel M. Crane and Thomas A. Breslin, *An Ordinary Relationship: American Opposition to Republican Revolution in China* (Miami, Fla., 1986), highly important; Dennis L. Noble, *The Eagle and the Dragon: The U.S. Military in China, 1901–1937* (Westport, Conn., 1990), especially on the Boxers. Akira Iriye, *Pacific Estrangement: Japanese and American Expansion, 1897–1911* (Cambridge, Mass., 1972), and Charles E. Neu, *The Troubled Encounter: The U.S. and Japan* (New York, 1975), both standard accounts; W. G. Beasley, *The Rise of Modern Japan* (New York, 1990); Yur-Bok Lee and Wayne Patterson, eds., *One Hundred Years of Korean-American Relations, 1882–1982* (University, Ala., 1986), key essays.

On Russia, the historical context is in Hugh Seton Watson, *The Russian Empire, 1801–1907* (Oxford, 1967); Dietrich Geyer, *Russian Imperialism . . . 1860–1914* (New Haven, 1987), stressing the domestic changes; Edward H. Zabriskie, *American-Russian Rivalry in the Far East, 1895–1914* (Philadelphia, 1946), still the best monograph; Frederick F. Travis, *George Kennan and the American-Russian*

Relationship, 1865–1924 (Athens, Ohio, 1990); John A. White, *The Diplomacy of the Russo-Japanese War* (Princeton, 1964); Raymond A. Esthus, *Double Eagle and the Rising Sun: The Russians and Japanese at Portsmouth in 1905* (Durham, N.C., 1988); Gary Dean Best, *To Free a People: American Jewish Leaders and the Jewish Problem in Eastern Europe, 1890–1914* (Westport, Conn., 1982).

For the Americas, important accounts include two books by Lester D. Langley, *America and the Americas* (Athens, Ga., 1989), which provides the broad context, and *The Banana Wars: An Inner History of American Empire* (Lexington, Ky., 1983); Barbara Stallings, *Banker to the Third World: U.S. Portfolio Investment in Latin America, 1900–1986* (Berkeley, 1987); David Healy, *Drive to Hegemony: The United States in the Caribbean, 1898–1907* (Madison, 1988), a superb overview; Warren G. Kneer, *Great Britain and the Caribbean, 1900–1913* (East Lansing, Mich., 1975), stressing the U.S. role also; Thomas Schoonover, "Imperialism in Middle America: U.S., Britain, Germany, and France Compete for Transit Rights and Trade, 1820s–1920s," in Rhodri Jeffreys-Jones, ed., *Eagle Against Empire* (Aix-en-Provence, 1983); Dwight C. Miner, *The Fight for the Panama Route* (New York, 1940), still helpful; J. Michael Hogan, *The Panama Canal in American Politics* (Carbondale, Ill., 1986), good on 1903–4; Michael L. Conniff, *Panama and the United States* (Athens, Ga., 1992); Richard L. Lael, *Arrogant Diplomacy: U.S. Policy Toward Colombia, 1903–1922* (Wilmington, Del., 1987), the best book on the subject, and important on the canal; Bruce J. Calder, *The Impact of Intervention . . . 1916–1924* (Austin, Tex., 1984), very good on Roosevelt's intervention and Dominican Republic's conditions; Brenda Gayle Plummer, *Haiti and the Great Powers, 1902–1915* (Baton Rouge, 1988), an important analysis; Schoonover, *The U.S. in Central America,* noted previously, an innovative and detailed analysis; José Joaquin Morales, *De la Historia de Nicaragua de 1889–1912* (Granada, 1963), has good sections on Zelaya from a Nicaraguan point of view.

On U.S.-Mexico relations, David M. Pletcher, *Rails, Mines, and Progress: Seven American Promoters and Mexico, 1876–1910* (Ithaca, 1958), remains important background; Ramón Eduardo Ruiz, *Triumphs and Tragedy: A History of the Mexican People* (New York, 1992), is a superb overview and sets the context; Alan Knight, *U.S.-Mexican Relations, 1910–1940* (San Diego, 1987), builds on Knight's two-volume work on Mexico and gives a different perspective; also, Dan LaBotz, *Edward L. Doheny: Petroleum, Power, and Politics in the U.S. and Mexico* (Westport, Conn., 1991); Gilbert M. Joseph, *Revolution from Without: Yucatan, Mexico, and the United States, 1880–1924* (New York, 1982); Gregg Andrews, *Shoulder to Shoulder: The American Federation of Labor, the United States, and the Mexican Revolution, 1910–1924* (Berkeley, 1991). Of special importance are two books by Friedrich Katz, *The Secret War in Mexico: Europe, the United States, and the Mexican Revolution* (Chicago, 1981), and *Riot, Rebellion, and Revolution: Rural Social Conflict in Mexico* (Princeton, 1988), which Katz edited.

Index